PREFACE TO FIRST EDITION

A famous Greek philosopher—it might have been Pythagoras, or maybe Heraclitus—once said, "We stand upon the shoulders of giants." No one can write a book such as this without relying upon the work done by many and various scholars, both past and present. It is just as well to admit as much at the outset, and to give thanks where due.

As I state several times in the course of the book, the notion that European witchcraft represented a survival of archaic shamanic practices is not my own. The Italian historian Carlo Ginzburg, currently at UCLA, has argued such an hypothesis in two major works, *Night Battles* and *Ecstasies*. The frequent citations to those books will indicate how much I owe to Ginzburg's research.

I have, however, tried to expand upon some of Ginzburg's points, and to demonstrate that the entire arcanum of European witchcraft can be shown to have shamanic roots. In so doing, I have wandered through almost all the major works of European mythology. My most constant companion, however, has been Mircea Eliade's classic work, *Shamanism: Archaic Techniques of Ecstasy.*

Beyond these scholarly acknowledgments, there are personal debts as well. I owe the greatest of such debts to the professors who first opened my mind and soul to the study of comparative mythology—Dr. Dorothea Kenny and Dr. Otto Sadovsky, both of California State University Fullerton.

Also, a special thank you to Marguerite for putting up with the writing of this book, which has been my constant obsession for the past year.

When I began this book, I sought simply to define the shamanic components of witchcraft. I had no idea that my research would lead me to conclusions that are likely to be controversial—if not downright inflammatory—to some contemporary Pagans. Harm was meant to none, and those who disagree with me are welcome to speak as loudly and as long as they wish.

—Kenneth Johnson
Cochiti Lake, New Mexico
The Autumn Equinox, 1994

INTRODUCTION

Witches and Shamans

GREENLAND, A.D. 1,000

Eric the Red's fledgling colony in Greenland had fallen on hard times. The hunters had not been successful, and the colonists hovered on the brink of famine. They decided to consult the sibyl.

Her name was Thorbjorg, and she was one of nine sisters, all of them priestesses of the goddess Freya who practiced the rites known as *seidr*. Thorkel of Herjolfsness prepared a great winter feast and had a high seat erected for her; on top was the traditional cushion stuffed with hen's feathers.

Thorbjorg wore a blue mantle which was studded with gemstones all the way down to the hem. Around her neck was a string of glass beads, and her head was covered with a hood of black lambskin lined with white cat's fur. Her staff had a big brass knob on top, and the brass was encrusted with stones. From her belt hung a pouch full of runes and other charms. She wore calf-skin shoes with the hair still on; there were big tin buttons on the ends of the shoe laces. Her gloves were of catskin, with the white fur turned inside.

The morning after the feast, she agreed to practice the *seidr*. She looked around the hall at the women who were present, and asked them if they knew the old songs and spells.

One called Gudrid answered: "I'm no sorceress, but I know the songs. My foster mother Halldis taught them to me in Iceland."

"Timely wisdom for the present," said Thorbjorg.

"But I can't sing for you," said Gudrid. "I'm a Christian."

"You would be helping the community—that won't make you any the worse a woman. Anyway, I leave it up to Thorkel. This is his house."

Thorkel persuaded the reluctant Gudrid to sing for them. Thorbjorg mounted her platform; the women gathered round. Gudrid took up the drum and began to sing—later it was said that no one had ever heard the old songs sung so beautifully.

On the wings of the music Thorbjorg flew away. Her eyes closed, she quivered and hummed. At last her voice came back to them, echoing from some world far away.

"The spirits are here. They have come for the singing, though they would not come before. I see many things now, things that were hidden. Now they are clear. The famine will pass; by spring it will be over. The sickness in the colony, that too will pass, and sooner than anyone thought."

She looked down from the platform and turned her distant gaze on Gudrid, standing there holding the drum.

"Gudrid, I shall help you for the help you have given us, for now I see your destiny, the life that you shall live. Married you shall be, and with the best marriage in the colony. But you shall not linger long here, for your roads all lead back to Iceland. There shall you be the mother of a great and noble line; a light shines upon all your descendants. And now, my child, farewell."

Then all the folk in Thorkel's hall crowded round the platform, begging for answers to their questions. Thorbjorg's voice echoed out of the Otherworld, and told them many things, and there was but little which did not turn out as she had said....

NORTHERN ITALY, 1600

Lucia woke in the middle of the night to find her husband Giacomo lying face up, breathing deeply. Rising on one elbow, she shook him experimentally. He did not move or respond in any way. Very well, then, he had taken the benandante road and gone upon one of his spirit journeys. He might be gone for many hours yet.

Of course, she had expected he would go. They were in the Ember Days, and last night had been a Thursday. On such nights, for nearly ten years now, Giacomo had departed on his nocturnal wanderings to fight for the village harvest. She remembered when the benandante "captain," Matteo the miller, had first come to Giacomo's house and told him, "You've been called." And Matteo had beaten upon his spirit drum, and sure enough Giacomo had fallen into a deep trance. And Matteo had seen Giacomo's spirit leave him, exiting between his lips in the shape of a mouse. And though Lucia was not especially gifted in matters of the Otherworld, there were times when she too had seen the little silver shape of a mouse squeaking through her husband's lips.

She rose and lit the candles on the mantel shelf. She lit one for St. Anthony and another for St. Simon, the friendly saints the common folk called *folletti*. The priest disapproved of them, saying they were not worshipped in the right and proper way, but more like "goblins." Well, so be it, she thought: the priest did not approve of Giacomo's spirit journeys, either.

Lucia pulled up her chair and sat down. For all these years now, she had kept a kind of vigil over Giacomo's wanderings, making sure that no one—even the children, still fast asleep in the trundle bed near the hearth—should disturb him. She must take special care that he should never get turned face down and risk being unable to return to his body. She noted that the little charm containing the dried remains of the caul in which he'd been born was round his neck, as usual. That was his protection as well as the mark of his gift, for the benandanti had chosen him at birth on account of his being born with the caul, waiting quietly till he reached his twentieth year when they had sent Matteo with the drum.

On the Ember Days, and especially on Thursdays, the hosts of the dead came close, so close, to mortal folk. Sometimes they moved quietly down the village streets like a soft gray mist, while sometimes they swept along furiously and were called the Wild Hunt. Many a man and woman slipped out of the body at those times, and went to join the ancestors. Giacomo had told her how they all met in a shining meadow of flowers which the benandanti called Josaphat's Field. There the benandanti joined with those of their ancestors who were still well disposed toward humankind. Armed with stalks of fennel, they went to battle against the wrathful dead who sought to blight the village harvest. Sometimes angry people, those who had quarrels with the other villagers, joined with the fearsome armies of the night and wielded sorghum stalks against the benandanti. There were cuffs and blows given and received, but at last Giacomo and his companions would find their way home again, and hopefully they would prevail, hopefully the harvest would be safe for another season.

For the name benandante meant "good walker," and men like Giacomo were good men and true, for they did battle for the sake of the crops, and thus for the safety of all who lived in the village. Who cared, then, what the priest might babble, or how he might complain? For Lucia knew that it was not the prayers of any priest, but the courage of the good walkers, which kept the village safe and the crops growing high....

The stories of Thorbjorg and Giacomo are separated by a gap of 600 years. The first one is recorded in *The Saga of Eric the Red*,[1] which, like most of the Icelandic sagas, constitutes a blend of fact and fiction. The second tale, that of Giacomo the benandante, is a fictional reconstruction pieced together from the records of witchcraft trials held in Italy during the late sixteenth century.[2] For although Thorbjorg—who may well have been an historical personage—lived at the far edge of the Christian world and hence would never have been tried for witchcraft, our more fictional Giacomo may well have found himself hauled up in front of the Inquisition.

The witchcraft trials constitute one of the saddest and strangest chapters in the history of the Western world. Though the Christian Church had always had its prohibitions against witchcraft, there were few actual witch trials until the last years of the fifteenth century. There had been isolated instances during the Middle Ages, it is true; most of these involved individuals accused of murmuring spells or incantations against a neighbor's fields or livestock. What began to happen in the early 1400s was quite different.

The 1300s had been a tempestuous era, characterized by a breakdown of the old medieval order. Feudal kingdoms gave way to new nation states, though not without a great deal of war and bloodshed in the process. Thousands died of the Black Death, which burst upon Europe in 1348. The common people, having lost their faith in the great edifice of Christendom, rose up in peasants' revolts and banded together in radical religious movements. The adherents of one such movement were called the Waldensians. They flourished in the western part of the Alps, where Italian auto factories, pristine Swiss cities, and trendy French ski resorts now hold sway. Meanwhile, in the Pyrenees Mountains that formed the border of France and Spain, there still remained a few surviving Cathars, practitioners of a dualist "heresy" which had been almost eradicated in 1244 during a bloody— and blatantly political—"crusade."

Beginning in the late 1300s, the Waldensians and the remaining Cathars attracted the attention of that darkest of medieval and Renaissance institutions, the Inquisition. This band of zealous Dominicans, originally formed to hunt down the Cathars, began to spread a wider net, roaming through the mountain hinterlands of Europe in search of questionable religious doctrines. As the inquisitors probed the collective mind of the European peasantry, they found something quite unexpected and much more unsettling than a few surviving Cathars or mere backwoods heretics such as the Waldensians.

There was, claimed the inquisitors—and the secular judges who aided them—an epidemic of witchcraft afoot. This phenomenon was no longer just a matter of a few isolated individuals putting spells on the cows. This, said the arbiters of heresy, was an actual cult, formed about 1375, which called upon demons who often bore the names and attributes of old pagan divinities, and which met by night in ceremonies called Sabbats. In the form of animals, anointed with hallucinatory herbs, the witches flew in spirit or on broomsticks to these lascivious revels, where they danced with a horned or antlered figure that the inquisitors believed to be "the devil."

Thus began a panic that seized Europe like a new plague for almost three hundred years. The mass burnings of suspected witches spread like a cancer across the continent in three distinct waves. The first outbreak, which began in the Alps during the 1420s, took almost eighty years to abate. Then, in the 1560s, a whole new siege of witch trials, much more ferocious and widespread than the first, shook the European continent, fading out only around 1600. Finally, a third, and even more brutal, wave of persecutions began in the 1620s. By the end of the century, however, the fury was spent, and the events at Salem, Massachusetts in 1692 were almost its last gasp.

No one will ever know for certain how many European peasants died during the Burning Times—a holocaust that, we should remember, took place not during the so-called Dark Ages, but during the more "enlightened" age of the Italian Renaissance and the early years of the scientific revolution. What had actually happened? There have been many "interpretations" of the witchcraft trials, their meaning and significance. The Church fathers, of course, saw witchcraft as a genuine heresy, the work of a very real and present devil, and as late as 1948 the Catholic historian Montague Summers was still supporting this traditionalist point of view.[3] Skeptical modern scholars, however, regard the witch persecutions as an exercise in illusion and paranoia. There was never any danger to Church or Christianity because there were never any witches. So argue the academics such as Norman Cohn[4] and H. R. Trevor-Roper.[5]

In the twentieth century, the victims of the witch trials have had a number of defenders who profess to agree with them on spiritual matters. The British Egyptologist Margaret Murray saw the witches as members of a Pagan resistance movement in the undercurrent of European history[6]—an argument which she reiterated with ever greater ferocity, beginning in the 1920s and continuing until her death at the magnificent age of one hundred. Gerald Gardner, often called "the founder of modern witchcraft," was in substantial agreement with Murray, but added that the witches, worshippers of Nature and sexuality, were quite alive and well—that they had, in fact, been quietly carrying on their ancient ways in an underground fashion since medieval times. Gardner's outlook suited the social and spiritual climate of the 1960s and spawned a whole generation of practitioners of Old European Paganism or Wicca, "the craft of the wise."

In the late 1970s and early '80s, Pagan feminists, taking their cue from Robert Graves' influential (and controversial) book *The White Goddess*,[7] came to see witchcraft as essentially a woman's religion with its roots in the Neolithic Era, and the women burned during the witchcraft trials as victims of a deep misogyny and fear of woman's spiritual power. This point of view was perhaps most popularly articulated in Starhawk's *The Spiral Dance*.[8]

It is possible that these changing points of view reveal more about our own times and issues than they do about the beliefs of our ancestors. Perhaps we are doing nothing more than seeing our forefathers, the peasants of medieval and Renaissance Europe, through our own eyes, projecting our own social and moral concerns upon them. Their own way of seeing things may have been quite different, and our nostalgic beliefs about their world view badly askew. We must ask ourselves if a European peasant woman of A.D. 1420, gathering herbs by the light of the moon and hoping the local priest wouldn't see her, would have recognized herself as the Pagan anarchist, feminist heroine, free love advocate, and proto-hippie that we would have her be?

In the light of so much uncertainty, it might well be asked why it should be helpful to set forth yet another reconstruction of the witch trials, or argue yet another theory. Nevertheless, we shall make the attempt, for we believe that even though the experiences of Thorbjorg the Sibyl and Giacomo the benandante were so widely separated in time and space, the two of them had much in common, for they were both practitioners of shamanism.

The notion that the European witch trials reveal to us a substantial body of spiritual or magical practice that can only be called shamanic is one which has already enjoyed some discussion among scholars—the idea has been especially well argued by the Italian historian Carlo Ginzburg.[9] These academic works, however, have so far remained outside the range of the general public, despite the extraordinary surge of popular interest in shamanism.

What, exactly, is shamanism? According to the definition of religious scholar Mircea Eliade, it is a "technique of ecstasy."[10] It is a form of spiritual practice that runs like an undercurrent through many of the world's religious traditions. It is also a spiritual *experience* or process that is so widespread it may well be fundamental to the human soul itself.

The shaman is a religious specialist whose gift and whose duty it is to serve his people and his tribe by mediating between them and the Otherworld. He travels to the Land of the Gods in search of visions. He journeys to the Land of the Dead to help and assist those members of the community who must take the fearsome road to those shrouded realms. He is part magician and part physician. He possesses the knowledge of herbs and other traditional healing arts. His ceremonies and rituals are typically undertaken to cure the sick.

The word "shaman" is Siberian in origin, for shamanism was first defined and described among Siberian tribes, but it is universal in character. It can be found in a more or less "pure" form among Siberian and Native American tribes, but it also appears as an element in the spiritual practice of the Chinese, Tibetans, Polynesians, Hindus, and—as we shall see—among the pre-Christian mythologies of Europe. It may well be the oldest of humankind's religious practices, for it was almost certainly fully formed by the time the present-day Native Americans left Siberia and wandered into the New World. This suggests that it may have been the "religion" of the Ice Age hunters, and that it has been part of our common human heritage since Paleolithic times.

Inasmuch as shamanism represents one of the most ancient and fundamental experiences of human spirituality, it is also one of the most persistent. Among traditional peoples, various shamanic practices often continue, as a kind of spiritual substratum, long after the missionaries have supposedly "converted the natives." This process can be observed in our own country. Anyone who has traveled extensively in the Southwest has seen thoroughly Pagan Native American ceremonies practiced in the central plaza while the Catholic church stands nearby with its doors open, accommodating the old ways by hosting kachinas on the altar, right alongside Jesus and Mary.

Something similar may have taken place in Europe. Because shamanism is a spiritual experience rather than a formal religion, it continues and endures while specific faiths come and go. Shamanism was practiced among the cave painters of France; it was practiced by the Neolithic farmers who raised the megaliths; and it was a strong force in the Indo-European religions of the Greeks, the Celts, and the Norse. What we shall be examining here is the idea that shamanic practice survived the Christianization of Europe as well, and that many of the victims of the witch trials were in fact practicing some form of shamanism.

If this is true, the European peasants who suffered during the Burning Times died for the sake of the world's oldest spiritual path.

PART I

Otherworlds

Everything is full of souls.

Guillaume Belibaste,
Cathar preacher, circa 1325

CHAPTER 1

The Shaman's Cosmos

THE NORTH STAR

Look up into the sky. Watch the constellations as they rise and set, as they circle around. Always, the sky is in motion. One star, and one star only, remains unmoving. That is the North Star.

According to the cosmovision of the shaman, the North Star is the axis around which all things revolve. It is the center of the universe, the "pivot of the four quarters." In Siberia, it is often called the "nail of the sky."* The sky itself is a gigantic tent, and the stars are merely holes in its covering. The North Star is the central pole that holds up the tent. The Buryat people of Siberia imagine the stars as a herd of horses; the North Star is the stake to which they are tied. Other tribes think of the pole star as a pillar, sometimes of iron, sometimes of gold. In any case, the human world is perceived as a world in

---

* The Taoists of ancient China remembered the nail of the sky, for their astrology is based on the constellations that revolve around the unmoving axis, the North Star, pivot of the four quarters.

constant motion, a constant state of change. Only one thing never changes, and that is the center of the universe.

When shamans depart upon their spirit journeys, they often take the road to the North Star. For countless centuries, the North Star has been watched through the smoke hole of many a yurt and teepee, and it is upon this small flickering light, seen through the smoke of the fire on cold wintry nights, that the shaman focuses his attention. The drum is beaten; the shaman falls into a trance. His spirit takes flight through the smoke hole, heading up the North Star road to the center of all things, the land of the spirits and the gods.

This, at least, is the simplest form of the shaman's journey to the center. But shamanism has had many and various concepts of the center and the road that leads thereto. In fact, the center is everywhere.

Tribal and traditional peoples live always at the center of the universe. No matter where they go, the still point at the midst of the universe goes with them. The familiar teepee of the Plains Indians is a model of the universe, for it is a tent of sky supported by a central pillar. When the great Lakota shaman Black Elk experienced his initiatory vision, he traveled out through the smoke hole of his family's teepee—he climbed the central pole of the universe to the world of the gods. The Plains Indian believed that *everywhere he pitched his tent became, at least for the time being, the actual center of the universe.* Thus the center of all creation is everywhere, and we always dwell within it. As we shall see, this concept has had a far-reaching influence on the history of world religions, especially yoga.

THE WORLD TREE

Because the center is everywhere, it can be expressed in many different metaphors. It may be the North Star, the central pillar, the World Mountain, or the World Tree. Perhaps the most important of these central images is the World Tree and the cosmos associated with it.

According to Siberian shamans, we live in a cosmos with three layers: Heaven, Earth, and the Underworld. The World Tree, the central axis of the universe, has its roots in the Underworld and its topmost branches in Heaven, almost touching the palace of the Sky Father. This great tree—in many Siberian traditions it is a birch tree—mediates between the worlds, and forms a pathway from one to the other. The souls of children yet unborn—and most especially the souls of future shamans—nestle in its branches, ready to climb down into incarnation. A Bird-of-Prey Mother, a fierce feminine bird spirit whom we shall meet again later on, also lives in the branches of the great Tree. So does an eagle, the totem bird of shamans, who resides in the uppermost branches. Above all, at the apex of the world, like the North Star itself, lives the Lord of the World, perceived as a detached, contemplative Sky Father.

The shaman is privileged to be able to travel up and down the World Tree. Climbing upward, he visits the palace of Sky Father or perhaps one of the other heavens along the way (sometimes there are seven heavens, sometimes nine). Here he receives transcendent messages or snatches of prophecy, important information concerning the proper performance of rituals. These messages he will communicate to the tribe. Climbing down toward the roots of the World Tree, the shaman takes the fearsome road to the Underworld, where dwell the souls of the dead. He does this for several reasons. Sometimes the soul of a sick person has already started on the hard cold journey to the land of the dead, and the shaman, by pursuing the wandering soul and intervening with it, may coax it back to the land of the living. At other times, the soul of one recently dead may become confused, reluctant to quit his former habitation or uncertain as to how he should proceed. The shaman assists the ghost of his tribesman by showing him the proper path to the Otherworld, and guiding him there.

Thus the World Tree is of vital importance to the shaman, for it is the symbol of his road, the road between the worlds, the road to the North Star and the center of the universe. Many Siberian shamans paint representations of the World Tree on their drums, while others decorate the central pole of their tent or yurt like a world tree. Some erect a pole just outside the tent and occasionally, during ritual, they actually climb the pole—a topic we shall investigate later on, when we chronicle the shaman's ascent in more detail.

The World Tree and the threefold cosmos appear everywhere, in mythologies throughout the world. The religions of Native American peoples are quintessentially shamanistic, and often embody shamanic ideas in a very pure form.

Take, for instance, the Sun Dance. This ritual is performed by many Plains Indian tribes, sometimes with rather different features. The version given here comes from the Wind River Shoshoni of Montana, Idaho, and Wyoming.[1]

A large cottonwood tree is selected to become the center pole of the Sun Dance Lodge. The lodge itself is shaped like a tent or teepee, with twelve support beams. That the Sun Dance Lodge represents the shamanic "tent of the sky" is clear from the terminology, for the central pole is "the backbone of the sky," a Shoshoni term for the Milky Way—which frequently serves as a metaphor for the shaman's path to the North Star. In more recent years, Christian influence has crept into the old ritual, and the central pole is now said to represent Christ, while the twelve support poles are the apostles. A buffalo head is fastened to the middle of the central pole, facing west. One of the lodge's rafters, anchored in the forked central pole and oriented east-west, contains a symbolic eagle.

In the old days, the Shoshoni constructed small stone hideaways in the mountains, concealing themselves inside and placing bait for the eagles on the roof. They caught the eagles barehanded, so that the carcass of an actual eagle was used in the Sun Dance. In more modern times, the tailfeathers of an eagle are used to symbolize the entire bird. The eagle, they say, is the greatest of all birds because it soars so high. It represents purity.

The Sun Dance lasts several days. After fasting and prayer, the dancers circle round the central pole of the World Tree. One of the purposes of the ritual is healing, and the clothing of those who seek healing is often left to decay in the sun after the dance is over. The central pole, too, must be left to decay naturally.

The Shoshoni Sun Dance is deeply reminiscent of Siberian rituals involving the world axis, but the same cosmology may be found among urban civilizations as well. The Classic Maya, for instance, conceived a superbly shamanic cosmos. In their tradition, the World Tree is a great ceiba or wild cotton tree.* This tree grows from the back of a great crocodile who slumbers in a pool of water at the bottom of the Underworld.† The Mayan Underworld itself is perceived as an inverted pyramid of nine levels. Above it is the Earth, the middle world in which we live. The roof of our world is the sky, which is held up by four great spirits called the Bacabs, who are sometimes represented as iguanas and sometimes as bees. They stand at each of the four cardinal directions. The World Tree continues up past our world, into the sky, the world of the gods.

Heaven is another pyramid, this one pointing upward and comprised of thirteen levels. At the apex of the pyramid or the top of the World Tree is the highest, the thirteenth, heaven. On the great branches of the Tree wait the souls of those unborn, ready to experience new birth in our world. In the topmost branches dwells a mythical bird called the muan.

Let us pause for a moment and note some of the characteristics of this Mayan shamanic cosmos:

- A world with three layers: Heaven, Earth, and the Underworld;
- A great tree at the center of all things, its roots in the Underworld and its branches in Heaven;
- A magical bird at the top of the tree;
- Thirteen heavens and nine hells (as compared with seven or nine heavens and hells among Siberian tribes);
- A sky held up by four monumental figures, one at each of the cardinal points;
- A pool of water at the bottom of the Underworld, with a reptilian creature therein.

---

* Even today, Mayan Calendar shamans select their divining seeds from the ceiba tree.

† In more northerly climes, where crocodiles are nowhere to be seen, the reptilian creature at the root of all things is a turtle—hence the term Turtle Island, the aboriginal name for the North American continent.

7

The similarity between the cosmos of the Maya and that of Siberian tribes is evident, but if we are to establish any connection between the shamanic world view and the witch trials, we must identify this same cosmos among European peoples.

In A.D. 1220, two hundred years after Thorbjorg the Sibyl spoke her prophecies in the distant Greenland colony, a learned citizen of Iceland decided to preserve the ancient mythologies of the Norse, the old legends that were fast disappearing as Christianity spread throughout Scandinavia. Snorri Sturluson, though himself a Christian, was also a bard, a lawgiver, and a politician, an erudite man with a great respect for the ancient ways. In a book history calls *The Prose Edda*, Snorri details the old Norse cosmos.

The center of the world is a great ash tree called Yggdrasil.[2] Its branches stretch over Heaven and Earth, while its roots are deep in the Underworld. There are three such roots, for there are three levels of the Underworld. One of these levels is simply called Hel (the origin of our own word "hell") and houses the ghosts of the dead. Another level belongs to the frost giants, and beneath it there is a pool called the Well of Mimir, which means "well of memory." Under this pool is buried the head of Mimir the Dwarf, a prophet who knew all things. To drink of this well is to acquire all the knowledge vested in collective humanity. A third level of the Underworld belongs to the gods, and houses another pool, called the Well of Urd or "fate." Here live the Three Norns, the wise sisters who weave the fates of humanity. Every day the gods travel on horseback over the rainbow bridge and come to the Well of Fate (not unlike the Buryats' herds of star horses who are tethered to the North Star). Here they meet to hold council.

Beneath the World Tree is a great serpent who gnaws continuously at the roots of Yggdrasil. But the World Tree continues to grow high, into the world of men, the middle world which is called Midgard. This world, too, is surrounded by another great serpent, the Midgard Serpent. The middle world was fashioned from the body of a great giant called Ymir; his domed skull is the dome of the starry sky. Four dwarves, one at each of the four directions, hold up the sky.

The World Tree Yggdrasil

Above our world, at the top of the World Tree, is Asgard, the land of the gods—though in fact the Norse heaven has three layers, including the kingdom of the Elves. The gods have their palaces at the top of the World Tree, where a great eagle—as among the Siberians and the Shoshoni—also resides.

Let us, then, compare the Mayan cosmos with that of the Vikings (see Table 1 on page 10).

The mythologies of the Maya and the Norse, though widely separated in terms of geography, share features that are too similar to be coincidental. They derive from a single source, and our brief survey of Siberian beliefs indicates that the common source is shamanism.

9

Though the Norse example brings us into the European cultural sphere, we may be left wondering whether or not the Scandinavian countries were unique, anomalous, and somehow different. Were they more deeply shamanic than other European peoples? The Norse were in close proximity to the Finns, renowned shamans and magicians closely related to the Siberian tribes. Was Norse myth influenced by the Finns? We may also remember that the far northern regions of Scandinavia were occupied by a shamanic people—the Lapp tribes. Did they, too, influence the Vikings in such a way as to render them unique?

COMPARATIVE COSMOLOGIES

MAYAN	NORSE
A world of three layers: Heaven, Earth, and the Underworld.	A world of three layers: Heaven (Asgard), Earth (Midgard), and the Underworld.
A great ceiba tree at the center of all things, its roots in the Underworld and its branches in Heaven.	A great ash tree (Yggdrasil) at the center of all things, its roots in the Underworld, and its branches in Heaven.
Thirteen heavens and nine hells.	Three heavens and three hells.
A sky held up by four monumental figures (iguanas or bees), one at each of the four cardinal directions.	A sky held up by four dwarves, one at each of the four cardinal directions.
A pool of water at the bottom of the Underworld, with a reptilian creature (crocodile) therein.	Two pools of water in the Underworld, with a reptilian creature (serpent) at the bottom of the Underworld.
The magical muan bird at the top of the World Tree.	An eagle at the top of the World Tree.

Table 1

Although it is true that the Norse retained the most powerful and striking shamanic world view of all Europe's pre-Christian peoples, they were not alone in that world view. We can find evidence of the same complex in other mythologies as well. An old Irish story tells us how the hero Finn MacCool became a poet. He went to study the bardic arts under an old fellow who lived by a pool that bubbled up beneath a great hazel tree. Hazelnuts dropped from the tree into the pool, where they were eaten by a salmon. Hazelnuts were symbolic of wisdom, and thus this salmon was the wisest creature in the world. The old man instructed young Finn to catch the salmon of knowledge and cook it for his master, but not under any circumstances to taste of it himself. Finn dutifully caught the salmon and cooked it—but the grease splattered on his thumb, which he quickly placed in his mouth. From that moment on, all Finn had to do was place his thumb upon his tooth and he was instantly able to understand all things.

We may easily recognize the great hazel tree as a World Tree—in fact, some Celtic myths specify nine hazels and place singing birds in their branches. The pool at the bottom of the hazel tree is the Well of Memory, and the salmon may represent the same primordial wisdom as is symbolized by the Mayan crocodile or Norse serpent.

The Celts are not the only European peoples whose cosmology closely resembles that of the Norse and of shamanism in general, for we may find the same world view even among the ancient Greeks.

The Greeks are perhaps the last European people we would suspect of practicing shamanism. After all, they are known to us primarily as the supreme rationalists of the ancient world, the forefathers of our own scientific civilization. Throughout the history of Classical Greece, even during the age of Pericles, Plato, and the West's first "scientific" thinkers, there was always an undercurrent of mysticism in Greek civilization. There were oracles (the most famous being that of Delphi), ecstatic cults like that devoted to Dionysus, and religious mysteries, as at Eleusis, but the mystical undercurrent in ancient Greek thought most important to our own study is the cult of Orpheus.

Some historians—especially those who regard mysticism as a kind of social disease—would have us believe that there never was an Orphic cult. It was all a literary fabrication, they tell us, concocted by a charlatan with the tongue-twisting name of Onomakritos. Other scholars believe that there was indeed an Orphic cult, one that was very alive and healthy,* and which was concerned principally with the journey to the Underworld.

Those who are familiar with classical mythology may remember that Orpheus was a great poet who descended into Hades in search of his wife Eurydice. This, of course, is the archetypal shaman's journey—the descent into the Underworld to help or even to retrieve the spirits of the dead. We shall have occasion to examine Orphic practices and beliefs in some detail during the course of this study. For the moment, we shall simply content ourselves with drawing a portrait of the Orphic Underworld.

Some of our best material on the Orphic cult comes from the graves of its devotees. Most of these graves were uncovered in the south of Italy, which, of course, was the home base of Pythagoras (himself probably an Orphic) and which seems to have been one of the centers of the cult. The Orphic initiates were buried with tablets—sometimes of gold—which were intended to serve as guides or road maps for the soul's journey to the Otherworld.

Let us quote from one such tablet:

> I am parched with thirst—
> dying.
> Drink from me, the eternal spring
> on the right by the cypress.
> Who are you?
> Where are you from?
> I am a child of earth
> and starry heaven,
> but my race is of heaven.[3]

---

* This author is aware of an oral tradition, circulating in contemporary Greece, that affirms that the cult of Orpheus is still "alive and healthy."

The same theme is reiterated, in somewhat more detail, in another of the tablets:

> *To the left of the house of Hades*
> *under a graceful white cypress*
> *a well offers spring water.*
> *Don't drink there.*
> *Find the well by the lake of memory.*
> *Guardians protect the cold water.*
> *Tell them:*
> *I am a child of earth*
> *and of starry heaven,*
> *but my race is of heaven.*
> *This you know.*
> *I am parched*
> *and perishing.*
> *Give me cold water*
> *from the lake of memory.*
> *They will give you water*
> *from the sacred spring*
> *and you will live*
> *a lord among heroes.*[4]

A very clear picture of the Otherworld emerges from these tablets. In the Land of the Dead stands the World Tree, in this case a cypress. To the left of the cypress is a well from which the Underworld traveler should not drink, and we know from other sources that this is the Well of Lethe or Forgetfulness. To drink therefrom deadens the soul and plunges it into oblivion. On the right, however, is another well, and a lake or pool, and these bodies of water go by the collective name of Memory or Mnemosyne. From this pool—which bears exactly the same name as Mimir's Well in more northerly regions—the soul is enjoined to drink, for to drink from this "sacred spring" awakens the soul to its heavenly or "starry" origins. The tablets, therefore, play the role of the shaman, guiding the soul of the initiate on its Underworld journey.

Clearly, then, the old shamanic cosmos comprised of World Tree, sacred pools, and three-tiered universe was prevalent throughout ancient Europe as well as among Native American and Siberian tribes. We are still a long ways from the witch trials of the fifteenth and six-teenth centuries. Did vestiges of the old world view survive into medieval and Renaissance times?

A search through European folklore yields numerous examples of the veneration of special trees, as we would suspect, for the World Tree, as we have seen, is everywhere. But what about the combination of sacred tree with sacred well? Can we establish that many villages and regions of Europe had their own World Tree and Well of Memory?

In 1810, an elderly Irish peasant patiently explained to a folklore collector his peculiar habit of frequenting wells near "old blasted oaks" or megalithic standing stones, where he would spit on the surrounding trees or hang rags upon their branches. He affirmed that such customs protected one against sorcery, helped the cattle to thrive, and kept the fairy folk happy. The old man and his companions often crawled sun-wise on their knees around the wells and stones, sometimes three or nine times. In County Armagh and County Carlow, the people rever-enced "fairy thorn trees" near holy wells until the first part of the twentieth century, often hanging medals, crucifixes, rosary beads, or strips of cloth on the branches to acknowledge the curative properties of the wells. In County Wicklow, a thorn tree called Patrick's Bush stood over a sacred well, and those seeking healing tied scraps of clothing to the tree, leaving them to decay naturally (precisely as in the Shoshoni Sun Dance).

The same complex of trees, wells, and healing power is attested to with thorn trees on the Isle of Man, as well as in the case of a yew tree in Scotland. If we were to extend our field of inquiry to consider holy wells and sacred trees separately rather than together, we would quickly find a surfeit of information, including such well-known pieces of folklore as the Holy Thorn of Glastonbury and the Major Oak of Sherwood Forest.

The practice of tying scraps of cloth or talismanic objects to such trees also seems to be more or less universal, and this author has seen similar objects (including cigarettes as well as the more typical rosaries and cloth) tied to an old juniper in New Mexico. The objects are affixed to the tree by the Indians of Cochiti Pueblo, whose ancestors once lived in the ruined Anasazi cities nearby.

Victorian folklore scholars were prone to regard the Maypole of medieval and Renaissance times as a purely phallic symbol. And though the May games of merry old England drew a great deal of disapproval from the clergy (especially those of Puritan persuasion), we must remember that the inhabitants of a prurient society are likely to see sex everywhere—even in matters more nearly cosmological. For the Maypole was as much a World Tree as it was a phallus. The following description of the rituals surrounding the Maypole was helpfully provided in 1595 by a rather sour Puritan who clearly does not condone the custom he so vividly describes:

People of many different cultures leave offerings at sacred trees

But their chiefest jewel they bring from thence [i.e., from the woods and groves] is the Maie-pole, which they bring home with great veneration, as thus—they have twentie or fourtie yoake of oxen, every oxe having a sweete nosegaie of flowers tied to the tip of his hornes, and these oxen drawe home the May-poale, their stinking idol rather, which they covered all over with flowers and hearbes, bound round with strings from the top to the bottome, and sometimes it was painted with variable colours, having two or three hundred men, women, and children following it with great devotion. And thus equipped it was reared with handkerchiefes and flagges streaming on the top, they strawe the ground round about it, they set up summer halles, bowers, and arbours hard by it, and then fall they to banquetting and feasting, to leaping and dauncing about it, as the heathen people did at the dedication of their idolls.[5]

The Maypole is decorated with "flowers and herbs" as if it were a vital, still-living tree. The same author goes on to report that the celebrants of the May games ended by running off into the woods to make love—a practice well attested in other literature of the period—and thus it must be admitted that even if the Maypole is in fact a World Tree, there is nevertheless something distinctly sexual about dancing round it. We shall return to this topic a little later on, but for now we may say that the practice of dancing around the World Tree was certainly conducive to states of ecstasy, for as late as the 1760s (and in puritanical Boston) the revolutionary adherents of Samuel Adams could still be roused to a state of wild intensity by dancing around the Liberty Tree.

But were these customs—the honoring of the great World Tree and the Well of Memory—actually cited as evidence of witchcraft?

In fact, they were, upon at least one occasion. The trial of Joan of Arc, which took place in 1431, has typically been ignored by students of the Burning Times (with the exception of Margaret Murray). Joan's trial, we are told, was a purely political affair—her English judges were concerned only with eradicating a military threat, and witchcraft, the official charge against Joan, was simply an excuse. Nevretheless, the trial records reveal a great deal of material relevant to our own inquiry, for one of the evidences of witchcraft against Joan was that she had, in her youth, danced around a "fairy tree."

During Joan's trial, she was questioned concerning a certain tree that grew near her home village of Domremy. She admitted that the tree in question was, in fact, known as the Fairy Tree or Ladies' Tree. Nearby was a fountain which was believed to have healing properties. After drinking of its waters, the sick rose up restored and circled the Fairy Tree, which was a large old beech. As a girl, Joan had often woven garlands for Our Lady of Domremy and gone with other village girls to the tree to hang the garlands there. Some of the villagers (though not her own family, Joan insisted) claimed that the fairies danced there. As for Joan herself, she had forsaken the Fairy Tree and the beliefs associated with it when she went to France to become a warrior.[6]

Twenty-five years later, when the French had regained the upper hand in their long war with the English, Joan was becoming a religious legend throughout the country. Her countrymen decided to re-open the investigation into her alleged practice of witchcraft, with a view to clearing her name (which they did, thus placing her firmly on the road to sainthood). The inhabitants of Domremy, her native village, were asked to clarify the matter of the "fairy tree." In so doing, they provided yet more material regarding the survival of shamanic customs in late medieval Europe. Joan's godfather testified:

> As for the tree that was called the Ladies' Tree, I have sometimes heard that ladies who cast spells—fairies they used to call them—used to come in the old days and dance under that tree.[7]

He went on to say that the fairies had disappeared after a priest read the Gospel of St. John aloud in the presence of the tree. But on certain holidays and saints' days, and especially on the holiday called

Fountain Sunday, people still danced beneath the Fairy Tree and feasted there. Then they returned home by way of the healing fountain, which was called the Frogs' Spring. They drank of the waters, gathered flowers, and sang and danced around the fountain.

A childhood friend of Joan's named Hauviette, about forty-five years old at the time of the re-trial and married to a peasant farmer in Domremy, remembered dancing with Joan around the tree:

> ...That tree had been called the Ladies' Tree since olden times, and they say that long ago the ladies they call fairies went there. But I have never heard of anyone who saw one.[8]

She too noted that the boys and girls of the village had a custom of going to the tree and the Frogs' Spring on Fountain Sunday, taking bread with them. Hauviette had gone there with Joan of Arc and other village children to dance around the Fairy Tree; they often brought gifts of nuts for the tree and fountain.

One of Joan's godmothers testified that "gentlemen and their ladies" often went to "stroll under the tree, because it is a fine tree." Like everyone else, she too remembered the fairy ladies, for she said that "in the olden days ladies that cast spells, who are called *fairies* in French, used to go under that tree. But because of their sins, as they say, they do not go now."[9] This woman, whose name was Beatrice, was eighty years old at the time of the re-trial, and hence must have been born about 1376. The fairy women, apparently, had disappeared somewhat earlier.

The picture that emerges is quite vivid. Near Domremy stood a great beech tree, the local World Tree, called the Ladies' Tree or Fairies Tree because long ago (or at least before 1375) it had been frequented by ladies, known as fairies, who cast spells and who danced under the tree. The ladies were no more, but people still danced under the tree. On Fountain Sunday, and also on certain saints' days in the spring and summer, the young people of the village brought bread and nuts to the tree. They hung garlands for Our Lady of Domremy on its branches. Then they "played games" and danced and sang around the tree. Afterward, they headed back toward the village by way of a spring called the Fountain of Frogs, where they drank water from the spring and danced again. The fountain (like the Well of Memory in the Orphic Underworld) was believed to have curative powers, as was the tree.* Even when there were no festivals in progress, "gentlemen and their ladies" went to the tree to stroll at their leisure.

THE WORLD MOUNTAIN

Trees were not the only objects around which European peasants sometimes danced. The standing stones and stone circles erected throughout the British Isles during Neolithic and Bronze Age times were, in the minds of the countryfolk, associated with dancing. For instance, the so-called "Merry Maidens" circle of Cornwall supposedly came into being when a group of young women was turned to stone for dancing on the Sabbath, while the Rollright Stones of Oxfordshire have long been rumored to be frequented by "witches" who dance round them in the moonlight.

Though the purpose of the megalithic monuments may never be fully understood, we may at least surmise that they too were images of the *axis mundi* or world center, the still point around which all things revolve.

Though the World Tree is the image of the universal center that is most often met with in shamanism, it is not by any means the *only* image. The pivot of the universe is sometimes envisioned as a pillar, or, more frequently, as a great mountain at the center of all things. In Hindu myth, the World Mountain is called Mt. Meru, and among the Norse it was Himmingbjorg, or "Heaven Mountain." The ziggurats of ancient Babylon were probably intended as images of the World Mountain, as were the pyramids of the Maya. Regarding the Maya, we may also remember that their universe was imaged in terms of two

---

* It would be interesting to know whether there were actually any frogs in the Fountain of Frogs, or whether the name comes from some local legend about a magical frog (the primordial reptile or fish or amphibian at the base of the Underworld pool).

great pyramids as well as in terms of a World Tree. One pyramid ascends to Heaven, while the other, which is inverted, reaches into Hell. The pyramid, then, is yet another World Mountain or center of the universe.

Some traditions make the identity of the World Mountain as a central axis even more clear by placing the North Star at its summit, as with the Hindu Mt. Meru and the Persian Mt. Demavend. We may also note that Mt. Demavend is an actual peak in the Elburz Mountains. Traditional peoples often regarded some local summit as their own World Mountain, just as various trees and wells throughout Europe became localized versions of the World Tree or Well of Memory—after all, the center is everywhere. Perhaps the best known of such physical "world mountains" is Mt. Olympus in Greece.

Standing stones may have represented the axis mundi, *the pivot of the universe*

Among the Maya, standing stones often doubled as symbols of the World Mountain. Mayan cities are filled with carved stone monuments that archaeologists call stelae and that record the deeds of the Mayan kings. The Mayans themselves, however, called these monuments *te-tunob* or "tree stones," indicating that they were regarded as images of the World Tree. By carving their deeds on such stones, the Mayan kings rather egotistically tried to place their own regal careers at the center of all things.

The World Mountain makes its appearance in the witchcraft trials as well. In 1630, a native of Hesse in Germany confessed that for several years he had been traveling in spirit to a mountain called the Venusberg during Ember Days. Here "fraw Holt" (i.e., the goddess Holda or Holle) had caused him to gaze into a basin of water, where he had seen splendid horses as well as the dead, in the form of men sitting at feast or in the flames.[10] A century earlier, in the early 1500s, an Italian peasant named Zuan delle Piatte had also confessed to visiting the "mount of Venus where lived Donna Herodias." He had traveled until he reached a lake, where a dark figure in a friar's habit prevailed upon him to renounce Christianity. The door to the mountain itself had been guarded by a serpent and by an old man called Ekhart who warned him that if he remained within for longer than a year he would never return. There were people inside the mountain, including "the Tonhauser and Donna Venus." It was a Thursday during the Ember Days of Christmas, and Venus had taken Zuan delle Piatte to the Sabbath; they rode black horses through the air and in five hours had circled the whole world. At the Sabbath he had encountered yet another female figure called "the woman of the good game."[11]

The story of "Tonhauser and Donna Venus" to which Zuan delle Piatte referred was in fact a well-known medieval legend, commemorated in Richard Wagner's opera *Tannhauser*. According to Heinrich Kornmann, whose *Mons Veneris* (*Mt. Venus*) was published in 1614, Tannhauser was a medieval minstrel who, on his way to a singing competition, passed near the Horselberg, a mountain in Thuringia. There he encountered a beautiful woman in the moonlight. The minstrel recognized her as none other than the goddess Venus, and followed her into the Horselberg, where he passed seven years in passion and in revelry. In time, however, he became weary, and called upon the Virgin Mary. The mountain split open and Tannhauser emerged. Throughout the world he went seeking Christian absolution, but no one, not even the Pope, would give it to him. Finally, he returned to the Venusberg to stay.

In this story, the World Mountain is localized, appearing as the Horselberg in Thuringia. There were other local Venusbergs throughout Germany, as well as the Italian version that appears in the trial of Zuan delle Piatte.

The presence of Venus *inside* the World Mountain may remind us that Joan of Arc's companions dedicated their garlands to "Our Lady of Domremy," and that some standing stones, notably the "White Wife" of County Antrim in Ireland, are named for females. And just as Tannhauser encountered Venus at the World Mountain, the Scottish bard Thomas of Erceldoune (hero of the ballad "Thomas the Rhymer") encounters the Queen of the Fairies while sleeping beneath the Eildon Tree—which, in Scottish dialect, means "fairy tree." Is there any significance to the fact that the spirit associated with the World Tree or World Mountain is typically feminine?

There is, in fact, a great deal of significance in all this, for it opens to us the *interior* cosmos of the shaman.

THE INNER COSMOS

The World Tree or World Mountain is typically believed to be endowed with a vital energy, a power that nurtures and sustains the world itself. The Mayans and Aztecs, for instance, imagined a channel of energy emanating from Heaven and spiraling *down* the World Tree, and another channel of power emanating from the earth (or Underworld?) and traveling *up* the tree. This energy or power was known in Nahuatl, the language of the Aztecs, as *malinalli*. The World Mountain was also endowed with a primal force or vital power, called *teyolia*.

Since the peoples of ancient Mexico usually perceived the World Mountain as a volcano, the vital force in the mountain is analogous to the fire in the center of the volcano.

The same image is found in Kabbalistic Hebrew writings.[12] The Tree of Life in the Garden of Eden becomes, in Kabbalah, an image of the universe as a whole. The power that rises from the base of the Tree is a feminine potency, in fact God's feminine half, known as the Shekinah. She ascends the World Tree in order to be united with God in mystical marriage at the summit of the Tree.

Most important to our purposes, however, is the fact that the Kabbalists also regarded the Tree of Life as existing *within* us. In almost all traditional spiritual systems, the image of the outer cosmos is reflected inside humankind, for our own inner world corresponds precisely to the universe around us. This symbiosis of cosmos and humankind found its way into Greek thought with the Hermetic axiom "As above, so below."

And yet it is to India that we must look to define more precisely the relationship between the inner and outer cosmos.

In yoga, it is said that the World Mountain, Mt. Meru, is inside the human body and that it represents the spinal column. The god Shiva himself becomes, in Tantrism, a kind of World Mountain, the still point around which all things move. In this aspect, he is symbolized by the lingam, a phallic stone that resembles nothing so much as the standing stones of old Europe. The power that moves through the spinal column, from its base to the crown of the head, is the shakti or kundalini, a vital energy perceived as a goddess.

In Tantra, it is Shakti, the Great Goddess, who dances around Shiva in a rhythm that is both cosmic and sexual. All our images of the Goddess in the Mountain or Tree are ultimately metaphors for the kundalini or "serpent power," a feminine energy both sexual and spiritual that has its origins at the base of the spine and, during spiritual practice, travels up our own internal World Tree or Mountain to the crown of the head—at which point we experience enlightenment.

Now we understand why the power within the World Tree or World Mountain is typically feminine, associated with the Goddess of Love or the Queen of Fairies. Traditional peoples, including Europeans, have always recognized that the shaman's universe exists within us, that the spinal column is in fact our own *axis mundi*, and that the acquisition of magical or shamanic power consists of "traveling up the World Tree" in more ways than one (i.e., the visionary or ecstatic journey of the shaman up the Tree is precisely analogous to the control and training of kundalini, the inner power). In this sense, as Eliade has pointed out,[13] yoga itself developed out of shamanism and constitutes a highly sophisticated, completely "internalized" rendering of the old shamanic techniques.

It is, of course, this vital power—depicted as a feminine potency and also as the "serpent" or other primal figure at the base of the World Tree—that makes all things live, that gives juice and sap to everything in the universe. This energy is primarily sexual. Now we may understand why the British Maypole is both World Tree and phallic symbol at one and the same time, or why peasant women in both England and the Breton peninsula of France rub themselves against standing stones in hopes of conceiving a child. For the Tree of Life contains the power that makes all things grow and flourish, just as sexual activity causes the human species to grow and flourish.

We have seen that medieval Europeans still retained vestiges of an extremely ancient cosmos—a cosmos known all over the world and which has its probable origins in shamanism. We have seen that a belief in this ancient cosmo-conception was frequently cited during the Burning Times as evidence of witchcraft. This, however, does not prove that the victims of the witch trials were themselves practicing some form of shamanic activity. In order to establish that, we must embark upon a deeper exploration of the shaman's traditional path—his call and initiation, his totem animals, and the details of his Otherworldly journey.

Though a powerful memory of the shaman's cosmos survived until the late Middle Ages, it has now virtually vanished. As we shall see, the ancient world view was in fact eradicated during the Burning

Times. The ordinary European no longer dances around trees—even if he can find a nice old one which is not the product of recent reforestation. The English Maypoles are now purely ceremonial, trotted out for the eager tourist at folklore festivals. We cannot leave the subject, however, without mentioning one last anecdote of particular interest.

The Pilgrims and Puritans were not the only discontented Englishmen who came to American shores during the 1600s. Not too far from Plymouth Rock stood the colony of Mt. Wollaston (present-day Quincy, Massachusetts), a community of indentured servants who had dreamed of becoming free men in a new world, but who, for the most part, wound up being sold to Virginia tobacco planters by their own leaders. One prominent member of the Wollaston colony, an aristocrat by the name of Sir Thomas Morton, who seems to have been a competent classical scholar as well as a former drinking companion of the poet Ben Jonson, decided to stand against his business partners and liberate the indentured servants.

Under Morton's leadership, Mt. Wollaston became "Merry Mount," a prodigal community where nought but feasting and drinking ever took place. Morton erected an eighty-foot Maypole of pine, surmounted with a pair of antlers, and invited the local Indians to join in the revels. (He most especially invited the Indian women, with bad poetry such as: "Lasses in beaver coats, come away/ Ye shall be welcome to us night and day....") The Pilgrims at nearby Plymouth Rock could scarcely tolerate such sensual license—especially since their own servants were running off to Merry Mount as fast as they could go. Miles Standish, gloomy hero of the poet Longfellow, was sent to drive Morton away, which he did with a small regiment of men. The Maypole was, of course, pulled down, and Nathaniel Hawthorne (a far more perceptive soul than Longfellow) later wrote that a shadow of sadness fell over New England when Morton was driven out.

Although Massachusetts is a long way from the lands of the Wind River Shoshoni, we must assume that the Algonquins understood Thomas Morton and his Maypole far better than Miles Standish or the Pilgrim fathers ever could.

The exercises below and throughout this book are not intended as exact reconstructions of ancient European shamanic techniques. Some have been couched in very contemporary terms—though others, like the first one given below, are probably quite similar to archaic practices. Essentially, these meditations and practices are intended simply to give you a feeling for the kind of spiritual techniques that were common among shamans and witches from the Stone Age until the end of the Middle Ages.

FINDING YOUR TREE OF POWER

Ancient Europe was covered with a vast deciduous forest—the forest of our ancestors, which figures in so many fairy tales. It was into such a deciduous wilderness that King Arthur's knights wandered in search of mystical adventure; it was in such a forest that Hansel and Gretel became lost. Because they were forest dwellers, European shamans had a special affinity for trees. Each tree had its special magic and meaning, its special lore—much of which has been preserved in the Ogham system of writing, the magical or divinatory alphabet of the Celtic peoples.

The last living European shamans—folk healers who live in the isolated villages of Russia, Rumania and Ukraine—still practice a technique that helps you to identify your own particular power tree. The version given below has been provided courtesy of Olga Luchakova, M.D., Ph.D., and Igor Kungurtsev, M.D.

1. Select a location with a lot of trees. Ideally, this should be a national park or forest where you can hike far away from other people or any kind of disturbing influence. If you live in an urban environment far from any national parks or forests, a simple public park may have to suffice.

2. Find a quiet outdoor spot near the stand of trees you have selected. This should be a place that is as free as possible from other people; you need to feel completely relaxed, not worried about whether anyone is going to see you and think you're crazy.

26

Close your eyes and take a few deep breaths.

Empty your mind of all thoughts. If you've practiced meditation before (especially of the yogic variety), you will be able to achieve this without difficulty. If not, you may have some trouble stopping the chatter in your mind. In many Eastern techniques, one is taught to observe the chatter dispassionately until it stops of its own accord. In Western techniques such as Hermeticism or Eastern Orthodox meditation, the thoughts that arise are assertively driven away until they stop.

Here is a gentle way to banish unwanted thoughts: If a thought arises to trouble you, try turning it into a visual image instead. Imagine that you are sitting on the top of a high mountain peak, watching the sky. The bit of mental chatter that annoys you is simply a cloud crossing the clear blue sky. Watch as the wind blows it into tatters and its remnants float away.

3. Now shift the focus of your attention to your physical self. You may do this by simply dropping your clear and cloudless mind down into your body. Let your awareness flow like light throughout your body, vitalizing it so that your unclouded mental state becomes an equally clear state of physical awareness.

4. When your body is fully empowered with clarity and calmness, begin walking through your forest or park. Walk among the trees, but without actually looking at them. In fact, do not look attentively at anything in particular. Keep your vision free and unfocused.

5. In time, you will find yourself attracted to a particular tree. Take a few deep breaths so as to increase your field of clarified mental-physical awareness. Then begin to approach the tree. Your heightened sense of perception will soon make you aware of the tree's consciousness. This means that you have entered into its aura.

Take time to feel a sense of oneness with your tree. Will it allow you to approach it now? If so, feel free to embrace it, to sit or stand with your back against it.

6. When you are at last able to make physical contact with your tree, surrender yourself to it altogether. Feel its calm, healing energy wash over you. No matter how many visits it takes you to achieve this, or how many times you go to the woods to commune with your tree, always begin with the meditation detailed above, so that you can maintain your sense of heightened awareness whenever you are in contact with your tree. Use that awareness to answer these questions: To what part of your body is the tree speaking? Which spiritual centers does it activate?

Like yoga, shamanism has always recognized distinct foci of spiritual energy within the body, the so-called chakras or psychic centers. Though different traditions vary as to the exact location and number of these chakras, the most commonly agreed upon ones are:

- The crown of the head, governing consciousness and the higher self;
- The "third eye," governing psychic perception and the higher mind;
- The throat, governing intelligence and communication;
- The heart, governing love and compassion;
- The solar plexus, governing anger, ego, and the power of assertiveness;
- The generative organs, governing sexuality;
- The coccyx or base of the spine, governing the survival instinct and the physical plane at its most basic level.

Different trees activate different psychic centers. The type of tree that speaks to you, the type of tree with which you have bonded, will give you a clue as to the nature of your own shamanic gift, because it will activate a particular psychic center. The center thus activated will tell you where your own personal power comes from. According to Celtic lore, for instance, the oak was the tree of kings and Druids, and symbolized regal and spiritual power. Its power helps to provide energy and dispel fatigue. The hazel was a tree of poetic wisdom and magic. According to Slavic shamans, pine trees share with oaks a vital, energy-giving power, while aspens "suck" away negative energy, and are used to drain off fevers or inflammations.

GROWING THE INNER TREE

As we have seen, the World Tree lies within us, as well as forming the center of the cosmos all around us. As the shaman, in ecstasy, travels up and down the cosmic World Tree to communicate with the world of the gods, so we may encourage our own life energy to travel up and down our interior World Tree, and thus communicate with our own higher self. In this metaphor lies the shamanic origin of yoga.

For this exercise, you may either sit or stand. The important thing is to keep your spine straight. Breathe in and out deeply and with regularity.

Imagine that your tree of power lies within you; your spine is its trunk. If you have worked with your tree of power and learned to know it, you will be able to visualize it with great clarity. Imagine its roots reaching down into the earth below your feet. Imagine your arms as branches; see the topmost branches crowning your head and the leaves or pine needles surrounding you.

Now breathe in, very deeply. A channel of life-giving energy is moving up your spine, just as the life-giving sap moves up the trunk of a tree. You may wish to visualize this energy as white light.

When the energy reaches the topmost branches of your tree, you will be able to feel its glorious light swirling around the crown of your head. You may even feel a tingling at the top of the skull, the place that Hindus and Buddhists call the "crown chakra" and that, when you were a baby, was the soft spot on top of your head.

Breathe out, again very deeply. Feel the energy sweeping down your spine, merging with the earth beneath you. When you breathe in once more, bring the energy back out of the earth and up your spine again.

Keep doing this until you are at one with your inner World Tree, and filled with a deep and abiding sense of calm.

Chapter 2

Initiation Rites

North Dakota, 1832

George Catlin, once a prominent portrait painter in Philadelphia, had for the last two years been engaged upon an extended ramble through the little-known lands of western North America. His purpose was to record in paint the lives and rites of American Indians.

In the course of his artistic odyssey, upon which he had been accompanied primarily by mountain men and fur company officers, he had witnessed a great many peculiar sights. None so peculiar, however, as what he witnessed in the villages of the Mandan Indians in the summer of 1832.

For several days, the tribe had been performing the annual ceremonies of initiation for young men. Bull dances had been held in the central square; the creation of the universe had been re-enacted. All this time, the young male candidates had been secluded in the medicine lodge, fasting and praying. Now the time had come. The climax of the great ritual had arrived.

Catlin sat in the lodge with his sketchbook, accompanied by the mountain man Abraham Bogard and the leading officer of the local fur company trading post. He watched as each young man, already weak from fasting, was cruelly pierced with bone hooks inserted in his flesh underneath the shoulder muscles, sometimes in front, sometimes in back. The hooks were long, sturdy, and notched to induce greater pain.

But even that did not constitute the full measure of the initiate's suffering. Each man was pierced in the arms and legs as well, and heavy buffalo skulls were attached with rawhide thongs to each bleeding limb.

Catlin gazed up through the central smoke hole of the lodge, from which two more rawhide thongs trailed down. These thongs were attached to the hooks which had pierced the young candidate's shoulder muscles, and he was hoisted up, up toward the central smoke hole. Catlin noted that this part of the ritual was endured with great fortitude. Each young man clutched his medicine bag in his hand as he was raised toward the sunlight; at last he swung some six or eight feet off the ground.

The older men who were in charge of the proceedings then began to spin the candidate round and round. Faster and faster he whirled until at last he could endure no more and began to cry out to the Great Spirit. The older fellows left off their spinning. In time, the young man ceased his whirling and hung there in the stillness, illumined by the sunlight which shone like white gold through the smoke hole. Finally, the candidate's medicine bag dropped to the ground as he began to lose consciousness. At that point, he was cut down.

Even that, however, was not quite the end. As soon as the candidate began to regain consciousness, he forced himself to crawl out of the lodge, into the light of day. Outside, Catlin observed, each young man was seized up by two strapping braves who tied him with rawhide thongs once again and forced him to race alongside them. The initiate stumbled along, still dragging buffalo skulls from his bloody limbs, until at last he fell and had to be dragged. Then the braves let him go.

At last it was finished. The initiation had been accomplished.

George Catlin recorded, in words, several sketches, and a full-sized painting, the details of the Mandan ceremony. What he had seen impressed him as so bizarre and unbelievable that he obtained signatures from his two white companions as evidence that the ritual had, in fact, taken place in the manner he described.

George Catlin and his companions were the only outsiders ever known to have witnessed the Mandan initiation rites. Five years later, the tribe was virtually eliminated by an epidemic of smallpox.

SHAMANIC INITIATION

The ceremony described by Catlin[1] was, in point of fact, a rite of passage into manhood rather than an initiation into the shaman's vocation. But the Mandans, like other Plains Indian tribes, were a shamanic society, and the ritual detailed contains many features that are common to the initiatory experiences of shamans throughout the world.

Though one may be born to a shamanic vocation, one attains power and mastery only through initiation. In some cultures, there are physical signs and peculiarities that mark one as a shaman at birth—notably, being born with a caul. Sometimes the future shaman is recognized by certain psychological traits that appear during childhood. A boy or girl who is sickly, or introverted, or who shows no interest in the tribe's traditional pursuits—for instance, a male child who doesn't care for hunting—is regarded in many cultures as a potential shaman. This is especially true when the individual in question is physically unable to take part in such traditional activities, as when a male child suffers from a lame leg. Such a person attracts the notice of older shamans and, when he or she reaches the right age, is trained by them in the techniques and traditions of the North Star Road.

Sometimes, however, potential shamans are called to the Otherworld by a spiritual experience that is solitary, lonesome, and usually terrifying. The shaman's path may even begin with what, in our own society, would probably be described as a psychotic episode. Among the Tungus of Manchuria, even one who has been carefully trained as a shaman may undergo a siege of wild madness. He may run away to the mountains for seven days or even longer, catching animals with his teeth, ripping them apart and eating them raw. He returns to the village bloody and crazed, his clothes torn and his hair matted.

At other times, a terrible illness marks the beginning of the shaman's path. Black Elk, the famous Lakota medicine man, suffered such an initiatory illness. Since the age of four he had been hearing spirit voices calling to him, but he had told no one. Then, when he was nine, he was eating at a friend's teepee when he heard a voice that said, "It is time; now they are calling you." Walking outside of the teepee, he found that his thighs hurt so badly he could scarcely walk. The next day, his band moved camp. During the course of the day's journey, Black Elk dismounted from his horse and, suddenly, his legs gave out entirely. He crumpled to the ground. He soon became feverish. Later, as he lay sick and delirious in his parents' teepee, he saw two "men" swoop down through the smoke hole with lightning on the tips of their spears and shout: "Hurry! Come! Your grandfathers are calling you!" Black Elk's spirit got up and walked outside, where a cloud seized him up and carried him to the center of the world. There he received the vision that made him one of the most renowned medicine men of his tribe.[2]

Whether a shaman is trained by the elders or receives an initiatory vision during illness or some other altered state of consciousness, there is more often than not an experience that embodies the theme of death and rebirth. Typically, the shaman is reduced to a skeleton and his flesh is torn from his bones. Yakut shamans fall into a trance and lie for three days in their yurts without eating or drinking. In their trance state, they experience their limbs being torn off by demons with iron hooks. Their bones are scraped clean. Sometimes the demons remove their heads and force them to watch their own dismemberment. Finally, their bones are gathered up, given new flesh, and restored to life.

A detailed record of such an initiatory vision was provided by a Samoyed shaman in Siberia. The man lay in a trance for three days, sick with smallpox. In a vision, he was carried to the middle of a great sea, from which he emerged and climbed a mountain (the World

Mountain of the shamanic cosmos). He met two great spirits, the Lord and Lady of the Underworld, who were also the Lord and Lady of the Waters. The Lady suckled him and called him her child; the Lord gave him two animal guides, an ermine and a mouse. He came to a high place with seven tents, where the inhabitants of the Underworld taught him about the various diseases that torment humankind.

Next, his animal guides led him to a place called the Land of the Shamanesses, where women strengthened his voice and throat. He then crossed more oceans, and came to an island where a great birch tree, the World Tree, grew. The Lord of the Tree gave him one of its branches, from which he was instructed to make three drums. The three drums were to be kept by three women and were to represent three powers—the ability to help women in childbirth, the ability to heal the sick, and the ability to find men lost in the snow. (The shaman who experienced this vision later cured three orphan girls of smallpox, married all of them, and gave each of them one of his drums.)

The sick man's journey continued. He entered a great mountain, where he saw two women, naked and covered with hair like the reindeer. Each woman gave birth to two reindeer, giving the shaman a hair from one of the deer, to be used when he attempted to locate reindeer for his people. Finally he came to yet another great mountain, where a blacksmith worked a bellows and a gigantic cauldron boiled on the fire. The smith cut off the man's head, chopped up his body, and boiled everything in the cauldron. The severed head was forged on an anvil and cooled and tempered in a pot of cold water. The bones were set floating in a river, from whence the smith retrieved them, put them back together, and covered them with flesh. The smith bestowed more powers upon the man, who at last awoke in his yurt, a fully empowered and initiated shaman.[3]

These same themes may be found in shamanic cultures around the world. Among the Mandans, the initiatory candidate was pierced and torn in actual reality, and draped with old bones in the form of buffalo skulls. He was hoisted up toward the smoke hole, as if he were ascending the World Tree or hanging tormented on its branches. The Mandan ritual has clear analogues to the Sun Dance common among most

Plains Indian tribes. As we have seen (in Chapter 1), the Sun Dance Lodge is itself a tent of sky with a World Tree or cosmic axis in the center. Those who seek initiation pierce their pectoral muscles with eagle talons. The talons are attached to rawhide thongs which, in turn, are tied to the central pole. The Sun Dancer then proceeds to dance around the central lodge-pole or world axis until his ordinary consciousness takes flight and he experiences an initiatory vision.

These rites of death and rebirth have their correspondences in India as well. One form of Tantric Yoga involves meditating in graveyards or on cremation grounds. The yogi observes the bodies being burned and turning to ash and dust.

Like the Samoyed initiate or the Yakut shamans who were forced to watch their own dismemberment, the yogi meditates upon his own death; he can feel his body dying, the skin dissolving or decaying until only a skeleton is left. Having thus confronted his mortality and symbolically died, he may then experience a vision of Kali or one of the other goddesses common to Tantra—a vision of renewal or rebirth.

We have identified four distinct patterns of shamanic initiation—though in some individual cases a shaman may undergo an initiatory experience that contains elements from several different modes. These patterns are as follows:

- The shaman is called by spirit voices, as was Black Elk;
- The shaman suffers an experience of madness or temporary derangement, as among the Tungus shamans;
- The shaman undergoes a visionary experience, sometimes brought on by illness in which he or she suffers death and dismemberment, only to be resurrected and reborn. This process may sometimes be embodied in ritual, as with the Mandan initiation ceremony or the Sun Dance;
- Either before or after the initiatory experience, the shaman often learns elements of his or her craft directly from elder members of the tribe.

Let us transfer our field of attention to the European mythologies and the various processes of shamanic initiation that are found there.

INITIATION RITES IN EUROPEAN MYTH

One of the most common "initiation stories" in European myth involves the "call by spirits." This is typically described as a transcendent, ecstatic, even somewhat sensual, experience. An excellent example may be found in an old Irish tale called "The Adventure of Bran." Bran was walking near his home when he heard a strange, sweet music behind him. His attempts to locate the source of the music failed, and at last he fell into a trance-like sleep. He awoke to find a silver branch with white flowers beside him. Bran took the silver branch home with him, and there appeared before all those assembled in his hall a beautiful woman, strangely garbed, who sang of the joys of an Otherworld she called the Land of Youth. The woman vanished, and Bran set sail across the sea in search of the Land of Youth. He came at last to "the Island of Women"—a common Celtic term for the Otherworld that may remind us of the Land of the Shamanesses visited by the Samoyed shaman during his initiatory vision.

A similar story concerns Connla the Fair, who was standing on the Hill of Usnach when he saw a woman in "unfamiliar dress." She identified herself as coming from the Land of the Living, where there is immortality and perpetual feasting. This Land of the Living lay inside a great fairy mound. Before vanishing, the woman tossed an apple to Connla. He returned home, but fell into a sulk and became incapable of taking any food or drink save the apple itself, which was always renewed as soon as he consumed it. Finally, unable to bear the realms of mortals any longer, he encountered the mysterious woman once again and set sail with her for the Land of the Living.

This type of initiatory experience was remembered well into medieval and early modern times, for it is recorded in the "Ballad of Thomas the Rhymer."* Thomas was asleep beneath a fairy tree when the Queen of the Fairies came riding toward him and carried him

---

* Though Thomas himself was alleged to have been a genuine historical personage who lived in the thirteenth century, the ballad that bears his name is in its present form no earlier than the seventeenth century.

away to the Otherworld. Here the shaman* is initiated while in a trance state (asleep) beneath the World Tree, in a manner very like the Otherworld travelers in the old Irish epics.

The siege of madness that afflicted some Siberian shamans seems to have been known in Europe as well, for it figures in a group of Welsh tales, the protagonist of which is none other than Merlin. The white-bearded enchanter of Arthurian legend has a long ancestry that leads back to Pagan times. Oxford professor Nikolai Tolstoy[4] has drawn attention to a very old body of Merlin stories which has nothing to do with King Arthur and which seems to center on a real personage, a historical Merlin who lived, in fact, some fifty years *after* the time of Arthur.

This Merlin was a warrior as well as a bard. He fought in the army of one of the few remaining Pagan kings of Britain, a local monarch who ruled in what is now southern Scotland. During a battle with the Christians in which his king was slain, Merlin experienced a vision and went mad. He vanished into the woods, living like a wild animal and eating the bark of trees—in other words, behaving in precisely the same manner as Tungus shamanic candidates undergoing their initiatory siege of madness. After this temporary sojourn in the wild, the Merlin of the old story took up residence on Hart Fell (a local World Mountain) next to a natural spring (a local Well of Memory), where he began his career as a prophet. His madness, then, may unquestionably be described as an initiatory experience, for it results in the ability to see the future.

It is also possible to discover, in a European context, the death-and-rebirth experience so common in other cultures. A good example may be found in *The Mabinogion*, a collection of Welsh stories that (although the original manuscript dates only from the twelfth century and shows clear signs of "Christianization") preserves a wealth of ancient British mythology. In the Fourth Branch of *The Mabinogion*,

---

* Thomas was a bard in the old Celtic sense, a profession much closer to that of the seer than to today's poet.

the hero Llew Llaw Gyffes nearly meets his death under some very peculiar circumstances—he is standing inside a temporary wooden shelter with one foot perched on a cauldron and the other on the back of a goat when his enemy thrusts a magic spear into his back. Yet Llew is not quite dead—he changes into an eagle and, though wounded, manages to fly away.

The eagle, of course, is the totem bird of shamans which resides in the top branches of the World Tree. It is precisely in such a World Tree that we next encounter Llew. His mentor, Gwydion of the Magic Harp, has set out in pursuit of him. He follows the path of a sow (in Celtic myth, swine were pre-eminently the totem animals of the Underworld) until he comes to a great oak tree. In the tree is a wounded eagle, shaking a stream of maggots from his wounded flesh. Gwydion begins to sing a magic song, and slowly the eagle makes its way down the tree to rest in his lap. Then Gwydion sings another spell that restores Llew to health and to his former human shape.

The story, though deeply garbled and confused by centuries of Christian redaction, reveals several important shamanic themes. Llew is wounded unto death in circumstances so unusual as to imply some sort of initiation ritual—we even meet with the boiling cauldron that appears in the Samoyed shaman's vision and that will concern us at greater length a bit later on. Llew becomes an eagle, which is the bird generally associated with shamans. Most importantly, he is discovered lying wounded at the top of the World Tree, which may remind us of the Mandans, the Lakota, the Samoyed shaman, and of all those who must be tormented and crucified, even dismembered, on the great trunk of the World Tree.

Llew is charmed down from the Tree by Gwydion of the Magic Harp, a character who is also rich in shamanic associations. As noted in Chapter 1, the Milky Way is regarded in many shamanic cultures as a road or pathway to the North Star; it was once called Caer Gwydion (Gwydion's Castle) among the Welsh. Gwydion is an enigmatic and somewhat mysterious figure, for he occurs nowhere save in *The Mabinogion* itself and, very briefly, in several other old Welsh poems.

One of these poems, "The Spoils of Annwn," concerns King Arthur's raid upon the Otherworld, and contains many poetic allusions to that mystic locale. One such allusion speaks of Caer Sidi, "the Revolving Castle," where Gwydion was once imprisoned in the "bone fortress." Is this a tantalizing fragment of some longer tale, now lost, in which Gwydion journeyed to the Otherworld and was "imprisoned"— or perhaps actually tormented—in a "bone fortress" that corresponds to the shaman's experience of dismemberment and reduction to a skeletal state?

Though Gwydion is, as we have noted, mysteriously absent from most Celtic myth collections, there is a distinct possibility that he is the Celtic equivalent of the Norse god Woden or Odin—there may even be a linguistic connection between them (wo = gwy, den = dion). Scholars acknowledge that Odin is one of the most genuinely shamanic figures in European mythology. He suffers a dramatic initiatory torment on the World Tree which is chronicled in an old Norse poem entitled *Havamal* ("The Song of the High One"):

> *I know I hung*
> *on the windswept Tree,*
> *through nine days and nights.*
> *I was stuck with a spear*
> *and given to Odin,*
> *myself given to myself....*
> *They helped me neither*
> *by meat nor drink.*
> *I peered downward,*
> *I took up the runes,*
> *screaming, I took them —*
> *then I fell back.*[5]

Odin has been wounded by a spear (like Llew) and—a mystical paradox—sacrificed to himself. Bleeding, he hangs from the branches of Yggdrasil, the World Tree, with none to give him food and drink. He peers downward, perhaps into the depths of Mimir's Well, which lies at the roots of the World Tree, for we are told in another place that Odin is privileged to converse with the prophetic head of Mimir because he sacrificed an eye for wisdom. And indeed, wisdom is what he seeks, for to the Norse the runes were not simply a secular alphabet—they constituted a body of lore, each letter rich with magical correspondences and esoteric meanings. Odin wins his goal and grasps the runes, but screams with the pain of knowledge acquired.

The subject of the *Havamal* sounds too much like Christ's crucifixion for some scholars, who have argued that the poem must be a late one, reflecting Christian influence. But, as we have seen, it embodies a mystical experience that is far older than Christianity and that may be traced all over the globe. It is, in fact, far more likely that Christ himself is but another shaman, hanging on the World Tree in the death-and-rebirth experience of initiation.*

Myths and legends that embody various forms of shamanic initiation are found throughout the pre-Christian mythologies of Europe—but do these initiatory experiences make an appearance in the witchcraft trials as well? Did the medieval and Renaissance peasants who retained such powerful memories of the old shamanic cosmos also undergo experiences that were, in themselves, shamanic, and that attracted the paranoia of the inquisitors?

A rite of initiation does appear—and often—in the records of the witch trials, but it is entirely different from the experiences under discussion here. Regarding the witches as members of a heretical or demonic cult, the inquisitors sought information about how the members of that cult were initiated. They elicited tales of kissing the devil's backside during Sabbat orgies and of being scarred with an awl. The records, however, have little or nothing to say about receiving an inner spiritual vocation through vision, training, or a profound death-and-rebirth experience. In this author's opinion, these "initiation rituals" (and the term is used guardedly, for it is here, more often

---

* After being tormented on the World Tree, Christ descends into Hell. He journeys to the Underworld during his initiatory experience and remains there for three days (in accordance with the shamanic preference for odd numbers like three, seven, and nine). The shamanic associations of the Christian myth become even clearer in the light of medieval legends which claimed that Golgotha was the place where the world was created (i.e., an *axis mundi*) and that the cross was carved from a tree descended from the Tree of Life in the Garden of Eden.

than elsewhere, that we meet with the preconceived fantasies of the inquisitors) arise from Pagan hunting and fertility rituals having little to do with the visionary experience of shamanic initiation. This is a subject we shall explore in a later chapter.

Let us return to our initial question: Do echoes of shamanic initiation experiences appear in the records of the witch trials?

BAVARIA, 1579

For most of his thirty years, Chonradt Stocklin had cut his winter wood amidst the grove of fir trees that lay just behind his house at the edge of the village. Fir made good firewood, and Stocklin, a shepherd, had a wife and several children to keep warm during the winter months. The forest had turned a glorious red and yellow some time back, and now the eastern winds were becoming more biting; the leaves were beginning to fall. Soon the first snow would come. It was time to cut wood.

This year Stocklin approached the grove of firs with some trepidation, for the spot was no longer simply a source of firewood; it had become a magic circle, replete with unsettling visions.

A year ago, Stocklin had been walking down the path to the grove when Jakob Walch, a drover and fellow villager, appeared on the path before him. This, of course, would not ordinarily be a remarkable event, for Jakob, like everyone else, cut his wood in the forest at the edge of town.

The remarkable thing was that Jakob Walch had died eight days previously....

Chonradt Stocklin had slipped into a kind of trance; time and space had disappeared down a windy tunnel, leaving only an eerie focus on an intense present during which Chonradt heard Jakob speak to him. He had been compelled by the powers above, complained Jakob, to spend three years wandering, after which he would be consigned to the flames of Hell for his sins. Therefore, intoned Jakob's ghost, Chonradt must strive to live a pure and holy life, lest he suffer the same fate....

What bothered Chonradt Stocklin today, as he walked down the familiar forest path he had avoided all year, was the preternatural stillness. The autumn woods might *always* seem silent to a city dweller, but to a villager like Chonradt they were ordinarily very much alive—with the song of birds, the sound of the brook, and the voice of the wind shaking down the golden leaves.

But today, even the voices of Nature were still....

And suddenly, the figure of Jakob Walch stood before him, as if in a burst of light. He who had once been a cowherd was now robed in spotless white, and a bright red cross flamed upon his breast.

"Come.... Follow me...follow me," intoned the voice of Jakob Walch.

The apparition struck Chonradt Stocklin with such power that he felt himself falling, losing consciousness, and as he tumbled to the ground, he knew that he would follow....

Chonradt Stocklin followed Jakob Walch on a visionary journey to the Otherworld, where he saw the dead in states of both suffering and joy. Walch instructed him to pray, go to Mass, and honor the sacraments. Over the next seven years, Jakob Walch would appear to Stocklin many times, always with similar instructions. Then, in 1586, Chonradt Stocklin was accused of witchcraft.[6]

Inasmuch as the testimony of Chonradt Stocklin is gleaned from the witch trials, we may be struck by the pious Christian overtones of his visionary experience. This is a matter to which we shall return, but for now, it is enough to note that Stocklin's piety availed him but little—the judges, who disregarded the Christian character of the dead cowherd's advice, subjected Stocklin to torture until they succeeded in forcing him to say that he was a witch who went regularly to orgiastic Sabbats. They also succeeded in compelling him to implicate several village women, who were eventually burned at the stake along with Stocklin.

THE OTHERWORLD CALL IN EUROPEAN WITCHLORE

What is important to our purposes is the shamanic nature of Stocklin's experience, for it is clear that he was "called by the spirits" in a manner reminiscent of Bran the Voyager, Connla the Fair, Thomas the Rhymer, or for that matter, of Black Elk, the Lakota shaman.

Stocklin was not entirely unique. Let us return to the trial of Joan of Arc. She, too, heard "spirit voices," which she took to be the voices of angels and saints. Her inquisitors attempted to imply that these were, in fact, the voices of demons. Whether or not Joan's judges were motivated largely by political concerns matters little in this context; what is important is that individuals who heard such voices could be and sometimes were accused of witchcraft.

But what, precisely, was Joan's experience? She said that at the age of thriteen she had heard a voice from God which came to guide her:

> And this voice came towards noon, in summer, in her father's garden.... She heard the voice on her right, in the direction of the church; and she seldom heard it without a light. This light came from the same side as the voice, and generally there was a great light....
>
> ...She said that if she was in a wood she easily heard the voices come to her.[7]

At first, Joan believed that the voice came "from God," but when she heard it for the third time, she recognized it as the voice of an angel. She testified that the voice always protected her and that she understood its directives. She further testified that the voice told her "once or twice a week" that she should leave Domremy in Burgundy and go to France. And because the voice had told her to go, she could no longer remain where she was. The voice also told her that she was destined to raise the siege of the city of Orleans—which in fact, she succeeded in doing.

This, at least, is what Joan said of herself. But even during her own time, a number of legends had begun to circulate concerning her voices:

There is also a wood, called the oak-wood, in French le
Boischesnu, *which can be seen from her father's door, not
more than half a league away. She does not know, nor has
she ever heard, that the fairies repair there; but she has
heard from her brother that in the country around it is said
she received her message at the tree; but she says she did
not, and she told him quite the contrary.*[8]

We may remember that Thomas the Rhymer received his
"shamanic call" while sleeping beneath a fairy tree. Joan, like Stocklin, heard her voices easily when she was in the woods, though she
assured her judges that she did *not* receive the call while standing
beneath an oak tree, magical or otherwise. The country people, however, seem to have believed that she *should* have done so—that a magical tree was the right and proper setting for someone to receive the
initiatory call from the spirit world.

Like Black Elk, Chonradt Stocklin and Joan of Arc were summoned to their shamanic vocation by spirit voices. The actual content of the experience is quite similar: what is vastly different is the
outcome. Black Elk's vision gave him an honored status in his community. The visions of Stocklin and Joan resulted in their being
burned at the stake.

Nevertheless, there is some evidence that at least a few rural communities valued those village members who were capable of undergoing shamanic experiences. Earlier in this book, we met a fictional
peasant by the name of Giacomo, who described himself as a benandante. The benandanti or "good walkers" lived in Friuli, a region in
the extreme northeast of Italy, and their activities appear in the court
records of the witch trials during the 1500s and 1600s. These individuals, most of whom were born with a caul and thus selected for their
vocation, left their bodies during the Ember Days, when the doors
between this world and the Otherworld were believed to be open.
They joined the hosts of the wandering dead and, aided by those who
were still well disposed toward the living, fought astral battles against
"witches" and ghosts who might seek to blight the harvest.

*During her trial for witchcraft, Joan of Arc was
accused of dancing around a sacred tree*

Like Joan, whose voices instructed her to save her people by going into France and driving the English out of the land, the benandanti were concerned with protecting their communities, serving the people and the land. Perhaps it is for this reason that their neighbors seldom accused them of witchcraft until well after the persecutions had become a general mania that affected almost everyone. It is also interesting to note that the benandanti, even when accused, were almost never convicted.

In fact, the "good walkers" constituted a brotherhood (and sisterhood), initiation into which involved selection and training by other shamans. Those born with the caul were duly noted by the older benandanti and, when they came of age, were approached by senior members of the group and thus called to their vocation. In 1591, a cowherd named Menichino della Nota testified that fifteen or sixteen years previously another peasant by the name of Giambattista Tamburlino had invited him to walk to the next village in search of "some fun." It was a winter night, and the two peasants were walking single file through the snow. Then Tamburlino informed Menichino that both of them were benandanti, and that Menichino must "go with him." When Menichino replied that he would not go, Tamburlino told him: "When you have to come, you will come." Menichino stubbornly insisted that no one would be able to make him do so, to which Tamburlino replied: "You will have to come anyway. One goes as though in a smoky haze; we do not go physically."[9]

There even seems to have been some initiation rite that involved being called by a drum. (Do we see here an echo of shamanic spirit drumming?) In 1580, a Friulian town crier named Battista Moduco gave the following testimony:

> Questioned: how long have you been involved with this, and are you now? he replied:
>
> It is eight years and more that I have not participated. One enters at the age of twenty, and is freed at forty, if he so wishes.

Questioned: how does one enter this company of benan-danti, he replied:

All those who have been born with the caul belong to it, and when they reach the age of twenty they are summoned by means of a drum the same as soldiers, and they are obliged to respond....

Questioned: who is it that comes to summon you, God, or an angel, a man, or a devil? he replied:

He is a man just like us, who is placed above us all and beats a drum, and calls us.[10]

Two traditional modes of shamanic initiation—training by older shamans and a call from the spirits—appear to be present in the context of the witch trials, but we are still missing any evidence regarding that all-important death-and-rebirth experience which is so fundamental to shamanic initiation.

It is possible, however, that the mythic images associated with that process—and a provocative hint of the process itself—may in fact be found in one of the most grotesque and puzzling elements in European witchlore.

THE CAULDRON OF REBIRTH

It was often alleged against the witches that they indulged in cannibalistic orgies, cooking and eating the flesh and bones of slain children during Sabbat rituals. Between 1435 and 1437, a German Dominican named Johannes Nider spent time at an ecumenical council in Basel, Switzerland. He was at that time in the process of composing a book entitled *Formicarius*—a theological treatise which compared the customs of men and ants. At Basel he had the opportunity to meet with a number of inquisitors who were then hard at work burning Swiss peasants; these individuals supplied Nider with the information contained in Book V of the *Formicarius*, which deals with witchcraft and magic. Nider tells us that it was the custom among witches to wage magical attacks upon children in their cribs, and thus to murder them. After the children had been buried, the witches dug them up and cooked them in a pot until the flesh turned into a pulp and fell from the bones. The more solid part of this repulsive substance was used as an ointment which, when rubbed onto the witches' skin, assisted their transformation into animals. The liquid part was drunk during initiation rituals into the so-called "sect" of the witches.[11]

Most scholars have seen, in Nider's rantings, a long tradition of persecution and paranoia which had nothing to do with the witches themselves. It has been pointed out that, during the days of the Roman Empire, Pagans accused Christians of cannibalistic feasts; later, Christians made similar accusations against Jews. During the heresy hunts that immediately preceded the witch trials, the same stories were revived against the Cathars and Waldensians. Therefore, if we hope to see in these accusations anything save the paranoid distrust of a mainstream group against outsiders, we are probably on the wrong track.

Or so it would seem, save for one very interesting story that has a direct bearing on our search.

We have seen, in the previous chapter, that the Orphic mystics of ancient Greece retained a world-view that was essentially shamanic, including the World Tree and the Well of Memory. The Orphics also maintained traditions that were quite different from the "standard" versions of the Greek myths, and one of the most important of these was "the dismemberment of Dionysus."

In the Orphic myth, Dionysus was not the child of Zeus and the mortal maiden Semele; rather, he was the son of Zeus who, in the form of a lion, coupled with the Underworld goddess Persephone. Fearing the wrath of his wife Hera, Zeus hid the child somewhere in the wild. But the Titans, the old deposed earth gods of Greek myth, found him anyway and, at Hera's instigation, tore him to pieces. They placed the fragments in a cauldron and boiled them. Whether or not the fragments were eaten or intended to be eaten is not altogether clear from the surviving fragments of the myth; however, Dionysus was rescued by his grandmother Rhea, mother of the gods and the

Cretan form of the Great Goddess. She reconstituted him and brought him back to life (and, as we shall see, she probably did so by singing over his bones).

In this story, we recognize a typically shamanic initiation process that is comprised of being:

- Torn to pieces by "demons";
- Reduced to a skeletal state;
- Cooked in a cauldron;
- Resurrected.

This myth became the basis of an initiation ritual among the Orphics, for we are told that initiatory candidates had their faces powdered white with ashes, representative of the "earth-born Titans."

The story has some interesting particularities. Dionysus, like the supposed infant victims of the witches, is stolen from the cradle and cooked in a cauldron. The Orphics embodied all this in an initiation ritual, and the broth allegedly made from the bones of dead children was likewise said to be consumed by witches as part of an initiation ritual. What, then, lies behind the paranoid ramblings of Nider and his wild surmises about the habits of men, witches, and ants? It is impossible to believe that villagers of late medieval Europe actually stole their neighbors' children for horrid cannibalistic feasts. There is no question that the fantasies of the inquisitors were largely responsible for this gruesome scenario. And yet the lineaments of shamanic initiatory practice can be perceived here, and in a formula not dissimilar to that of the Orphic myth.

Is it just possible that the ecclesiastical fantasy of boiling children in a cauldron contains some kernel of fact, deeply misunderstood and twisted by the minds of the inquisitors?

To make such an argument based only on Nider and the Orphics would be somewhat far-fetched, but the cauldron that appears in both sources is well-known in European lore, and it is clearly linked with the shamanic cauldron of rebirth and regeneration that appeared in the Samoyed initiate's vision. We have already noted the presence of a cauldron in the tale of Llew Llaw Gyffes, which is found in the

Fourth Branch of *The Mabinogion*. This, however, is not the only such vessel that appears in that collection of tales. The Second Branch contains a cauldron that King Bran gives to his sister Branwen and the King of Ireland as a wedding present. Whenever slain warriors are tossed into it, they are immediately reborn, ready to fight again. When the King of Ireland mistreats his wife Branwen, her brother Bran collects his champions and heroes, invades Ireland, and fights a war replete with feats of magic (much garbled by the Christian redactors of the old story) which ends with the cauldron exploding and Bran suffering from a fatal (and hence magical) wound in the heel.* He instructs his men to cut off his head, which then, like the head of Orpheus or Mimir, becomes an oracle.

In *The Mabinogion*, the cauldron given by Bran is said to have come originally from Ireland. The King of Ireland is himself already familiar with it, and claims that it was first seen among mortals when a giant man and woman emerged from a lake, the man bearing the cauldron on his back. This, then, must be the same cauldron that is known in Irish myth as the Cauldron of the Dagda, for that god is also said to have borne the vessel upon his back.

The Cauldron of the Dagda was one of the four treasures brought to Ireland by the Tuatha de Danaan (i.e., the gods), and it had the same properties attributed to Bran and Branwen's Cauldron of Rebirth—the bodies of the slain, if thrown into it, would be regenerated. The four treasures of the Tuatha de Danaan appear in later myth as the four treasures of the Grail, with the cauldron itself recast as a mysterious "grail," said to be the cup from which Christ drank at the Last Supper. Thus the shamanic cauldron of rebirth was transformed into a Christian symbol as well as a "hellish cauldron" in which witches mixed their "foul brews."

A tale similar to that of Bran's invasion of Ireland is found in "The Spoils of Annwn," which, as we have already seen, places the shaman

---

* Shamans are often lame or, in myth, suffer a "magical wound" in the heel or thigh. Notable examples are Chiron, Achilles, Hephaestus, and the Biblical Jacob.

Gwydion in an Underworld "bone fortress." In this poem, King Arthur and his knights invade the Land of Annwn (the Otherworld), bringing back the "spoils," which include a magic cauldron. As we have already noted, the Land of Annwn includes that "Revolving Castle" wherein Gwydion was "imprisoned in the bone fortress." The cauldron of rebirth, then, is to be found right where initiatory shamanic visions usually find it—in the Otherworld.

Irish myth sometimes calls this vessel of rebirth the Cauldron of the Dagda, but it is more often associated with a goddess than a god. Another Irish tale records the journey of King Cormac to the Otherworld, where he meets the Lord and Lady of that land; it is the Lady who holds the magic cup and extends it to Cormac. Similarly, the Fisher King may be the lord of the Grail Castle, but the Grail itself is carried by a maiden called Repanse de Schoye (Chosen Response). A Welsh folktale, sometimes attached to *The Mabinogion*, concerns the "cauldron of Cerridwen," which is a cauldron of inspiration rather than of rebirth (i.e., a Well of Memory rather than a Well of Forgetfulness); its possessor is the hag or witch Cerridwen, who was probably once a goddess. Another one-time goddess is the Irish saint Bridget, depicted in pious legend as a slave girl in charge of her master's pantry. When she gave of the pantry's bounty to passing strangers, the pantry always became full again, so that her master never noticed any lack. Bridget's pantry is one more redaction of the Cauldron of Rebirth.

As we have seen, it was Rhea, the Cretan Great Goddess and mother of the gods, who brought Dionysus back from the dead; she too is a "mistress of the cauldron." It is one of the primary functions of the Goddess to restore the dismembered shaman to life—a magical feat accomplished through spells, chants and songs. And we may find evidence, in the witch trials themselves, that she still performed that function in the late Middle Ages.

Let us proceed, then, to meet the Old Bone Goddess.

DEATH AND REBIRTH

The death-and-rebirth experience that shamans undergo in vision may also be accessed through meditation. In fact, practitioners of Tantric Yoga have been doing precisely this for centuries: meditating, often in graveyards or on cremation grounds, on their own deaths. The exercise below is a variant on this age-old tradition. It has been given a contemporary flavor, however, because to envision ourselves dying as our distant ancestors died has a great deal less impact than envisioning our own deaths as they might actually occur.

DO NOT ATTEMPT THIS EXERCISE IF YOU ARE DEPRESSED OR PHYSICALLY UNWELL!

1. Lie down flat on your back, with your hands folded across your chest—the position that, in our society, corpses generally occupy in their coffins. Ideally, the room should be almost (but not quite) dark. Imagine that the walls of a coffin enclose you; you are trapped inside, and cannot move. Allow the feeling of claustrophobia full range, uncomfortable though it may be.

2. When you have grasped the feeling that your physical body is trapped inside a coffin, start breathing deeply. With each breath, fill yourself with light. With each breath, realize that the body is transient and that your essence is immortal.

3. When at last your body is filled with light, imagine yourself rising up, walking away from the coffin, from the imprisoned carcass. Walk to the door and gaze back at yourself through the dimness of the room. You should be able to fully envision your body lying there, perfectly still, your eyes dull, your skin ashen and waxy.

4. Using all the powers of your imagination, envision your friends and family carrying your coffin to its final resting place. Watch with a quiet sense of detachment as they decorate the casket with flowers and wreaths; watch as you are laid in the earth.

Continue watching as time goes by; the crowds have vanished; the flowers fade, then blow away. If you have a vivid and fearless imagination, you may be able to imagine your body decaying beneath the earth; you may be able to smell it, to feel the quiet, industrious work of the worms.

5. Now let your mind soar free. The light that fills you, that continues to grow stronger with each breath, has become an all-encompassing flame. Mentally, shout out "I AM!" and leap into that blazing light.

6. When you have been entirely absorbed into the light, you may open your eyes. Take your time. Feel that the light is still within you, regenerating you, filling you with power, energy, and renewed vitality. Give thanks.

THE SPIRIT DRUM

The Samoyed shaman who underwent his initiatory vision during three days of illness journeyed to the World Tree; there, the Lord of the Tree gave him a great branch from which to carve the three drums that would aid him in his magic.

Shamans all over the world have used drumming to induce a trance state and thereby begin the Otherworldly journey. Though evidence for shamanic drumming in Europe is sparse, there are a few provocative hints; we have seen how Battista Moduco, the benandante, testified that he and his spiritual cohorts were summoned with a drum.

A shaman typically acquires his or her drum after successfully completing the initiatory experience. When you feel you have mastered the death-and-rebirth exercise detailed above, you will want to acquire a drum to aid you with some of the other exercises in this book. Traditionally, shamans carved their own drums. If you are skilled with crafts, this is a marvelous thing to do, for it makes the drum your own in a way that nothing else can.

However, it is easy nowadays to buy a drum in any "New Age" store. Some of these are made by Native American peoples who have their own shamanic practices; others are not. Buy whatever kind of drum you please, but try to avoid huge pieces that are difficult to haul around; this could inhibit your practical work later on. A drum whose head is about ten inches in diameter is nice and handy.

In any event, you must somehow make the drum a magical object that is entirely your own. One of the best ways to do this is by decorating it. You may wish, for instance, to hang objects from it—Native Americans typically attach feathers, stones, etc. to their drums. Though the possession of eagle feathers is illegal in the United States (unless you happen to be a "card-carrying" Native American), you might consider using swan feathers, for the swan was one of the principal shamanic birds of old Europe. The favorite stone of European shamans was amber. If you wish, you may attach objects to your drum with red cord or thread, for most ancient European peoples regarded red as the color of vitality and of the life force.

Shamans often decorate the heads of their drums with magical symbols and pictures. You may wish to paint a simple line drawing on the head of your drum.

After you've found your drum, just practice beating it.

CHAPTER 3

The Old Bone Goddess

THE SHAMANIC BONE MOTHER

Among the Yakut shamans of Siberia, the World Tree is a great fir that grows in the farthest north. In the branches of the tree nests the Bird of Prey Mother, who has iron feathers, an iron beak, hooked claws, and the head of an eagle. Shamans are born from the eggs she lays in the World Tree.

When the shaman, now in the world of men, is ready to undergo his spiritual birth, he will meet the Bird of Prey Mother again. She will carry his soul in her iron beak to the Underworld and leave it to ripen on the branches of a pine tree. When the soul is ripe she will bring it back to this world, tear the shaman's body to bits, and distribute the pieces to the various demons of death and disease. The demons will consume the pieces of the shaman's dismembered corpse. When they are done, the Bird of Prey Mother will gather together the shaman's bones and restore them to life—at which point the shaman himself, dreaming in his visionary trance, will awaken to the world again.

57

This female figure, whom we shall call the Old Bone Goddess, appears in various forms throughout the mythology and spiritual practice of Europe, Tibet, and India (she is less often to be found among the shamanic cultures of North and South America). In Tibet, she takes the form of the various female demons who torment the initiate during the *bardo* state which occurs between lifetimes. In India, we may trace her physiognomy through Kali and other goddesses associated with popular Tantric worship. These goddesses dance on the corpses of men and gods, their fangs dripping with blood, skulls around their waists. One of them, Chinnamasta, is even headless, like the shaman in his or her initiatory ordeal.

We have noted that Tantric adepts undergo the process of death and rebirth meditatively, contemplating their own death and dissolution in graveyards and on cremation grounds. In time, they will be graced with a vision of one of the Tantric goddesses who will appear, no longer in her dark and fearsome aspect, but as a creature of great beauty.

In ancient Europe, the Old Bone Goddess is to be met with almost everywhere, in a splendid variety of shapes and characters. The predominance of the old shamanic goddess in Europe—as opposed to her relative scarcity in the Americas—suggests a fundamental orientation in the myth systems of ancient European peoples. Marija Gimbutas, professor of archaeology at UCLA, has devoted a large part of her career to tracing the goddess through Neolithic Europe. She draws attention to the great number of goddess images and figurines in the oldest settled communities of that continent, the farming villages of the Balkans, which flourished from the eighth to the third millennia B.C.[1] The majority of Pagan feminists regard witchcraft, or Wicca, as quintessentially a survival of such an ancient Neolithic religion, one based primarily on worship of the Goddess. In this book, we consider the victims of the witchcraft trials as participants in a shamanic world view, one which includes, but is not exclusively centered on, the Goddess. Nevertheless, it is clear that the Goddess had a stronger presence in Europe than she did on other continents; it is also clear that she is one of the star performers in the witchcraft trials.

To detail the various forms of the Old Bone Goddess would fill several books; only the merest suggestion of her vastness can be hinted at here. Let us, then, examine those aspects of the goddess which have the most direct bearing upon European shamanism and upon the witch trials.

THE WHITE LADY IN EUROPEAN MYTH

Digging among the Neolithic villages of southeastern Europe, Dr. Gimbutas often came upon stylized female figurines—stiff, austere, carved in white, and perforated with holes. She believes these figurines represent a deity she calls the Old European Goddess of Death and Rebirth, and in whom we may recognize the even older shamanic Bone Mother. Gimbutas points out that, even up to the present day, death appears in European folklore as a spectral "white lady." This archetypal image, she declares, goes all the way back to the Neolithic.[2]

Some Pagan feminists, following the argument of Robert Graves in his influential book *The White Goddess*, regard the White Lady's color as signifying that she is primarily a goddess of the moon. Indeed, the moon, in its waxing and waning, is a universal metaphor for the inner spiritual process we call death and rebirth—the spiritual process that forms the core of the shamanic experience. But spiritual metaphors exist on a number of levels, and the White Goddess takes her color from the whiteness of skeletal bones as much as from the moon.

The White Lady is perhaps most familiar to us as the banshee of Irish folklore, the spectral female figure whose appearance portends death, and it is quite possible that the Old Bone Goddess has a long history in the British Isles, for she is often associated with megalithic monuments. In Chapter 1, we mentioned the "White Wife," a great standing stone, painted white and personified as female. Various dolmens around Ireland are named "Grania's Bed," ostensibly in reference to the beautiful Grania, snatched from a loveless marriage to the aging Finn MacCool by her lover Dermot, an early Irish incarnation of Sir Lancelot. Among these dolmens, we are told, the lovers paused to rest while they fled through the land, pursued by Finn. The word *grania* literally means "hag," an unlikely name for a beautiful princess. "Grania's Bed," then, is the "Hag's Bed," another suggestion that the megaliths were associated with the Old Bone Goddess.

As we may see from the Orphic myth of Dionysus, as well as Yakut shamanic tradition, the Old Bone Goddess is primarily concerned with gathering up the bones of the dead and restoring them to life. The earliest megalithic structures, great chambered tombs like Newgrange and West Kennet, were repositories of bones—the skeletons of village members were collected and stored in individual cists or chambers within the tombs. Often enough, they were painted with red ocher—red, as the color of blood and, hence, of vitality, symbolized life and rebirth. Most tombs from this period (3,500 to 2,000 B.C.) face west, and in later Celtic myth the west was the direction whence lay Tir-na-nog, the Land of Youth, sometimes called the Island of Women (like the Land of Shamanesses in the Samoyed shaman's initiatory vision, described in the previous chapter). These early megalithic tombs all contain forecourts, enclosed areas in which rituals are believed to have been held. Were the bones of the dead, painted with the color of life and rebirth, carried into these forecourts to serve as

Megalithic tomb

the focus for rituals of communal regeneration? And was the Old Bone Mother the principal deity in such rites?

Whatever her history may be in the Neolithic, the Bone Goddess is abundantly present in the later mythologies of Iron Age Europe. The collector of bones appears in a variety of forms, typically bird-like, for after all, she is the Bird of Prey Mother. As recently as 1976, an Irish woman described the banshee as "a bird, you'd hear the flutter of the wings...And they say it is a bird, not a woman, a bird."[3] More specifically, the banshee was often said to be a crow or raven. The Irish goddess of battle, called the Morrigan or Morrigu, likewise appears in animal form as a raven who gathers up the bodies of slain warriors. In later medieval legend, she becomes the enchantress Morgan le Fay, much lovelier but still performing her archetypal task, for it is she who bears the mortally-wounded Arthur across the water to Avalon (equivalent to the Celtic Otherworld, Tir-na-nog, or the Island of Women), where he will be healed and restored.

In Norse myth, the Old Bone Goddess appears in multiple form as the Valkyries, who, like the Morrigan, haunt the battlefields, riding forth on winged horses to gather up the bodies of the dead. The pretty girls on winged horses, however, constitute a later and much softer image than did the original Valkyries, who, in very early Scandinavian carvings, are depicted as bird-like creatures with great claws. Often, they swoop down on their own dark wings rather than on attractive white steeds, although sometimes they ride on wolves, or in a great boat sailing through blood-drenched skies.

In the Icelandic *Saga of Burnt Njal*, there are twelve of them, and they appear in one man's vision just before the Battle of Clontarf, weaving upon a loom that is made of men's entrails and weighted with severed heads. The dead warriors whose bodies are retrieved by the Valkyries will later be brought back to life in Valhalla, where they will enjoy an existence comprised of eternal feasting. (This Feast of the Dead is a matter of extreme importance in the history of the witch trials, as we shall see.)

Shamanic initiation

The spectral Valkyries who appear in *The Saga of Burnt Njal* bear a strong resemblance to the Three Fates of Greek myth, as well as to the Norns, who played the same role in Viking lore. These three wise women—Past, Present, and Future—weave the destiny of human beings, just as the Valkyries in *Njal's Saga* weave the fates of those who will fight in the coming battle. Even Odin (a great shaman in his own right, but a newcomer among the gods when compared to the Old Bone Mother) cannot change their decisions. And where do the Norns sit as they weave? At the Well of Fate which lies at the root of the World Tree. In the three worlds of the shamanic cosmos, the Bone Mother dwells below.

The Bone Mother, then, is primarily an Underworld goddess, and it is to her dark, mysterious realm that all of us—whether we be shamans or not—must one day travel in order to experience rebirth. Thus Ishtar, the love goddess of ancient Babylon and Sumer, traveled to the Underworld to seek her dead lover Tammuz. In the depths she encountered Ereshkigal, a terrifying Queen of the Dead, with leeches in her hair. The Old Bone Mother hung fair Ishtar on a meat hook in the coldest cavern of hell, precisely as the souls of Yakut shamans are draped on the branches of the World Tree by the Bird of Prey Mother.

Aphrodite, another goddess of love, made a similar journey in hopes of rescuing her slain lover Adonis. She was, in fact, able to win him resurrection of a sort, though only through bargaining with Persephone, the Queen of the Greek Underworld and the principal goddess of the shamanistic Orphic cult. Like the Valkyries, Persephone has been cleaned up by later generations of mythographers—she is most familiar to us as the sweet virgin who was carried off by dark Hades while innocently gathering flowers in the fields of Eleusis, but her name means "she who is to be feared," suggesting that she, too, was once a fearsome death mother with serpents in her hair.

More often than not, the Underworld (or, more accurately, Otherworld) Queen works in consort with a mate. Ereshkigal shared her throne with Nergal, and Persephone with Hades. The Celtic Lady of the Cauldron who makes her appearance in tales of Otherworld journeys (some of which were quoted in the previous chapter) also has a male counterpart, whose name varies from story to story, but is most often Mannanan mac Lir, the old Irish god of the sea. Sometimes, however, the Otherworld Goddess reigns alone, like the Norse Hel (the Mother Hulda of *Grimms' Fairy Tales*).

One way or another, it is to her realm that we must travel to be stirred and regenerated in the Cauldron of Rebirth. Though we may simply be dropped into the goddess' cauldron in order to be made new again, it is equally likely that she will sing magic charms over us in order to restore us.

The *Kalevala*, a group of magic tales and shamanic chants collected in Finland, tells the story of Lemminkainen (Lover Boy), who journeyed to the far northern regions of Lapland to woo the daughter of the Old Woman of North Farm. But the Old Woman set three tasks for Lemminkainen, feats of heroism and magic which he must accomplish before she would even consider giving him her daughter. Lemminkainen succeeded in his first two labors, but then the Old

Woman set him the most difficult task of all—he must shoot the swan that swims in the River of the Dead. Lemminkainen lay in wait by the Underworld river, awaiting the swan, and it was there that he came to grief. One of his old enemies, a grubby cowherd named Soppy Hat (reminiscent of the strange, sometimes silly names given to demons in many aboriginal traditions), was also waiting there. He shot Lemminkainen with a magic dart. Lemminkainen tumbled into the River of the Dead and was engulfed by a great whirlpool, wherein the son of the Underworld King sliced him into eight pieces with a sword.

Finally, Lemminkainen's mother (who had warned him against going to North Farm in the first place) went to look for her son. She dredged the River of the Dead with a rake and brought up all the pieces. She reconstructed the body and tied all the veins together. Then she sang. She called upon various gods and spirits to fill Lemminkainen's veins with vital energy. She called upon a humble bee to travel to the three realms (a familiar shamanic theme) and bring back honey, which she smeared upon Lemminkainen's corpse. Finally, he awoke to life again. This is essentially the same story as the Egyptian myth of Isis and Osiris, wherein Isis gathers up the dismembered pieces of Osiris and sings him back to life again with magic chants.

The Old Bone Mother's rejuvenation therapies are not limited to human beings—she performs the same operation on animals. This is fitting, for in one of her other incarnations she is the Animal Mother, another familiar figure in Siberian shamanic lore. Many goddesses who embody the death-and-rebirth process are associated with specific totem animals: Welsh Rhiannon or Gallic Epona with the horse, Greek Artemis with the bear, Norse Freya with the cat, and Irish Morrigan with the raven or crow.

Deities associated with the Underworld (and, as we have seen, the Old Bone Goddess is essentially an Underworld goddess) often tend to have dominion over the earth which lies immediately above them, perhaps because everything that grows on the earth emerges from *underneath*, from the realm of the Underworld King and Queen. Thus the animals, as creatures of the earth, fall under their jurisdiction. The Greek goddess Artemis, who appears frequently in the witch trials under her Roman name of Diana, is a classic Animal Mother, roving through the wild forests accompanied by bears, dogs, wolves, and other creatures. Even "smiling Aphrodite" occasionally manifests as the Animal Mother, for she came to meet her lover Anchises trailed by a whole menagerie of critters, including lynxes and bees.

Thus we find that it is part of the Bone Mother's business to resuscitate the bodies of slain animals. She undergoes some fairly peculiar metamorphoses in the process. One of the names given to the Goddess during the witch trials was Pharaildis, in reality, the name of a fairly innocuous German saint. Saint Pharaildis, however, was said to have resurrected a goose by collecting its bones. The Old Bone Goddess does not act alone in this regard—her spouse, the Underworld Lord, performs the same service for members of the animal kingdom.

The Norse goddess Freya with her cats

According to a work composed by Danish missionaries in the 1700s, Lapp shamans gathered up and arranged the bones of sacrificed animals with great care, placing them in a basket of birch twigs and then erecting above them a carved tree trunk portraying the lightning god Horagalles with his hammer. This Horagalles, claimed the Lapps, would restore life to the animal victims, and they would become even fatter than they were before. The name Horagalles is clearly related to the Norse Thor, who (according to the *Prose Edda*) resurrected several rams by striking them with his hammer. The semi-legendary Saint Germanus, evangelist to the Celts, performed the same "miracle" with slaughtered oxen.

The Old Bone Mother's ability to resuscitate dead animals shows up in some very unlikely places—for example, in the fairy tale of Cinderella.

There are literally hundreds of versions of the Cinderella story, for it is one of the most widespread folktales in the world. The version familiar to most of us, which is French and almost insufferably cute, was written down by Charles Perrault in 1597. But even in this version, there are several clues that remain to indicate that Cinderella is engaged in the shamanic journey to the Otherworld. First of all, there's her name: she is Ella of the Cinders, and ashes appear in many versions of the story. And as we have seen, they also appear on the faces of Orphic initiates, symbolizing the Otherworldly journey. We should also remember that many shamans are lame or have some sort of magical wound involving feet or thighs—witness Chiron, Achilles, Hephaestus, King Bran, the Fisher King, and the Biblical Jacob. Sometimes the motif of "being shod in only one sandal" is substituted for the wounded foot, as with Jason, Perseus, and (at the Villa of the Mysteries in Pompeii) Dionysus.* This explains Cinderella's unusual problems with her footwear.

---

* Why should a shaman have only one sandal? It has been speculated that this theme has to do with shamans who took the crane as their totem animal. However, this author believes it is more properly linked with the idea of asymmetry, an adjunct of the Otherworld journey. As we shall see, shamans come back from the Otherworld all mixed up, or asymmetrical.

Then there is the matter of her fairy godmother, who, in some versions, is not at all the good-natured bumbler of the Disney cartoon. In a Scottish tale recorded in the late nineteenth century and entitled "Rushy Coat" (a humble coat of rushes has been substituted for the face full of cinders), the Cinderella character cherishes a calf that has been left to her by her real mother. The evil stepmother kills the calf. But then the slain animal magically speaks, instructing Cinderella to *gather up and arrange its bones*. She does this, placing them under a stone. From that moment on, the animal is, for all purposes, resurrected, for it performs magical wonders on her behalf throughout the rest of the story. Cinderella, then, is none other than the Old Bone Goddess herself.

In fact, the Bone Goddess makes frequent appearances in European folklore, just as Marija Gimbutas has claimed, and appears in a variety of guises. The Brothers Grimm tell the tale of "Mother Hulda," which chronicles the adventures of two girls. One, like Cinderella, is a stepchild; though she is beautiful, her stepmother hates her and favors her own daughter, an ugly, lazy creature. The beautiful stepdaughter is spinning by a well one day. So industrious is she that her fingers begin to bleed; the spindle becomes slippery and she accidentally drops it down the well.

Her evil stepmother is infuriated, and orders the girl to find the lost spindle. Thus the girl dives into the well and winds up in a beautiful land—the Otherworld. There she encounters an old woman named Mother Hulda, who at first strikes terror into the girl's heart on account of her huge teeth (suitable for a Bird of Prey Mother). But the old woman is kindly, asking only that the girl do an honest day's work. So she does the household chores, making up Mother Hulda's bed and shaking out the feathers (which causes it to snow in the human world), and so on. In return, she is fed well, and, when she at last becomes homesick, she is rewarded: a shower of gold falls upon her as she walks out Mother Hulda's door, and the gold is still with her when she returns to the world above.

Now the stepmother is determined to win some gold for her own daughter. She sends the lazy girl down the well to Mother Hulda. But the shiftless creature only pretends to do the work; in reality, she wastes her time all day (as a result of which it fails to snow in the human world). When she is ready to go home, she stands hopefully in Mother Hulda's door, only to be covered with black, greasy pitch, which will stick to her for the rest of her life.

Of all European countries, Russia retains the most nearly complete portrait of the Old Bone Mother, which is not surprising, inasmuch as many of Gimbutas' "white lady" figurines came from what is now the Ukraine. One of the most popular figures in Russian folklore is the witch Baba Yaga. Her revolving hut in the forest stands on a pair of chicken legs, and the fence around it is made of human bones, the spikes topped with grinning skulls, the doorway of the house fashioned out of human leg bones. Around the hut circle three horsemen; a white horseman who

Baba Yaga with her mortar and pestle

brings the early dawn, a red one who brings the sun, and a black one who brings the night.

Baba Yaga herself is called the "boney-legged," and she sports a huge nose. She travels through the sky in a mortar and pestle, and sweeps her footprints away behind her with a broom. More often than not, she is malevolent—she tries to eat everyone who comes to her home by popping them into her oven. But, like Mother Hulda, she rewards those who have the courage to serve her well and die the internal death that leads to spiritual transformation.

Vassilisa the Wise is sent to her hut by a typical evil stepmother; the fire in the house has gone out and Vassilisa is to seek "light." Baba Yaga tests her with a number of seemingly impossible, heroic tasks, but when Vassilisa accomplishes them all, she carries home the light in a flaming skull. Those who shirk their work or try to trick the old witch suffer a somewhat darker fate than the lazy girl whom Mother Hulda coated with pitch; their bones are sent home in a basket.

Finally, it is worth noting that the Old Bone Goddess is still with us, alive and well, in the folklore of contemporary Mexico.[4] There she appears as La Loba, the Wolf Woman, a wild crone who is occasionally seen by the local folk, chauffeured through the hot desert night in a black limousine whose back window has been blown out by a shotgun blast, headed for Oaxaca. Somewhere in the hills she has a cave, and there she gathers up the bones of wolves who have died. She reconstitutes them and sings over them. The wolves rise again and lope out into the desert where they are transformed into beautiful women.

If the Goddess of Death and Rebirth has survived from Neolithic times until the twentieth century, then there should be no question that she was alive and well in the European imagination at the time of the witch trials.

And indeed, there is no question about it at all.

SCOTLAND, 1662

The judges were shocked. The beautiful red-haired farm wife had not been tortured or interrogated. For that matter, no one had even accused her of witchcraft! She had come forward of her own accord, she said, in order to confess.

And confess she did. Over and over again, from April all the way to June....

Isobel Gowdie, married to a dim-witted farmer in the village of Auldearne, had led an incredibly boring life, cutting peat and cooking stew on the cold moors near Inverness. Boredom didn't suit her, for she was clearly a woman of intelligence and imagination. Perhaps that was why she had turned to witchcraft....

Now she was talking about how she and a companion had traveled "in the spirit" one night. They had flown through a dark gray sky above an old barrow mound. Then the mound began to open below them, revealing a scene of brightness and great cheer within. Drawn by the joy of it, the women had swooped down into the barrow.

They knew immediately that they had entered the Downy Hills, the realm of the fairies. Inside the mound, it was bright daylight, just as it was night outside. The fairy animals were frolicking about: "There were elf bulls routing and skoiling there at the entry, which feared me," Isobel said.

Isobel Gowdie met the King and Queen of Elfland. "The King of Fairy is a brave man, well favored and broad faced," she told the judges. And as for the Queen, "She is bravely clothed in white linens, and in white and brown clothes."

And what had Isobel done during her night in the Hollow Hills?

She had feasted with the fairies. "I got meat there from the Queen of Fairy, more than I could eat," she said.

After the feast, there had been a hunt. The little elvish boys had plenty of elvish arrows, made by the Devil himself. Isobel and her friend took to the air again and went shooting with the elves. They were hunting human game. At first Isobel had a bit of trouble learning to throw the arrows properly, but in time she managed to bring down a ploughman with a fatal elf-shot. Annoyingly enough, however, she'd missed that damnable Laird of Park when she'd taken a shot at him....

The judges, however, were sitting up now. They had yawned their way through Isobel's yammering about the Queen of the Elves; peasant superstition was of no interest to them.

But now they'd heard the word they wanted to hear.

The sheriff of Auldearne rapped his gavel; the pastor cleared his throat. "You mentioned the Devil," said the sheriff, eagerly. "Tell us more about him."

Isobel had plenty to say about the Devil; we shall return to her revelations later on.[5]

After three centuries, Isobel Gowdie remains a bit mysterious. Why should she confess voluntarily, risking a hanging when no one had even accused her? Was she mentally ill?

No one knows. Isobel Gowdie implicated a number of other Auldearne women as fellow witches (incidentally, Isobel was the first person to use the word "coven" and fix its membership at thirteen). None of them tried to wriggle out of the accusation; they all backed up Isobel's testimony, word for word, and they did so with what the judges must certainly have regarded as "unseemly pride." But whether or not Isobel's brains were rattled, she was certainly well informed about peasant superstition—a matter of more interest to us than it was to her judges.

THE FAIRY QUEEN

The elvish rambles of people like Isobel Gowdie and Thomas the Rhymer were not isolated incidents; the common folk of the British Isles had been visiting the fairy realm for centuries, as this thirteenth century monk's complaint clearly shows:

> But, I ask, what is to be said of those wretched and super-
> stitious persons who say that by night they see most fair
> queens and other maidens tripping with the lady Diana and

*leading the dances with the goddess of the pagans, who in
our vulgar tongue are called Elves, and believe that the latter transform men and women into other shapes and conduct them to Elvelond, where now, as they say, dwell
those mighty champions...all of which are only phantoms
displayed by an evil spirit?*[6]

The appearances of the Fairy Queen or her associates are so
numerous, and she is known by so many names, that we can chronicle
only the most outstanding examples.

In the last chapter, we encountered a benandante named
Menichino della Nota who was initiated by a friend on a back country
road. He affirmed that during his nocturnal journeys to Josaphat's
Field (the name by which the benandante knew the Otherworld), he
encountered a lady who sat upon the edge of a well and who was
called the abbess. In 1619, another benandante named Maria Panzona
spoke of the same "abbess," and added that all the benandanti did
homage to her by bowing their heads. Writing in 1457, the Italian
theologian Nicholas of Cusa mentions two old women who worshipped a "good mistress" named Richella, who came to them at night
as a well-dressed woman, though they never saw her face clearly.

Sometimes more than one mysterious female figure makes an
appearance. In sixteenth-century Sicily, a number of women stated
that they periodically met with mysterious women they called "ladies
from outside" (or, variously, the Beautiful Ladies, Night Women, and
Mistresses of the House). They flew through the air with these "ladies
from outside" to feast in meadows or remote castles. The supernatural
women were beautifully dressed, like Richella, but had cats' paws or
horses' hooves. Their leader was called the Matron, Teacher, Greek
Mistress, Queen of the Fairies or simply the wise Sibilla.

We have already encountered Joan of Arc and her fellow villagers
who danced around the Fairy Tree at Domremy. The old beech tree
received its name because the fairies were said to appear there, but it
was also called the Ladies' Tree, for the fairies were perceived as mysterious, supernatural women. These fairies not only danced beneath

the tree, they also "cast spells." It was said that the actions of Catholic priests, notably the reading of the *Gospel of St. John*, had caused them to disappear.

As we noted earlier, the fairies departed from Domremy about 1375. One hundred years earlier, however, their visits were still regularly anticipated—and honored—by European peasants. A story from *The Golden Legend* (circa 1254) relates that country people were accustomed to setting a table for "the good ladies who ride out at night." In the story, the ladies are also called "our neighbors."

In Sicily, the visiting fairy women took mortals with them on their rambles. In point of fact, a fair number of European peasants—especially women—were prone to go riding with the fairy folk. A medieval theological tract called the *Canon Episcopi* (circa 900) warns priests and inquisitors to be on the lookout for such practices:

> *It is also not to be omitted that some wicked women perverted by the devil, seduced by illusions and phantasms of demons, believe and profess themselves, in the hours of night to ride upon certain beasts with Diana, the goddess of the pagans, and an innumerable multitude of women, and in the silence of the dead of night to traverse great spaces of earth, and to obey her commands as of their mistress, and to be summoned to her service on certain nights.[7]*

We must remember that the clergy had a Latin education. When country people spoke the names of their local goddesses, the priests wrote down "Diana," which they regarded as the Latin equivalent. But whatever the name, the archetype or pattern of belief was common throughout Europe.

Country people in the Middle Ages believed in supernatural women who were typically called "fairies" or "elves" and who were ruled by a queen. On certain nights, a table of food was set for the fairies, who were called the "good people" or "good neighbors," and their queen was often called (like Richella) the "good mistress." Some people could see the visiting fairies, perhaps dancing under a local tree. Others, who were not afraid to go journeying in Otherworldly realms, actually traveled with them "in the spirit" (i.e., in a shamanic trance, like the benandanti). Jean de Meung (circa 1270) refers to these journeys in his satirical additions to an old medieval epic called *The Romance of the Rose*.[8] Many people believe (though Jean, a skeptic, regards them as crazy) that they ride out at night with Dame Habonde; all those who are "third-born" must join them. Three times a week, their souls leave their bodies, pass through doors or other barriers, and, riding far and wide with the "good women," enter people's houses.

Fairies dancing near mounds and trees, from an old woodcut

THE WILD HUNT

To travel with the fairies was not a mere romp in the garden with charming and diminutive creatures like the fairies of Victorian folklore. One roamed the sky upon animals, accompanied by a host of spectral beings. The sight of this great gathering of spirits was a terrifying thing for many Europeans—they called it the Wild Hunt.

The Ecclesiastical History of Orderic Vitalis[9] records an event which allegedly took place in 1091. A priest was strolling along a path one night when he heard a clamor that sounded like an army on the march. He then beheld an enormous being with a club, and knew himself to be in the presence of the terrible Herlechin. This creature was followed by a crowd of men and women, some on foot and others on horseback, but all tormented by demons. These were the souls of those who had died in a state of sin, and they complained of their sorry fate.

The "fairies" who wander through the world on certain nights, and who are joined by certain individuals such as benandanti and witches, are, in one very important sense, equivalent to the souls of the dead.* The Old Bone Mother, after all, is an Underworld goddess, and her legions are comprised of those who have been gathered up and carried to the shadowy realms.

Sometimes, however, the doors between the worlds are open. The earliest trial records specify Thursdays (sacred to the god Thor or Jupiter), as well as the Ember Days in between Christmas and Epiphany. (Halloween seems to have emerged a bit later, and specifically in Celtic countries.) When the doors between this world and the next stand open, the spirits come pouring through, led by their king, or, more often, their queen. In southern Germany, the goddess of the Wild Hunt was called Perchta, Bertha, or Berta, also known as "the bright one"; she was a huntress, an Animal Mother. According to Tyrolese poet Hans Vintler,[10] writing about 1410, she had "an iron nose," not unlike the Bird of Prey Mother's iron beak. In central Germany, her name was Holt, Holle, or Hulda (who, as we have seen, survived in the stories of the Brothers Grimm). In those parts, she was essentially an agricultural goddess, and we may tentatively link her name with Hel, goddess of the Viking Underworld. In France, she is

---

* The connection between "the fairy folk" and the souls of the dead is a very controversial topic in folklore circles. W. Y. Evans-Wentz, before gaining fame as the translator of *The Tibetan Book of the Dead*, began his career as a folklorist with *The Fairy-Faith in Celtic Countries* (New York: Citadel, 1990), wherein he equated the fairies with the spirits of the departed. The eminent folklore scholar Katharine Briggs, in "The English Fairies", *Folk-Lore*, 68, (1957), 270–87, rejected such an identification; later, in "The Fairies and the Realm of the Dead", *Folk-Lore*, 81, (1970), 81–96, she changed her mind.

Abundia (the Habonde of Jean de Meung) or Satia, both of which mean "abundance"; and in northern Italy, we have met her under the name of Richella, which means precisely the same thing. In Scotland, the sixteenth-century "Ballad of Tam Lin" portrays the Queen of Fairies (who lives in a "green hill," just as Isobel Gowdie claimed) leading her cohorts on a fearsome "riding" on Halloween night.

But as we have seen, the Fairy Queen must have a Fairy King—the lord of the old European Underworld who shall occupy our attention at some length in a later chapter. He, too, is sometimes named as the leader of the Wild Hunt. He goes by various names, such as Herne the Hunter, Odin, or, in the tale told by Orderic Vitalicus, Herlechin (whence the name Harlequin, a nature spirit disguised as a Renaissance comedian). In the region around Glastonbury, in southwest England, the Wild Hunt is led by a certain Gwynn ap Nudd,* though the leader is also said to be King Arthur himself.

And what do the dead do when they enter our world? They look for food and drink. After all, feasting is the principal mode of activity in the Otherworld, is it not? The Valkyries carried warriors off to an eternal feast in Valhalla, and the fairies were feasting in a barrow mound when Isobel Gowdie went to visit them. Their food itself is magical, for it is well-known in Irish and Scottish lore that those who wander into the barrow mounds and feast with the fairies will probably return only hundreds of years later, if at all, and even if they return promptly, they will never be the same again.

The spirits of the dead can be treacherous; as Giacomo, our fictional benandante, knew, they are sometimes well disposed toward us and sometimes hostile. Therefore, it is the better part of wisdom to set a table for them. They like good food and wine, and a clean, well-swept house. William of Auvergne wrote in the thirteenth century that the "ladies of the night," led by Domina Abundia or Satia, fly through the air and invade people's cellars, where they eat and drink the provisions set out for them and in return bring prosperity upon the

---

* The name means "The White One, son of the god Nuada." The White Lady's color marks her as an Underworld deity, associated with old bones; so does Gwynn's.

house. If there is nothing for them to eat, they withhold their blessings. (They may do worse than that—some European peasants claimed
that they would defecate in your wine barrels if they were angry.)

Let us pause now and piece together everything we have learned
into a coherent portrait:

- Throughout the Middle Ages, European peasants continued to
  revere a Pagan Goddess of the Otherworld and her male consort. This practice was the subject of great consternation on the
  part of the Church.
- The Otherworld Goddess was known by many different names,
  depending on the region or locality: she was Abundia,
  Richella, Satia, Hulda, Perchta, or simply the Fairy Queen.
  Christian preachers with Latin educations tended to identify
  her with Diana.
- The Goddess and her consort reigned over the interior of the
  earth and the spirits of the dead. Their Otherworld realm was
  entered through particular mountains, like the Venusberg, or
  (in the British Isles) through old Stone Age barrow mounds.
- The spirits of the Otherworld—who are variously identified as
  elves, fairies, or simply as "the dead"—spend their time feasting
  eternally. They are fed from a cauldron or cup of abundance
  (the origin of the Holy Grail, the witches' cauldron, and the
  horn of plenty), which is the symbol of the Goddess.
- The Goddess beneath the earth rules all things associated with
  the earth. Many traditional peoples regard the world as receiving its sustenance from a primordial force which arises from
  beneath the surface of the earth. This power is the source of the
  crops, which is the single most important form of "abundance"
  for agricultural peoples. It is also the source of the metals that
  lie beneath the ground and that formed (and to some extent,
  still form) the basis of our units of exchange—we should
  remember that the word "plutocracy," meaning "rule by the
  wealthy," is derived from the name Pluto, the Underworld Lord
  of classical mythology. So the Goddess is responsible for both
  the growth of the crops and for material wealth—hence she is
  called Abundia or Richella.

- She is also responsible for the health and welfare of the animals, earth's creatures—which, for meat-eating societies, constitute yet another form of abundance. One of her ancient titles was the Animal Mother or Mistress of the Animals.
- Sometimes the doorways between our world and the Otherworld stand open. In medieval times, such interfaces were attributed to Thursdays, the Ember Days between Christmas and Epiphany, and, at least in Celtic countries, to Halloween. The spirits of the dead or the "fairy folk" ride forth as a Wild Hunt, sometimes led by the Goddess herself, and at other times by her mate, who was called Herne the Hunter, Odin, Harlequin, or even King Arthur. Mounted on various wild animals, the spirit members of the Wild Hunt race through the night and enter the houses of the living. What they seek is meat and drink, for the dead, who feast eternally in the Otherworld, have insatiable appetites. If unsatisfied, they can be treacherous and even cause property damage. Thus it is best to honor them by referring to them as "the good people" or "the good neighbors," whose leader is the "good mistress"; one should set a table for them, and keep the room clean and well swept.*
- Setting forth food and drink for the dead was a practice that the Church condemned and tried to eradicate; but worse still was the ability of some peasants, especially women, to actually join in the Wild Hunt. These individuals, including groups or associations of individuals such as the benandanti or "good walkers," would enter a shamanic trance and travel forth "in spirit"—leaving their bodies behind and passing through locked doorways in the process. They would fly through the air with the hosts of the dead, perhaps to accompany them in their quest for food and drink, or dance with them beneath a Fairy Tree, or (in the case of the benandanti) to join with their ancestors in taking up arms against the wrathful dead who might seek to harm their village communities.

---

* The practice of setting a table for the spirits or "the dead" seems to have survived until the very end of the witch trials; testimony from Salem, Massachusetts, mentions "a red feast." Food colored red was sometimes tabooed in ancient Europe, for it was associated with the dead.

- Those who possessed such shamanic abilities acquired knowledge of their own talents through an initiatory experience. A man you had known all your life might come to your house beating on a spirit drum, or approach you on a dark country road, as among the benandanti. You might hear and see spirits calling you to a mystical vocation, like Chonradt Stocklin or Joan of Arc. The goal of the initiatory process was this: one acquired the ability to undertake the trance journey common to all shamans, and hence to interface with the Otherworld, the original source of wisdom and abundance.
- Those who possessed such shamanic abilities, and who continued to revere the Lord and Lady of the old Pagan Otherworld, were often accused of witchcraft.

We have seen that shamanism is remarkably persistent. It has its roots in the religious experience of Stone Age man. This religious experience was carried from its original home (which was possibly, but not certainly, in Siberia) to Europe, Asia, the Americas, and even the islands of the Pacific. Different mythologies came and went throughout the course of human history, but shamanism remained essentially the same. Capable of endless adaptation and variation, its core experience was easily assimilated into any number of religions. In Europe, the earth-centered ancestral cult of the Neolithic was replaced by the sky-centered mythologies of the Indo-European peoples, which were in turn replaced by Christianity. Shamanism survived them all, and was still alive and well during the witch trials of the Renaissance and Reformation.

Pagan feminists are clearly correct in affirming that the Diana of the witch trials is, in fact, a most ancient and well-nigh universal goddess. As we have seen, she was Queen of the Otherworld and Lady of Abundance.

But can we say with certainty that she is really the Old Bone Mother of primordial shamanism?

NORTHERN ITALY, 1389

They had been coming, most of them, since childhood, traveling in the spirit on Thursday nights. They gathered in a place of mist and dream light, a place beyond time, a place beyond place. The living and the dead together, they gathered to greet their mistress, Madonna Oriente.

Pierina de Bugatis had come since she was sixteen, when her aunt begged it of her. "One must take my place," she had told her. "If no one takes my place, I will never be permitted to die." Her aunt taught her how to summon the friendly spirit who dwelt beneath the house and who would help conduct her on her spirit journey. Pierina had taken her aunt's place and had never had cause to regret it. She cared little for the sentence the inquisitors had placed upon her, five years ago. To wear two red crosses as a penance! What did that matter? For here, in the Society, she had learned finer things than any priest could ever teach her. She had learned the virtues of herbs, and how to heal the sick. She could divine the location of missing objects, or take a spell off a fellow villager.

The woman called Sibillia was equally gifted. She had earned her nickname because she had learned to predict the future—Madonna Oriente had taught her how. Sibillia had been traveling here since her girlhood. She, too, had been hauled up in front of the judges five years ago, and forced to wear the little red crosses. And during her waking hours, she played out her role, attended mass, and never mentioned Oriente.

But here, among Oriente's people, she never mentioned Christ. For Christ might rule the world, but Madonna Oriente ruled the Good People....

And now Oriente came, stately in her walking, stately and filled with grace. And those gathered there, the spirit travelers, living and dead, heard the rustling and lowing of the animals.

For she came with a great troop of wild beasts around her, all the beasts of the world, two of every kind—all except for the fox and the ass, who were forbidden. And they followed her like a great throng, and they were legion, for if any kind of beast were missing from her company, then certain it was that the world would end that minute....

And they gathered close, the living and the dead, to make their bows to her, their obeisance. And only the shadows of the dead who had been hanged or decapitated stayed behind, gloomy and ashamed for they could not bow their heads properly to honor her.

And the people bowed. And they said: "Be well, Madonna Oriente."

And she answered, "Be well, Good People."

And the people cried out to her, the spirits of the living, to ask their questions, to hear their fates. And Oriente sat, stately and strong by the edge of the well, and she answered each and every one. And she told them their fates, and she never lied—as Sibillia especially knew full well, for she had learned her own arts here in this school.

And now the feast. The Good People took up their axes and they slaughtered the oxen. The whole Society fell to feasting on the rich fine meat—especially the dead, the hungry ones.

And when they were finished, Pierina de Bugatis helped to gather up the bones of the oxen they had consumed. Sometimes a bone or two turned up missing; Pierina had learned to fetch a stick of elder wood to put in its place. She helped to place the bones back inside the skins, wrapping them up like that.

And then the miracle took place, the beautiful miracle. Madonna Oriente, in silence, approached the hides, and she lifted up her wand, and struck the hides three times.

And the oxen rose up, lowing and calling, and walking just the same as ever...Oriente's miracle.

And now the wild host, gladdened by the sound of life restored, set forth across the sky. They flew across the quiet valleys, the hills, down the village streets. They burst into the houses, hungry still. And in many houses, small and large, the floor was cleanly swept, the room neat and tidy. Candles flickered cheerily atop the tables, with food set out as for a feast. And when they found a house of joy like that, they blessed it, one and all. And when they saw houses dark and cold, they cursed them if the folk were rich, yet blessed them if they were poor, for the poor had nothing to give and needed all the blessing they could get.

And at last, as darkness faded and the first gray light began to grow along the shadow of the hills, they drifted off, in ones and twos, back to the realm of the dead or the village houses of the living.

Sibillia flew back across the stream that ran along the village edge, and as she did so she caught herself dropping a stone into the water.

And she watched, with the detachment of the spirit body but with a certain shock and sadness nonetheless, as the ripples grew and grew and she began to spin with them, down a circular tunnel. Now why on earth had she thrown that stone? Why had she witched the water? Now she would never return to the Good Society, never again....

And indeed, the woman named Sibillia never did return to the Society of Oriente. The very next year, in 1390, she and Pierina de Bugatis were once again arrested and tried for witchcraft.[11] This time the charge was more serious, for they had been punished once before but had not ceased in their nefarious ways.

Sibillia and Pierina were sentenced to death and executed in 1390.

THE FEAST FOR THE DEAD

Of the many shamanic practices we shall examine in this book, the Feast for the Dead has had the greatest longevity of them all—and, as a living folk custom, its practice is actually on the rise in contemporary America.

Throughout Mexico, the Days of the Dead are celebrated on Halloween and on the days immediately following—the "official" Day of the Dead is November 1. Altars are erected in homes and dedicated to departed members of one's family. Colorfully decorated, these altars contain religious objects as well as photographs of the deceased. Food is cooked and placed upon the altar to feed the dead. After the deceased have taken their invisible portion, the family will eat the actual meal. Candies made in the shape of skeletons are particular favorites among the children.

During the Days of the Dead, Mexican families visit the graves of deceased relatives in their local cemeteries. They decorate the graves, so that the cemeteries become colorful, magical places. Picnics are held, and in this way, too, families symbolically feast with their ancestors. The people say that the spirits of the dead will walk abroad at night during these days, just as the Celts once said that the Fairy Host would ride on Halloween, or just as medieval Germanic peoples said that the Wild Hunt would ride during the Ember Days. And just as European peasants believed that the Good Folk visited their cottages to eat the food and drink the wine, contemporary Mexicans believe that the souls of the dead will search for their previous homes. Paths of marigolds, the flowers of the dead, are often strewn in front of houses, for it is believed that a path of these flowers will assist the spirits of the deceased in finding their way home.

Whether this custom is entirely aboriginal, or whether it owes a debt to Spanish folklore, is unclear. Nor, for our purposes, does it make much difference, for, as we have seen, the spiritual traditions of ancient Mexico and of ancient Europe were both shamanic in origin. What is important is that this ancient custom—which appears so strongly in the early records of medieval witchcraft—is still strong and vital in the present day. It is, in fact, perhaps the only component of medieval witch belief that has retained its full vigor among large numbers of contemporary people, and because of the large Hispanic population in California and the American Southwest, more and more people (even Anglo-Saxons) are beginning to celebrate the Days of the Dead.

The medieval witches, like European shamans of Pagan times, believed that their devotions to the ancestors helped the dead and the living alike. To maintain a close and friendly connection with the ancestors was a way of assuring that the whole community—both living and dead—would maintain its spiritual health, and that a continuity with tradition and with the past would be preserved in the present. We may no longer live in small villages that constitute worlds unto themselves, but we all live in some kind of community, and we all have a duty to help our community maintain its spiritual health— even, or perhaps especially, if we have come to perceive that community as global in nature. After all, healing the tribe is the proper business of shamans. One of the most important ways that we can do this is to honor the ancestors.

The traditional time for this practice is Halloween or All Souls' Day, but it may be done at any time.

1. Establish a little bit of "magical" or "sacred" space in your home. Such a place need not be large—just large enough for a table. The table itself can be old, simple, or small—in Mexico, people use whatever is available, and peasants in medieval Europe undoubtedly did the same. This table is for the Good Folk, the Dead. This is where you will serve them their meals.

2. Next, you will need photographs or other mementos of your dead. In Mexico, the altars for the Days of the Dead are decorated with framed photographs, portraits, and personal objects owned by one's

departed parents, grandparents, siblings and so on. These mementos are set forth upon the altar as images and reminders of those who have passed beyond.

The notion of honoring your deceased relatives may be troubling for some of you, especially if you've gone through various kinds of therapy that encourage you to find the source of your own negative habit patterns in parental programming. Why pay homage to a mother who was abusively cold, or a father who was a chronic alcoholic? Why should you honor a grandmother who shattered the family structure for generations to come by running off with a carnival barker long ago? Aren't these the very people from whom you are attempting to liberate yourself?

But the Feast for the Dead is a much more ancient tradition than any current brand of therapy, and it may force you to see things in a different light. To honor the dead is an act of love which requires that we forgive our own past and all the people in it. What you honor in your father is not his alcoholism—it is his immortal soul, a soul in which you share simply by virtue of being human. What you honor in your cold or abusive mother is not her fierce rigidity, but the fierce fire of spirit that once burned within her and that burns within all living. Following a shamanic path means that you must learn to nurture a loving concern for the ancestors, for all the departed souls of your total human community, which goes beyond mere emotional attachment or aversion, and which can only be defined, as the Buddhists define it, in terms of compassion.

3. When you have selected photographs or other mementos of your "ancestors" and placed them upon the table, you may wish to continue with other forms of decoration. In Mexico, you will see truly marvelous displays on the altars of the dead, including candles, charms, popular religious pictures, flowers, and even an occasional black velvet Elvis painting or a string of Christmas tree lights! Suit yourself. Be creative.

4. Now you must feed the dead. What shall you feed them? Anything you like! In Mexico, it would not be unusual to cook up Grandpa's favorite enchilada recipe and place it on the altar next to his picture. In ancient Europe, food colored red was symbolic of the life force and of rebirth, and hence of the dead as well. Thus apples were regarded as the magical food of the Otherworld in Celtic lands, and so on.

5. When you leave food and drink on the altar, try to hold good thoughts for those to whom the food is dedicated. Contemplate, reflect, imagine. What was good about that person, or those people? What was beautiful, a part of their essential immortality of spirit? Sit and meditate on these things, and begin to visualize a rose-colored glow of love arising in your heart center. When your heart is filled with love for your particular ancestors, you may send forth that love, on rays of rose-colored light, all over the world, to all our ancestors, and to the living as well.

6. Leave the food on the altar for as long as is practical (considering the nature of the food, its perishability, the temperature of the room, etc.). Take it off the altar and eat it while it is still fresh and nourishing. If you can manage to share it with like-minded relatives who honor the same dead, or with friends who have their own ancestors to salute, then so much the better. Eat in silence, and in reverence for the souls and spirits of those who came before you. Cherish them with each bite, drink deep of their spirit with each sip.

CHAPTER 4

Totem Animals

SHAMANIC POWER ANIMALS

The Lord and Lady of the Underworld, those primordial figures who survived into the Burning Times, were, among other things, the special deities and protectors of wild creatures—the Master and Mistress of Animals, no less. Thus we might expect that the witch trials would preserve a great deal of shamanic lore and practice concerning the animal kingdom, and they do.

For most modern urbanites, the animal world is something separate and remote; a domestic pet plus the occasional pigeon or cockroach forms the extent of our interaction with animals. But to traditional peoples everywhere, animals are true contemporaries and close neighbors; the boundaries between their world and ours are blurred, indistinct. To traditional hunters, the animals they stalk are not simply mindless victims or pieces of meat; rather, there is a symbiosis, a spiritual bond between the hunter and the hunted—especially when a man stalks an animal large and aggressive enough to stalk him in return. The Greeks and the Celts may have given their gods human form, but the mythologies of aboriginal North America and tribal Africa are concerned primarily with animals (i.e., with the archetypes of the collective unconscious embodied in animal form).

An animal spirit may have an archetypal link or relationship with a whole group of people—a clan or other extended unit which takes its name or its character from a totem animal. In Siberia and North America, there is one particular animal which serves as a totem for that group of individuals we call shamans. This is the eagle, whom, as we have seen, dwells in the top branches of the World Tree, the land of the gods.

The Buryat say that in the beginning there were only the gods and the evil spirits. Humankind was created by the gods, but cursed with illness and death by the evil spirits. Therefore, the gods sent the eagle to act as a shaman for suffering humanity. The humans, in their ignorance, did not understood the eagle; nor were they able to accept a mere bird as their savior, so the eagle was given the power to grant shamanic abilities to the first person he encountered. This proved to be a young woman, sleeping beneath a tree. The eagle mated with her and she gave birth to the first shaman—which, symbolically, tells us that shamanism is "born" from the union of the enlightened consciousness which dwells at the top of our own internal World Tree with the feminine potency that sleeps at its base.

Many Native American tribes also recognize the eagle as the most sacred of birds. The Shoshoni place him at the top of the central pole in the Sun Dance Lodge, another metaphor for the World Tree. Because the eagle flies the highest, his is the purest spirit; thus he is most admirably suited to help the shaman journey to the land of the gods, the topmost branches of the World Tree. Eagle feathers are a vitally important part of healing ceremonies in many tribes, for, as we have seen in the Siberian example, the eagle was sent to humankind to help heal the diseases with which the demons have cursed us.

Individuals may also have their own totem or power animals, quite independently of their birth clan, and though the eagle serves as the

The eagle serves as the totem
of shamans in general

totem of shamans in general, an individual shaman or shamaness typ-ically has an individual power animal as well. As we have already seen, many shamans are called to their vocations by spirits from the Otherworld; often that call comes from a spirit who has taken the form of a particular animal, one which will later become that shaman's helper or guide, as both the ermine and the mouse guided the Samoyed shaman on his initiatory journey (Chapter 2). The famous Lakota medicine man Lame Deer received his call directly from the eagle, who tapped him on the shoulder with its wings and told him that "they" had been waiting for him, and that the eagle would now be with him always "as a ghost."[1]

Sometimes the call from an animal helper is an enormously rich and complex experience. Another Lakota, Crazy Horse (who was as much a shaman as he was a warrior), received a vision wherein his horse hobbled near the site of his vision quest, broke free, and began to run as if it were floating through light. It changed colors as it ran in a zigzag pattern, and Crazy Horse carefully watched its phantom rider, who wore a stone behind one ear, a lightning bolt painted on his face, and who had a hawk above him. From that time on, Crazy Horse always rode into battle in the same fashion—a stone behind his ear, a lightning bolt on his face, and a hawk feather in his hair. He rode his horse in a zigzag pattern, as in his vision. It was believed that no bullet could touch him as long as he was protected by his horse, his hawk and his stone. (In point of fact, he proved immune to bullets throughout his career; he was on foot when he was killed by a bayonet.)

A power animal may reveal complex messages and visionary phenomena of various kinds to a seeker such as Crazy Horse; it may play a unique and overwhelming influence in one's life. To the professional shaman, a power animal acts primarily as a guide upon the Otherworldly journey.

In the early 1800s, a horse sacrifice that took place among the Altaic peoples of Siberia was recorded in great detail.[2] The ceremony lasted for several days and took place in a specially constructed yurt, the center of which was a birch tree notched with nine steps. The shaman's assistants tended the horse selected for the sacrifice.

The shaman, after calling on the spirits with his drum, mounted a scarecrow shaped like a goose and, as he rode it to the sky, he sang and called out like a goose. He chased the soul of the horse, even while his assistants rounded up the physical horse and, with the shaman's help, sacrificed it.

On the second day, the shaman invited the spirits to a feast of horseflesh. The participants in the ceremony mimed the actions and behavior of spirits as they took part in the feast.* The shaman then invoked the gods, mounted the first notch of the central birch tree,

---

* The attentive reader will have noted, in the last chapter, a certain confusion among medieval writers as to whether the "feasts for the dead" associated with the Otherworld Goddess were attended only by spirits and astral travelers, or whether actual people took part. As we can see from this Siberian example, such close distinctions between the living, the dead, and the astral may simply be a mental construct of our rationalistic civilization, and relatively meaningless to traditional peoples.

and began his ascent to the ninth heaven. At first he rode upon the spirit of the sacrificed horse, which took him as far as the third notch on the tree, symbolic of the third heaven. Then the horse became weary, and the shaman summoned the goose once again, cackling like a goose as he climbed. Thus mounted, he ascended at last to the ninth heaven, the top of the birch tree.

ANIMALS IN EUROPEAN MYTH

Many elements of the Altaic shaman's experience appear in the mythologies of Europe. Odin, that enigmatic figure who gained wisdom through his self-sacrifice upon the World Tree, is also a traveler to the Otherworld; as such, he rides upon an eight-legged horse called Sleipnir. According to an old Eddic poem, Odin rode Sleipnir down the long road to the kingdom of the dead in order to rescue the soul of his slain son Balder. He was challenged by a fierce dog guarding the portals of the Underworld, but won his way through to consult the spirit of a dead shamaness.

*Odin and Sleipnir, from an eleventh-century
rune stone on the Isle of Gotland*

According to the somewhat later writings of Snorri Sturluson, the journey in search of Balder's soul was entrusted by Odin to his son Hermod, and it was Hermod who rode Sleipnir to the nether realms. His ride took him across a bridge that spanned the Resounding River (the bridge was guarded by a maiden, another dweller at the threshold of the Otherworld). Sleipnir leapt over the gates of Hel to bear Hermod into the hall of the Old Bone Goddess herself, where he found Balder sitting like a king next to Mother Hel. When Sleipnir is not engaged upon his Underworld journeys, Odin keeps him tethered to the World Tree—and, as the Buryats of Siberia would tell us, the stars are but a herd of horses tethered to the North Star, which is the center of the universe.

Odin was not the only figure in European myth to employ a horse for shamanic purposes. The Greek hero Bellerophon flew to Olympus, the land of the gods, mounted upon the most famous of all magical horses, the winged steed Pegasus.

When the Altaic shaman's horse became tired, he rode a goose. This particular bird is mentioned in a shamanic context in the *Brihadaranyaka Upanishad*:

> *Striking down in sleep what is bodily,*
> *Sleepless, he looks down upon the sleeping senses.*
> *Having taken to himself light, he has returned to his own*
> *place:*
> *That Golden Person, the Lone Wild Gander...*
> *He goes wherever he pleases, that Immortal,*
> *The Golden Person, the Unique Wild Gander.*
> *In the State of Sleep, soaring high and low...3*

Shamanic flight to the Otherworld is linked with various birds, a number of which play their part in European mythology. When the Red Branch champions of Ulster met to celebrate Samhain (Halloween), the great hero Cuchulain brought down a number of birds to give to the ladies of the court. The only woman who lacked such a prize was the wife of Cuchulain himself. He promised her a bird of her own, but the next winged creatures flying over the lake proved to be two birds bound together by a chain of reddish gold. Cuchulain's wife urged him to leave them alone, for they were obviously magical, but Cuchulain was not to be dissuaded. He made two unsuccessful attempts on the birds with a slingshot, then tossed a javelin which barely grazed the feathers of one of them. Afterward, he fell into a trance and journeyed to the Otherworld to make love to the goddess Fand, wife of the sea god Manannan mac Lir.*

The story doesn't tell us what *kind* of birds served as Cuchulain's guides to the Otherworld. Perhaps they were wild geese, as in the visionary experience of the Altaic shaman. Considering that the story is Irish, it is more likely that they were swans, for another old Celtic tale relates how the children of the god Lir were transformed into swans. In fact, swans were associated with the Otherworld journey in many parts of Europe—we have already heard how the Finnish folk hero Lemminkainen came to grief while trying to shoot the swan of Tuonela, who swims in the River of the Underworld. Like Cuchulain, he was led into a shamanic journey of death and rebirth when he unsuccessfully tried to bring down a magical bird.

Though horses and swans seem to be the most common Otherworld guides in European myth, they are not the only creatures to serve in that capacity. The three animals that appear most universally in shamanic traditions all over the world are birds, the bear, and the deer. In how many stories have King Arthur's knights followed a stag into the forest, only to be led not to a simple hunt but to a series of magical adventures? And in how many fairy tales are the heroes or heroines helped and guided through similarly magical exploits by any variety of friendly animals?

In fact, animal helpers and totems permeate European mythology. In addition to his horse Sleipnir, Odin also claimed the raven as his special helper, for his two ravens, Hugin and Munin (Thought and

---

* Manannan mac Lir is only one of the many names given to the Otherworld Lord in Celtic myth; he also appears as Pwyll, Bran, Pryderi and (probably) Cernunnos.

Memory), range far and wide over the world and bring information back to him. Early Scandinavian carvings depict Odin riding through the sky upon Sleipnir, accompanied by two ravens who fly overhead—a visual image that would do credit to Crazy Horse.

Odin was also the commander-in-chief of the Valkyries, sending them forth to the battlefields to gather up the corpses of the slain. As we noted in the previous chapter, the Valkyries themselves seem originally to have been birds of prey, and there is some evidence that they were specifically linked with ravens and crows, for an Old English poem

A wood nymph and her deer

names the raven as *waelcasig*, a word related to valkyrie and meaning "chooser of the slain."* The Morrigan, who, in Celtic myth, fulfilled the same function as did the Norse Valkyries, was also a raven or crow. Thus the Old Bone Mother herself occasionally appears as a shamanic totem animal—not only for Odin, but for the Irish hero Cuchulain, who had a special (i.e., totemic) relationship with the Morrigan.

Swine also played a significant role in European myth. The Norse god Freyr possessed a magical boar; this marks him as a deity of the Underworld and a probable "lord of animals," for swine in general are connected with the Underworld in Celtic myth as well, and it was a herd of swine that the Welsh shaman-hero Gwydion stole from Pryderi, the Underworld King, in the Fourth Branch of *The Mabinogion*. Freyr's sister Freya, the Viking Aphrodite whose female devotees, like Thorbjorg the Sibyl in our introductory chapter, practiced the shamanic rites known as *seidr*, rode about in a chariot drawn by cats, though she, too, possessed a magical boar.

Pagan Europeans, then, maintained a connection with the animal kingdom that was just as close as that enjoyed by Siberian shamans or Native American medicine men. The entire animal kingdom took part in that spiritual interconnectedness: Sigurd the Volsung slew the dragon Fafnir and bathed in its blood, which gave him the power to understand the speech of *all* animals.

THE WITCHES' FAMILIAR

When we turn once again to the witch trials, it is clear that animal helpers constitute one of the most deeply shamanic themes to be found there, for they are equivalent to the well-known phenomenon of the "witches' familiar."

---

* In Old English, the word we usually transcribe as "valkyrie" was written *waelcyrge* (*wael* = val, *cyrge* = kyrie), which also meant "chooser of the slain."

Animal familiars were especially popular in the British Isles. King James VI of Scotland (who was also King James I of England) had a positive horror of witchcraft, supported the witch trials, and even wrote a book called *Daemonologie*, wherein, commenting on the relationship between witches and the devil, he remarks:

> *To some of the baser sort of them he obliges himself to appear at their calling upon him…in likeness of a dog, a cat, an ape, or such-like other beast; or else to answer by a voice only. The effects are to answer to such demands, as concerns curing of diseases; or such other base things as they require of him.*[4]

It is not clear why James should characterize the "curing of diseases" as "base." One might, however, accurately characterize "the curing of diseases through the means of a spirit animal helper" as "shamanic."

Almost any animal could be a familiar. The Essex village of Chelmsford seems, during the late 1500s, to have been exceptionally rich in such communications with the animal world. Ursula Kemp kept two cats as familiars, and her neighbor Alice Mansfield kept four. Elizabeth Bennet had a black dog, and Agnes Heard had six white-speckled blackbirds; the familiar of Joan Prentice was a red-eyed ferret. Elizabeth Sowtherns of Lancashire (1612) preferred a brown dog, while Ellen Green of Leicester (1619) enjoyed the magical services of both a kitten and a mole. Jane Hott and Elizabeth Harris of Kent (1645) kept a hedgehog and a mouse respectively.

In northern Italy in 1387, an accused Waldensian named Antonio Galosna testified that a woman called Billia la Castagna had kept a toad underneath her bed, feeding it meat, bread, and cheese. She then made a potion from its excrement, and those who consumed the vile stuff were forever after incapable of leaving her heretical sect. In the late nineteenth century, also in Italy, the Tuscan witches known as *streghe* kept parakeets or canaries who would, for a few coins, pick a client's fortune out of a pile comprised of slips of paper. The term *streghe* (or, in the singular, *strega*) comes from the Latin *striga*, meaning "screech owl," suggesting that the original totem of the Italian witches was that nocturnal bird of prey. As recently as 1926, Mother Redcap, who lived near Cambridge, England, and was reputed to be a witch, was often seen roaming about accompanied by a rat, a cat, a toad, a ferret, and a mouse!

Many of these animals can be shown to be of significance in the mythology and folklore of ancient Europe. The cat, perhaps the most common of all familiars, was sacred to the Norse goddess Freya; she rode about, as we have noted, in a chariot drawn by those animals, and her priestesses, like Thorbjorg the Sibyl, wore gloves of cat skin. Freya was a goddess of both shamanic practice (Norse *seidr*) and unbridled sexuality; the cat may have symbolized either of these.

The dog was a well-known guardian of the Otherworld; the Greek Hades was guarded by the three-headed Cerberus, and Odin encountered a dog when he rode to Hel on Sleipnir's back in search of the soul of Balder. When, in the First Branch of *The Mabinogion*, Pwyll of Dyved encountered the Underworld King, that spectral lord was riding through the woods accompanied by his magical hounds. The association of the dog with the Underworld is extremely ancient, for it was the totem of Hecate, the goddess of the waning moon; earlier still, fierce howling dogs appear on pottery from the Ukrainian Neolithic, circa 3,500 BC. That the dogs mentioned as familiars in the witch trials are related to these Underworld guardians is suggested by the tale of John Law, a peddler who refused to give a free set of pins to one Alison Device, an alleged witch. The unfortunate peddler came face to face with a huge black dog whose eyes were like fire and whose teeth were fiercely bared; the apparition caused a stroke that left Mr. Law's left side paralyzed. This popular image of the "devil dog" forms the basis of Conan Doyle's famous story *The Hound of the Baskervilles*.

The toad, like the dog, also has associations that stretch back into the Neolithic, for it is a frequent subject for figurines from the early Balkan and Aegean cultures, and is found in contexts dating all the way back to 6,000 B.C. The toad is typically shown with its legs outspread and its pubic triangle accentuated, which suggests that it is linked with the Goddess as birth-giving mother. That this is indeed the case is indicated by the fact that, even now, similar carved toads can be found as votive offerings to the Virgin Mary in churches throughout Bavaria, Austria, Hungary, Moravia, and the former Yugoslavia; they are intended as charms against barrenness and as protection in pregnancy. In the Baltic, however, the toad was regarded as an evil creature that can cause madness and, like the vampire, suck the blood from humans while they sleep. As such, it may well be an aspect of the Old European Death Goddess herself. Thus the symbolism of the toad, whether positive or negative, links it to the Otherworld Goddess.

Interestingly enough, toad's meat was once eaten to aid in labor pains, which may remind us of the testimony of Billia la Castagna, who allegedly fed meat and cheese to a toad and then made potions from its excrement. The trial record itself is garbled, but we may wonder whether Billia was, in fact, eating—or at least licking—the hand-fed toad itself. Shamans in Siberia and the Americas often use psychotropic substances to induce the Otherworldly journey, and certain species of toads contain the chemical bufotenin, which makes it possible to obtain a six-hour psychedelic trip by licking their flesh! (The Maya seem to have employed this method.) There is, of course, an equal possibility that Billia's "toad" was in fact a "toad stool", perhaps a fly agaric mushroom, for medieval European peasants often used terms referring to animal excrement as idiomatic descriptions of hallucinogenic mushrooms.

The hedgehog kept by Jane Hott of Kent also has an ancestry extending back to the Neolithic, and is found as a carved figurine among the same cultures that favored the toad and the dog. In European folk medicine, hedgehog fat rubbed on the body is believed to be a rejuvenating tonic, and wounds rubbed with that substance are said to heal quickly. Like the toad, the hedgehog is associated with the birth-giving goddess. In the Tyrolean Alps, a cow's uterus, which, after the birth is over, remains swollen and covered with warts, is called a "hedgehog." Models of such uteri, carved of wood and called "spiky balls," were, like the carved toads from elsewhere in Europe, placed in Tyrolean churches as ex-voto offerings.

And last but not least, there is the humble mouse. The soul of our fictional benandante Giacomo (in the Introduction) left his body in the shape of a mouse; this mode of astral exit, occurring through the mouth, is mentioned in the testimony of several accused benandanti. The earliest witch persecutions, which date from the early fifteenth century and began in the Western Alps, insist that the "sect of the witches" was at that time but newly formed, having originated about 1375 with the teachings of an individual known only as Scavius, who was said to be able to take the shape of a mouse. Was Scavius, perhaps, a shamanic traveler whose soul left his body in the form of a mouse?

And indeed, if witches were shamans, then we should expect to find that their animal familiars were used primarily as guides or vehicles for spirit flight—for, as we remarked earlier, for the professional shaman the power animal is primarily a guide upon the Otherworldly journey.

Thus we return to the medieval ecclesiastical text called the *Canon Episcopi*, quoted in the previous chapter, "...some wicked women...believe and profess themselves, in the hours of night to ride upon certain beasts with Diana...and an innumerable multitude of women, and in the silence of the dead of night to traverse great spaces of earth..."

The Wild Hunt, led by the Underworld God or Goddess, was as much a procession of animals as of the dead, for after all, these deities are also the Lord and Lady of the Animals. Their human followers, who joined the furious journey, frequently rode mounted upon animals.

Almost any animal would do. Zuan delle Piatte, who, in Chapter 1, found the Goddess dwelling inside the World Mountain, rode with her round the world (in five hours, no less) mounted on black horses. The Goddess herself seems to have ridden horseback more often than not, for those regions of Western Europe wherein we find the tradition of the Wild Hunt most prevalent are also the regions where ancient Celts worshipped a goddess on horseback—Gallic Epona, Welsh Rhiannon, the Fairy Queen who figures in the ballads of Tam Lin and Thomas the Rhymer, and even (in folklore) Lady Godiva.

In Sicily and southern Italy, sheep were preferred. King Arthur, sometimes named as the leader of the Wild Hunt, is shown mounted on a ram in the cathedral of Otranto, and the Sicilian women who followed the "ladies from outside" rode mounted upon castrated rams. The Italian benandanti rode forth to their nocturnal battles upon a veritable menagerie of livestock—boars, dogs, hares, pigs, and cocks!

By far the most popular mount for witches, however, was the goat. Witches are shown riding on goatback as early as the 1300s, as depicted on a bas-relief at Lyons Cathedral. Similar illustrations appear in a print by the German artist Albrecht Durer (fifteenth century), then somewhat later in another print by Hans Baldung (1514), and later still in the *Compendium maleficarum* of Guaccius, published in 1626.

SHAPE-SHIFTING

Animals were not the only means of locomotion used by witches in their nocturnal rambles; we will consider the famous broomstick in the next chapter. But before we leave the subject of animals, we must touch upon the most intimate possible connection between humans and animals—the ability of some witches to actually transform themselves into animals.

This, of course, is the phenomenon known as shape-shifting, and it appears in many shamanic cultures around the world. In the American Southwest, for instance, the Navajo Indians still have a deep fear of certain witches called "skinwalkers," who can change themselves into animals, usually wolves. (In Navajo tradition, skinwalkers are invariably evil practitioners of malevolent or black magic.)

Shape-shifting is found in European mythology as well. Snorri Sturluson relates how three magic cauldrons holding the mead of inspiration were captured by a giant named Suttung. Odin set himself the task of reclaiming that potent nectar for the gods. He hired himself out as a manual laborer to Suttung's brother Baugi. The only payment he asked was a drink from one of the magic cauldrons, but Suttung refused to pay the worker; thus Odin changed himself into a serpent and bored into the side of the mountain, the giant's home.

Having arrived, he made it worth his while by sleeping with Suttung's daughter for three nights. In return, he demanded three sips of mead.

Odin drained all three cauldrons in three gigantic draughts, then changed himself into an eagle and flew away, back to the land of the gods where vessels had been prepared to receive the magical nectar. Odin spilled some of the divine fluid upon the earth as he flew home (thus poetic inspiration came to the world of humankind as the gift of a shaman disguised as an eagle). Odin's predilection for shape-shifting is remarked upon by Snorri Sturluson, who says, "His body lay as though he were asleep or dead, and he then became a bird or a beast, a fish or a dragon, and went in an instant to far-off lands."[5] Snorri's description of a shamanic trance could scarcely be bettered.

An equally remarkable shape-shifter is depicted in one of Russia's old medieval hero tales. Volkh Vseslavevich led an army of 7,000 men against a mythical "Tsar of India" who was threatening the kingdom of Kiev. While his men slept, Volkh changed himself into a wolf and went out hunting for meat to feed the army, as well as clothing for them from the skins of sables and panthers. On other nights he became a falcon, hunting birds so that his men would have a varied diet. He then changed himself into an aurochs, leapt high into the air, and, becoming a falcon once again, flew to India to spy on the Tsar. Shifting his shape once more and becoming an ermine, he chewed through the Tsar's bowstrings with rodent teeth and buried his weapons in the ground by digging with his sharp claws. Finally, when he and his army stood at the gates of the Indian palace, he turned himself and all his men into ants so that they could crawl through the interstices of the carved gates and thus, triumphantly, enter the palace.

Witches were likewise believed to be able to change themselves into animals. Our red-haired friend Isobel Gowdie, visitor to Elfland, had, as we have remarked, a peculiar desire to confess to everything in detail (this included confessing to crimes no one had accused her of). Isobel's totem animal was the hare, and whenever she desired to speed to the Witches' Sabbat she changed herself into that creature by chanting the following spell:

I shall go into a hare,
With sorrow, sigh, and mickle care;
And I shall go in the Devil's name,
Aye while I come back again.

Thus transformed, she flew to the Sabbat, along with her companions, some of whom favored the shape of cats. When she was finished with her spirit traveling, she chanted another spell to regain human shape:

Hare, hare, God send thee care;
I am in a hare's likeness now,
But I shall be a woman e'en now,
Hare, hare, God send thee care.

Isobel, always more than willing to volunteer information, went on to say that she and the other witches of Auldearne also transformed themselves into crows (totem animal of the Valkyries, the Morrigan, and the banshee). "When we will be in the shape of crows we will be larger than ordinary crows," she said, "and will sit upon branches of trees."[6]

Indeed, shape-shifting appears as an integral part of the witch trials almost from the very beginning. In the Valais trials, part of the first wave of persecutions, which date from the early 1400s and were centered in the Western Alps, the male witches said that they took the shape of wolves, and that "the devil" appeared to his devotees in the shape of a bear or a ram. A half century later, a German demonological text by Ulrich Molitor includes an illustration showing witches on the way to the Sabbat, midway through their transformation into animals. This brings us back to Scavius, the alleged founder of the witch cult who was said to be able to transform himself into a mouse (i.e., to leave his body in that form in order to do his spirit traveling).

Shape-shifting is a primary facet of the shamanic experience. The shaman, transformed into the shape of his or her animal helper, journeys to the Otherworld in that form. We may conclude that shape-shifting left its mark upon the "higher" mythologies of ancient Europe, and that it was still very much a part of surviving shamanic folk practice during the witch trials. European peasants with psychic or shamanic gifts kept animals or "domestic familiars" with whom they enjoyed a particular spiritual kinship. On certain nights, they laid out a feast for the spirits of the dead, fell into a trance, and either rode upon, or were in fact transformed into, animals as they journeyed in spirit to join the Wild Hunt, the procession of departed spirits that was led by the old Pagan Lord and Lady of Otherworld.

Shape-shifting may also explain certain folkloric phenomena that is connected with witchcraft in a more vague way. Take, for instance, the Viking warriors who called themselves "berserkers." The word means "bear shirt," and describes men who, during battle, became possessed by a war-like frenzy so intense as to constitute an out-of-body experience. Were they, in fact, "shape-shifting" into the consciousness of their animal totem, the bear?

Ordinarily, we connect the bear with the Mistress of the Animals rather than with her spouse. The Greek goddess Artemis, associated with wild places and wild creatures, is actually named "Mistress of the Animals" in Homer's *Iliad*, and many scholars believe that the bear was her totem animal.

Yet it is possible that the bear was connected with the Underworld Lord as well. The berserkers were dedicated to the worship of the shamanic god Odin in his aspect as Lord of Battles, and Odin was sometimes named as the leader of the Wild Hunt. Another leader of that spectral procession was King Arthur, whose name means "bear hero," and who was associated with the constellation called the Great Bear (i.e., the Big Dipper). This circumpolar star group was sometimes called Arthur's Wagon and regarded as the vehicle that enabled him to circle the pole star—thus placing Arthur and his Wild Hunt firmly on the North Star Road!

In the Alpine witch trials of the early 1400s, the devil was said to have appeared in the shape of a bear. This is unusual—in later trials, he typically reveals himself as a goat, but the trials in question were very early, probably containing more genuine folk elements and fewer inquisitorial fantasies.

These "folk elements" may well stretch back to an almost unimaginably distant horizon. The earliest form of religious expression of which we have knowledge is intimately connected with the bear. Stone sanctuaries filled with the skulls of gigantic cave bears have been discovered in archaeological contexts that appear to stretch all the way back to Neanderthal Man. Interestingly enough, the caves in which these sanctuaries were found are, for the most part, in Switzerland, not far from the Valais, where the trials that featured the Devil in the shape of a bear were held.

In addition to the berserkers, we may also wish to briefly examine the phenomenon known as lycanthropy—the magical ability to assume the form of a wolf.

In general, werewolves have a rather bad name—they are usually perceived as demented wild men, social outcasts who live in the woods, take on wolf-like characteristics, and consume farm animals or small children. A rather typical case occurred in the French Alps (point of origin for some of the other early witch trials) in 1598. A teenage boy was out picking fruit with his sister when she was attacked by a creature that seemed part human and part wolf. The boy defended his sister, but was mortally wounded in the process when the werewolf grabbed his knife and stabbed him with it.

The local villagers hunted down a whole family of alleged were-wolves, the Gandillons. Perrenette Gandillon, a semi-retarded girl, was immediately blamed for the crime and summarily executed. Her sister Antoinette, her brother Pierre, and his son George were all arrested for lycanthropy and jailed. Pierre in particular seems to have been deeply implicated, for his face was scarred with scratches and he confessed to falling into a trance on Maundy Thursday and attending a "Sabbat of werewolves." When the witch-hunting judge Henri Boguet visited the Gandillon family in jail, they were running about on all fours. The judge asked them to transform themselves into wolves for his benefit. They replied that they were unable to do so because they lacked their traditional ointment or salve (another suggestion that hallucinogenic substances may have been employed by some native European shamans).

There are also cases that are not so typical,[7] and that reveal a rather different side to the much maligned werewolves. One dates from the 1540s, and the other one, a very late example, is from 1692 (the same year in which the last major witch persecutions, the Salem trials, also took place). Both examples come from what was then called Livonia, and which now constitutes the independent Baltic republics of Lithuania, Latvia, and Estonia. This region was the last portion of Europe to remain "officially" Pagan; Lithuania was formally converted to Christianity only in 1386.

In the 1540s, Hermann Witekind, a Livonian by birth and a professor at the University of Riga, interviewed an imprisoned peasant accused of lycanthropy. The peasant danced joyfully about in his jail cell, and seemed inordinately happy. He informed Witekind that he had escaped from jail just the other night, transforming himself into a wolf, freeing himself from his shackles, and climbing out the window. He had then headed for "an immense river," but had ultimately returned to jail "because his master wished it."

More information is supplied by an eighty-year-old man known only as Thiess, accused of being a werewolf in 1692. He testified that he was transformed into a wolf three times a year—on December 13 (St. Lucy's Night), June 23 (St. John's Eve), and the Feast of the Pentecost (which is the seventh Sunday after Easter). On those nights, devils and sorcerers, armed with broomsticks wrapped in horses' tails, stole the shoots of grain from the local fields, and tried to make off with them. If they were successful, the result would be famine. But the werewolves were the defenders of the harvest; armed with iron whips, they pursued the evil ones even to the depths of Hell, which lie at the end of the ocean (an "immense river" indeed). There a great battle ensued for the sake of the harvest.

At the end of his testimony, Thiess declared triumphantly that the werewolves had been victorious that year, and that a fine harvest was assured. He refused to repent of his ways—in fact, he insisted that the werewolves were "the dogs of God" and the enemies of all evil, and that, whatever his interrogators might believe, he himself was certain he would go to Paradise. The old man was sentenced to ten lashes, but apparently survived to fight for the harvest again.

We may remember that the Alpine witches burned in the early 1400s affirmed that the male members of their sect were capable of changing themselves into wolves. We may surmise that the wolf was a well-known totem in Europe who originally protected the village with his fierce courage, and that it was only later, perhaps under the pressure of the witch trials themselves, that his image degenerated into one of evil.

The ability of witches to journey in the spirit mounted on animals, to transform themselves into animals, and the keeping of animal familiars by witches, all reveal yet another component of witchcraft that has its roots in shamanism—the use of animal totems. It was partly by means of an intense shamanic relationship with particular members of the animal kingdom that witches were able to leave their bodies, join the spirits of the departed on those nights when the doors between the worlds were open, and journey in spirit to the Otherworld, there, like Sibillia and Pierina of Milan, to learn the wisdom shamans have always learned—natural healing techniques and portents of the future.

We have now examined a number of shamanic elements in traditional witchlore:

- Initiation into altered states of consciousness through the medium of an intense spiritual experience, or, sometimes, through oral transmission from one's elders;
- The adoption of an animal familiar or, through shape-shifting, an animal persona;
- Travel with the Lord and Lady of the Otherworld as members of the Wild Hunt or procession of the dead;

- A journey to the Otherworld, there to participate in the eternal Feast of the Dead which, on certain nights of the year, was ritually imitated in humble cottages throughout Europe.

The ultimate goal of the witches' experience, therefore, was the Otherworld journey itself. Now it is time to accompany them on their travels.

FINDING YOUR ANIMAL TOTEM

1. This exercise is best performed outside, in Nature, for it is there, after all, that the animals reside. If you can manage it, pack your drum in a day-pack and hike out a ways. Find an isolated spot to sit. Bring a blanket or mat to sit on if that makes you more comfortable.

   There are many, however, who live in the city and do not have ready access to the great outdoors. Don't worry about it; this exercise can easily be practiced indoors as well. All you really need is some room to move and a place to sit.

   As you sit, you may wonder which way to face. There are, in fact, many shamanic traditions about the four cardinal directions. To the earliest European farmers of the Neolithic, the happy Otherworld and all its wisdom and grace was symbolized by the west. Most traditions that have emerged from shamanism maintain this symbolism, with west serving as the direction of transformation, death, and rebirth. The east, as the opposite direction, represents all the opposite qualities embodied in the notion of beginnings; thus Hermetic and Kabbalistic rituals typically begin with the practitioner facing east, and yogis face east each morning to honor the rising sun. The north is commonly regarded as a difficult direction; it is from the north that the winter snows descend upon humankind to chill the earth. The opposite direction, south, is symbolic of abundance and fertility.

   The answer to our question, then, is to face any direction you please, though east or south would be preferable.

   If you are working outdoors at night, you may wish to focus your gaze upon the North Star. If you live in the city and are working indoors, you can simply visualize the North Star shining above your head. The easiest way to find the North Star is to look for the Big Dipper. You probably know where it is already, for it is one of the best-known and most easily-identifiable constellations in the heavens.

Now focus on the Dipper's bowl. Note the end of the bowl farthest from the handle, and follow its line to the top or rim of the bowl. Then keep following that same line with your eyes until you reach the next star. This is Polaris, the North Star. You will know you've located it correctly if the star you're gazing at forms the top of the handle of yet another dipper—the Little Dipper.

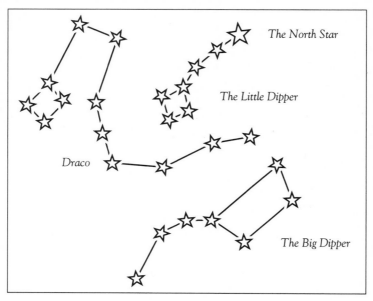

Finding the North Star

2. Indoors or out, begin this exercise with drumming. Drum slowly and rhythmically at first. If you can work with a partner, so much the better. Let your partner do the drumming for you, the better to focus your own concentration.

As you feel yourself become part of the drumbeat, build up your inner World Tree in your imagination. Breathe in and out with a deep and constant rhythm that harmonizes with the drumbeat. Breathing in, draw the energy up from the earth to the topmost branches of the tree; breathing out, circulate the energy back into the earth.

3. When you feel fully empowered with the energy of your own internal World Tree, stand up and increase the pace of the drumbeat. If you are working alone, you may need to get the hang of holding and beating your drum while moving around. (This, along with the difficulty involved in dragging a large object through the outdoors, is why it is best to work with a drum of relatively modest size.) Moving and drumming all at once may seem awkward at first, but Native American shamans do it all the time. Of course, if you are working with a partner, you won't have this problem; and when you stand up you will be signaling your partner that you are ready to dance, and that the pace of the drumming should increase.

   If you genuinely feel that dancing with drum in hand is likely to cramp your style, and if your powers of imagination and will are sufficient to keep the drumbeat pounding in your head without the aid of the physical instrument, then by all means you may set down the drum at this juncture.

4. Move around the room, or around the outdoor space you have selected, in a circular motion. For this kind of work, always move in a clockwise direction. Walking in the path of the sun symbolizes increase and beneficence, while moving counter-sunwise or widdershins produces the opposite effect (and is best left to experienced magical workers who know what they're doing). As you move, feel free to use any kind of footsteps you please, but try to keep your movements more or less in time with the drumming. If someone else is drumming for you, or if you feel sufficiently confident to work without the drum, then you can use your hands as well.

   As you dance, mentally call upon all the world's creatures to be with you in your circle. Send forth a voice from your mind, and see the sound waves traveling out through the universe. You will soon begin to sense the presence of the animal powers, to feel wings brush against your body, to hear the birdsong and the howling of wolves or coyotes, the neighing of horses, the scream of the jaguar—all the sounds and sensations of the animal kingdom.

5. As you dance in a circle, surrounded by the animal powers, be aware of how your footwork changes; be aware of your hands and arms, if you're using them. You will take on a particular gait, a particular stance, a particular set of motions. These movements are characteristic of your animal, whose presence you will now begin to feel.

When an animal has fully established itself within you, let it dance in your spirit for a while. Then, stop dancing. Stand still until your breathing is slow and rhythmic once again. Welcome your animal into your soul.

When working with animals, be open-minded. Most Americans want to have a really trendy animal for a totem—a wolf, a bear, an eagle. I remember a Native American poet who joked about attending a men's group where "all these white guys wanted the biggest animal they could think of for a totem. I told 'em just skip the small stuff and go with Tyrannosaurus Rex."

But the biggest or cutest or trendiest critter isn't necessarily the most powerful animal for you. In European lore, the little mouse was the spirit traveler par excellence, and hence an animal of great power. Don't try to bend the powers of the animal kingdom to your will; just let your animal come to you. Your animal totem may change over time, anyway, or you may find yourself hosting more than one. Records from the witch trials suggest that many witches had at least two or three animal familiars at one time.

Though rituals are both interesting and powerful, they aren't the whole story. More often than not, we acquire our familiars in the most ordinary ways—a stray dog or cat may approach you in the street, begging to be taken home; or, if you live in the country, your familiar may turn out to be the wild critter who's friendly enough to eat from a little bowl on your front porch.

Don't intellectualize about the qualities attributed to different animals—by so doing, you will only end up choosing an animal image of how you want to be, rather than finding the totem you really need. You can go and read about your animal totem after you've found it. The animals detailed in this book are, of course, native to Europe, since they were mentioned during the witch trials. If your animal turns out to be native only to the Americas, you may wish to find out what different Native American tribes believed about that particular animal and its powers. If your animal is native to both Europe and America, you may still wish to examine some of the relevant Native American animal lore, simply to acquire a fuller perspective. All lore and myth arises from the earth, and cannot be separated from the land out of which it was born.

CHAPTER 5

Traveling in the Spirit

THE OTHERWORLD JOURNEY

The World Tree that stands at the center of all creation is more than a monument; it is a highway. Its topmost branches twine around the palaces of heaven; above shines the North Star. Its roots descend into hell, where the spirits of the dead either feast in eternal joy or wander in a kind of vague, shadowy shuffle. It is the shaman's business to travel up and down the trunk of the great tree, bringing back messages from the gods or from the dead.

In many Siberian tribes, actual wooden poles are erected as part of the shamanic ritual; the ascent to the sky is a physical act performed by the shaman. For instance, the Altaic shaman in the previous chapter climbed such a pole on his journey to the sky. Let us follow him once again, on the concluding portion of his journey. A birch branch, notched with nine steps, formed the central pole of his yurt. After sacrificing the horse, he summoned "the mother of the nine eagles," then appeared to sink beneath the weight of gigantic wings. He circled the birch tree several times, then prayed to the Guardian of the Door to send him a guide, which he received in the form of a spirit horse.

Mounted upon his horse, the shaman took up his perch on the first notch of the tree, beating his drum with great vigor. Leaping down again, he straddled a bench covered with horsehide, riding it and exulting that he had reached the first heaven, the level of the full moon. Hurrying back to the tree, he climbed to the second notch, still singing, then the third. At this point his "horse" became weary, and the shaman paused—first, to water his horse, which he did by imitating the sound of a horse drinking, then to prophecy the next season's weather, sicknesses, and misfortunes, as well as the sacrifices the tribe would have to make in order to set things right. Then the shaman summoned the wild gander and continued his journey.

Through the heavens he climbed, miming various actions along the way. As he reached the fifth notch of his ladder, he had a long discussion with the Supreme Creator, giving forth more prophecies while keeping others secret, known only to himself. He reached the ninth heaven (some very talented shamans used a tree with as many as twelve notches) and spoke with Bai Ulgan, the god of the sky, who delivered, through the shaman, yet more predictions about the harvest and the coming season. Finally, the shaman collapsed, exhausted, to awaken a little while later.

The journey to heaven, however, is only half the story, for the World Tree also leads downward, into the depths of the Underworld, and it is here that the shaman must travel in order to communicate with the spirits of the dead, or, in healing rituals, to rescue the souls of those who may have begun to wander down that long dark road but who are still within reach of healing.

In some cultures, a professional distinction exists between "white" shamans who specialize in journeys of heavenly ascension, and "black" shamans whose skill consists of the ability to travel to the Underworld. Among the Altaians, at least, shamanesses undertake only the Underworld journey, which is thus a specialty of women.

Let us remain among the Altaic people for a moment longer, and follow one of their shamans to the land of the dead. According to Eliade,[1] a black shaman, departing from his yurt in a state of ecstasy, took the road to the south (as opposed to the North Star Road). By the power of magic songs, in which the entranced shaman was joined by the companions who were gathered in his yurt, he and his horse crossed vast mountains and deserts, and came at last to the great Mountain of Iron, which is littered with the whitened bones of unsuccessful shamans and their horses. Having climbed and crossed the great mountain, the shaman went on to descend through a hole in the earth. Arriving at last in the netherworld, he had to cross a furious ocean that was traversed by a bridge as narrow as a hair. In the roiling waves below lay, once again, the bones of unsuccessful spirit travelers.

Next, the shaman came to a region where the souls of sinners were tormented. Then, finally, he reached the yurt of Erlik Khan, Lord of the Underworld. The shaman needed to bribe the porter and his dogs with gifts of beer, beef, and polecat skins. Then, at last, he was able to enter the dwelling place of the King of the Dead.

Back in the shaman's own yurt, his audience watched as he rose up, still in trance, and mimed his conversation with Erlik Khan. Depending on the situation, the shaman might be pleading for the soul of a sick tribesman, or conducting a kinsman on the terrible journey, or simply trying to obtain Erlik Khan's blessings for the cattle (the Underworld Lord is, after all, the Master of Animals).

Whether the road led to the sky or to the world below, most Siberian shamans seem to have entered the trance state by way of drumming and chanting. Some, however, employed hallucinogens to induce the ecstatic state. In Siberia itself, the red-and-white fly agaric mushroom seems to have been the drug of choice. It has been suggested that fly agaric was the original *soma*, the ecstatic nectar described in the *Rig Veda*. The Scythians sniffed cannabis, while Native American shamans employed a truly vast pharmacopoeia: peyote in northern Mexico and the American Southwest, mushrooms among the Mound Builders and in ancient Mexico, the San Pedro cactus in the Andes, *ayahuasca* or *yage* in the Amazon.

In some cultures, all the elements of the shaman's quest—trance, hallucinogens, the heavenly journey, the world of the dead or the ancestors, and the blessing of the tribe or kingdom—were united in rituals of great symbolic and spiritual complexity. We may remember that the Classic Maya envisioned a superbly shamanic cosmos with two world mountains, a thirteen-step pyramid leading to heaven, and an inverted, nine-step pyramid leading to the Underworld. These two pyramids found their center in a common axis, a great ceiba tree. The recent decipherment of Mayan hieroglyphics indicates that the pyramids that now fascinate tourists from all over the globe were built as models of the World Mountain. The king of the Mayan city state— who, like an Egyptian pharaoh, was regarded as a divine being—prepared for public rituals by fasting, praying, and ingesting psychedelic chemicals within the confines of the temples that crowned the pyramids.* During the ritual, he emerged onto the top of the pyramid, often performing a sacred dance. Thus, symbolically, he stood atop the World Mountain, his own body aligned with the trunk of the World Tree. Indeed, the World Tree is always within us, and we may assume that the king's own inner World Tree was fully activated by a combination of meditative discipline and hallucinogens, and that he was thereby engaged in the shamanic ascent, linked to the heavenly world.

In the course of the ceremony, it would be necessary to consult the ancestors, the spirits of the dead (in this case, the spirits of former kings) who lived in the world below. To summon them, the king would light huge quantities of copal incense, slit his penis with a stingray spine, and bleed onto pieces of specially prepared bark paper. Soon, an ancestor spirit would emerge from the incense smoke and speak to the king, who would communicate his vision to the assembled people. Mayan women of royal lineage sometimes undertook these rites themselves, though instead of employing a stingray spine upon their genitalia, they passed lengths of thick, thorny yucca rope through their tongues.

---

* In many cases, the temple atop the pyramid may have been regarded as the mouth of the Earth Monster, a primordial reptilian deity who, like the Norse Midgard Serpent, encircled the world.

The themes that constitute the shamanic journey to the Other-world are so universal that they appear outside the cultural sphere of shamanism proper. They are the search for:

- Divine wisdom (especially involving healing or curing);
- Communication with the ancestors;
- Spiritual and material benefits for the tribe, harvest, kingdom, etc.

The shamanic ascent, or "journey to the sky," for instance, has even found its way into the so-called "higher religions." As noted earlier (Chapter 1), Mircea Eliade points out that yoga itself may well have developed out of shamanism. In Hindu mythology, the World Mountain is known as Mt. Meru, and each of us is said to have Mt. Meru within us, embodied in the spinal column. In yoga, the vital power called kundalini, perceived as a serpent coiled at the bottom of the spine (like the serpent, dragon, or other reptile at the bottom of the World Tree), rises up the spinal column, or internal World Tree, until it reaches the "thousand-petaled lotus," the crown chakra at the top of the head, which is the symbolic equivalent of the "world of the gods," the North Star, or the eagle that dwells at the top of the World Tree. This process of the "ascension" of vital energy, in addition to bringing enlightenment, also serves to endow the successful yogi with *siddhis*, magical powers that are essentially the same as the powers enjoyed by shamans.

Echoes of the shamanic ascent can even be found in the Bible, especially in the story of Jacob. We might suspect Jacob of being a shaman from the very outset, for he came into the world holding onto the heel of his brother Esau, and we know that heels and thighs are part of the shamanic mystique. Again, when Jacob wrestled with the angel, his thigh was "thrown out of joint" (i.e., Jacob suffered the shaman's magical wound). While he was on his way to find a bride, he lay down to sleep with his head upon a rock. He dreamed of angels *ascending a ladder to heaven*, and heard a voice that prophesied his future. When he awoke from his experience of shamanic ascent, he raised up the stone upon which he had slept and poured oil over it, as if he were erecting the model of a World Mountain upon the place that had become his own *axis mundi*, his universal center.

BEANSTALKS AND CORACLES

Inasmuch as the Otherworld journey is a universal theme, we would expect to find it among the mythologies of Europe as well. The Orphic cult of ancient Greece, mentioned earlier, retained many archaic features—an Orphic myth in which the world is created by the hatching of a world egg laid by the "bird of night" has been identified by Marija Gimbutas as part of the mythology of the most ancient Balkan farming villages.[2] The Orphic path revolved around obtaining special or occult knowledge of the Otherworld, primarily through an initiation ritual which itself contained shamanic elements such as smearing the faces of initiates with ashes, symbolic of the Underworld.

Orpheus, the mythic founder of the cult, was a great Underworld traveler himself. A poet from Thrace, whose singing charmed the animals (i.e., he is a Lord of Animals), Orpheus lost his beautiful wife Eurydice to the bite of a serpent. He set out to Hades to win her back—much as a shaman might pursue the soul of a sick tribesman down the Underworld road in hopes of reclaiming it. Orpheus' singing charmed the inhabitants of the Underworld, even impressing Hades and Persephone, but he failed to bring Eurydice all the way back into the light of day—he inadvertently looked back at her, which caused her to disappear into Hades once and for all. (Odin, too, failed to bring Balder back from the dead—for even the greatest shamans of all may fail to retrieve a soul from the Lord and Lady of the Otherworld.)

If the shamanic journey is found in the most sophisticated Greek myths, it is also found in the humblest of folktales. The British folk hero known only as Jack was, like many shamans, regarded as an impractical idiot—he traded a useful cow for a handful of silly magic beans, but the beans proved to be magic indeed, creating a gigantic "beanstalk" up which Jack climbed—another ascent of the World Tree. At the top he found a magical land—the Otherworld or land of the gods. The folktale, of course, comes to us from Europe's Christian centuries, and thus the lord of the sky has been transformed into a grumpy giant whose great desire is to eat Christians!* Nevertheless, Jack manages to rescue his father and win both a magic harp and a magic bird.

The tale of "Jack and the Beanstalk" suggests that European peoples had rites based upon the ascent of the World Tree, and we have already seen that they were aware of the Underworld journey as well. The story of Odin's (or Hermod's) journey down the World Tree to Hel, mounted upon Sleipnir, the shamanic horse, features some of the

Jack and the Beanstalk,
from an old woodcut

---

* The famous "Fee-fi-fo-fum, I smell the blood of an Englishman" was originally "I smell the blood of a Christian."

same elements as the Underworld journey of the Altaic "black" shaman—a guardian dog, a porter at the Underworld threshold, an ocean or "Resounding River," and a narrow bridge.

European peoples accomplished their journeys up and down the World Tree by various methods. We began our study with the Norse sibyl Thorbjorg, mistress of a rite called *seidr*, which was practiced exclusively by women,* and which involved journeying to the Otherworld in a trance induced by music and chanting; its object was to obtain information about the future. The fact that Thorbjorg sat upon a cushion of hen's feathers has suggested to some scholars that she may have taken flight in the shape of a bird. The bird as a shamanic guide was well-known among Celtic peoples as well. Nikolai Tolstoy draws attention to elements in the oldest Merlin stories that suggest that King Arthur's enchanter may have possessed a "cloak of feathers,"[3] and Cuchulain fell into a shamanic trance following his attempt to bring down two magical birds.

Cuchulain's trance is described as a "sleep," though some shamanic trance phenomena among the Celts was a good deal more dramatic. In 1188, the priest Gerald of Wales made an ecclesiastical journey through the land of his birth and gave this sketch of the Welsh soothsayers called *awenyddion*, which means "poets":

> *When you consult them about some problem, they immediately go into a trance and lose control of their senses, as if they are possessed. They do not answer the question put to them in any logical way. Words stream from their mouths, incoherently and apparently meaningless and without any sense at all, but all the same well expressed: and if you listen carefully to what they say you will receive the solution to your problem.*

---

* According to Snorri Sturluson, Odin was regarded as "less than a man" because he practiced *seidr*! The feminine emphasis in *seidr* suggests that it was oriented towards the world of the dead which lay beneath Yggdrasil rather than the heavenly world at the top of the tree. The art was practiced by priestesses of Freya, who was a goddess of fertility—she and her brother Freyr may be yet another incarnation of the Lord and Lady of the Otherworld. Odin, too, made a typically "feminine" shamanic journey—down the Road to Hel to seek Balder's soul.

Gerald went on to say that when it was all over and the soothsayers came out of their trance, they seemed just like ordinary people awakening from a deep sleep—though they required a good shake before they could regain control of themselves. Afterward, they remembered nothing of what they had said during their trance.

The awenyddion seemed to receive the divinatory gift:

> ...through visions which they see in their dreams. Some of them have the impression that honey or sugary milk is being smeared on their mouths; others say that a sheet of paper with words written on it is pressed against their lips.[4]

The techniques of these Welsh soothsayers have their correlations elsewhere in Europe. Another monk,[5] this one living in what is now Romania, recorded in the seventeenth century how Moldavian enchanters, both men and women, answered questions put to them about illnesses, future events, and so on. They whispered, rolled their heads, grimaced, and shook. Then they fell spread-eagled upon the ground, in a trance, for an hour or more. Before awakening, they rose up and behaved as if possessed by demons. Then they awoke and delivered their prophecies. In the Macedonian village of Velvendos, certain women, in a state of trance, received information from "angels" about the village dead; this custom persisted at least until the 1950s. Another village, called Duboka and situated in what is now Serbia, also maintained shamanic rituals until very recently; these were actually conducted in public. During the Pentecost, some of the village women fell into a trance state during which they made contact with the dead. Other villagers played the favorite songs of some of the recently deceased in order to invoke their spirits. While the women lay in trance, men danced around them. The leader of the dance held a special knife decorated with garlic and camomile. When the trance session was over, he sprayed a mixture of river water and herbs into their faces to awaken them.

The trance phenomena recorded by Gerald of Wales among medieval Celts, therefore, seems to have been fairly common throughout Europe and to some extent persists to this very day. But it is to the

Celts that the most unique form of the shamanic journey belongs, for some of them traveled to the Otherworld in boats.

In Celtic myth, the Otherworld frequently lies "over the waves." Perhaps the inhabitants of the British Isles had envisioned it as such for several millennia before the Celts ever arrived. Some of the most important Neolithic tombs are oriented toward the west, toward the setting sun and the vast ocean. In any event, the Otherworldly voyage is a common theme in Celtic legend. The most elaborate of such tales is "The Voyage of Maildun," in which the hero sets forth with sixty men to find the slayers of his father and, in the process, encounters a number of fabulous "islands" that bear the clear physiognomy of the Otherworld.

If Maildun set forth upon a vengeance quest, there were other Celtic heroes whose travels arose from motives that were more clearly shamanic. Bran the Voyager heard the song of an ethereal woman and could do naught but follow her, taking ship to a magic realm called the Land of Women. In a similar tale, Connla the Fair received an apple (the tabooed "red food" of the dead) from another mysterious woman, and the taste of mortal food or mortal joy was ever afterward insufficient for him. He sulked until the woman reappeared, at which point he set sail with her for the mystic west, where, according to the story, she lived in a "great fairy mound." And, most famous of all, King Arthur was borne away to the "Isle of Avalon" in a barge that was sailed by Morgan le Fay—a medieval redaction of the Old Bone Goddess!—there to await healing and rebirth.

But do such tales indicate actual shamanic practice and belief, or are they merely the result of literary convention?

In the middle of the sixth century A.D., the Byzantine historian Procopius[6] recorded a strange story that he himself labeled "superstition." Although his geography is vague, Procopius' tale seems to take place on the peninsula of Brittany, a Celtic enclave in northwest France right across the channel from Britain itself. Procopius says that some of the men there performed a special task, one which was inherited from "those who did it before them." On certain nights, they went to sleep with the knowledge that they would receive a call. A knock was heard at the door and a mysterious voice called them forth from their homes. Impelled by a power greater than their own will, they made their way down to the beach, where they found special boats waiting for them, always empty. But as they set sail, the boats sank almost down to the level of the water, for they were laden with the souls of the dead. A voice called out the names and stations of the invisible passengers, who were then ferried across the channel to "Brittia," which apparently means Britain. The journey thence, which would normally last a night and a day, took only an hour, and the boats were light and buoyant on the return voyage.

Because the Breton men were drawn forth from their beds, we may suspect that they were traveling "in the spirit," and that their voyages were, in fact, trance experiences. Oddly enough, there is evidence that such voyages were undertaken in reality—and by Christians, no less! During the time of Procopius, and for a century or two thereafter, monks in Ireland practiced a "Celtic Christianity" that was quite different from official Catholic doctrine (and hence eventually suppressed). Believing that God could most easily be discovered through communion with wild nature, Celtic monks lived as hermits on the rugged coasts of western Ireland. Some of them actually set themselves adrift on the Atlantic in sturdy little coracles, regarding this as an extremely powerful form of spiritual practice. St. Brendan the Navigator is the most famous of these Christian voyagers, for the story of his travels contains material that, some writers argue, reflects an accurate picture of North American geography. But whether or not Brendan ever reached present-day New England, the mystical and dreamlike quality of his tale indicates that at least some of its components were drawn from the myth of the Otherworld voyage.

THE JOURNEYS OF THE WITCHES

If we turn to the witchcraft trials, we may discover several different levels of communication with the inhabitants of the Otherworld. Some individuals, for example, possessed the ability to see the dead, though they did not claim to be able to journey with them into their realm. Anna la Rossa, of Udine in Italy, testified that she could see the dead. She told one individual that "master Battista" was going about looking worried, with his head cast down, and she informed someone else that his deceased mother was of good cheer and often visited the sanctuary of Santa Maria della Bella.

On another occasion, while she herself was praying in that same sanctuary, Anna la Rossa saw the dead daughter of a certain Lucia Peltrara, wrapped in a winding sheet and looking disheveled. The spirit asked Anna to convey to her mother Lucia the following request: that she should give a shirt to a woman named Paola, and that she should go on pilgrimage to several local sanctuaries. (Here again, as with Chonradt Stocklin, we see an individual accused of witchcraft whose "visions" have a seemingly pious Christian character.)

During a series of heresy trials held against the Albigensians in the Pyrenean village of Montaillou, between 1320 and 1325, a farmer named Guillaume Fort marveled at the ability of his neighbor, Arnaude Rives, to see the dead. Arnaude often saw demons leading the spirits of the deceased—which looked like living, fully fleshed bodies—across an isolated region in the mountainous wilderness of the Pyrenees. She then watched as the demons cast the souls over the edges of precipices, where they fell howling to the rocks below, though of course they could not die. This curious version of the Wild Hunt, or procession of the dead, was not witnessed by Arnaude alone—Bernard den Alazais, a blacksmith, could see it too.

In other instances, medieval European peasants used divinatory tools to see into the Otherworld and obtain information therefrom. The most common such practice was gazing into a simple bowl of water, a technique known as "scrying." Wyprat Musin, a woman of Tyrol, was tried for witchcraft in 1525. She confessed that she often followed a certain Fraw Selga (sister of Fraw Venus), in processions of the Wild Hunt that took place on Thursday or Saturday nights. Wyprat Musin upon occasion gazed into a basin of water, wherein she saw the flames of Purgatory and the images of various folk in her parish who were destined to die within the year.

In 1622, a Hessian peasant named Diel Breull lost his wife and children and fell into a profound depression. Sinking into a trance one day, he awoke to find himself inside the World Mountain, the Venusberg of medieval German lore. Here he encountered Fraw Holt (Mother Hulda), who instructed him to gaze into a basin of water. He saw magnificent horses, men who sat feasting in the midst of flames, and numerous people, now long dead, whom he had known in years past. In 1629, and again in 1630, Breull was tried for sorcery—but by this time he had taken up the practice of gazing into a crystal ball!

Perhaps the most elaborate testimony concerning the practice of "scrying" comes from Mantua, in Italy. Giuliano Verdena, a weaver, was tried for witchcraft in 1489. It was affirmed that he practiced a form of divination wherein he lit a candle, placed it next to a vase filled with water (sometimes holy water), and then enlisted the services of a child, whether boy or girl, to gaze into the vase and relate what he or she saw there. The child was taught first to invoke a spirit called "white angel" or "holy angel," while Giuliano read from a book. The children saw in that vase the spirits of the dead, some mounted, some on foot, some without hands, and most looking like "Muslims" (at least this is how Verdena and the children interpreted their appearance). Sometimes they saw a large man seated with servants on either side of him; this was Lucifer. When the inquisitors questioned Giuliano about this very suspect personage, he replied that he called upon Lucifer only in an attempt to persuade the "master of the arts" to reveal to him the location of certain treasures, which he intended to put to good Christian purpose by using them to finance a crusade against the Turks. When Giuliano himself gazed into the bowl of water, he saw a woman called "the mistress of the game," clothed in black and with a long chin hanging all the way down to her stomach (our old friend the Bone Goddess). She offered to reveal to him the secrets of herbs and animals.

Simple though the practice of "scrying" may seem to be, it is significant from the mythological point of view. Those who gazed into these ordinary bowls of water did so in order to observe the condition of souls in the Otherworld, and to learn knowledge of future events. We may remember two other pools of water that held in their depths the imprint of both the future and the past—the Well of Fate and the Well of Memory. These magic springs not only figure prominently in Norse mythology but appear in the Orphic cult as the Wells of Memory and Forgetfulness. Sometimes, as we have seen, there may be as many as nine springs, and sometimes only one. We have noted that, throughout Europe, a local tree and spring were often revered as regional manifestations of the World Tree and the Primordial Well. This author considers it very likely that the bowls of water into which the witches gazed owed their symbolic origin to the Well of Memory and Fate, the pool of water beneath the World Tree that is the source of *all* knowledge, both of the present and the future.

It is clear, then, that individuals accused of witchcraft had various humble methods of communicating with the Otherworld. Certain people, believed to possess a form of psychic perception or clairvoyance, could "see" the dead, who were, in fact, all around us at every moment—for as the heretical Cathar preacher Belibaste affirmed, "Everything is full of souls. All the air is full of good and evil spirits."[7] Yet other individuals, drawing on the ancestral memory of the Well of Fate, employed the use of a basin or vase of water in order to gaze into the Otherworld.

However, most witches or followers of the Wild Hunt practiced much more dramatic methods of traveling in the spirit, and these methods have become part of our collective folklore....

THE SAVOY ALPS, CIRCA 1420

The six of them were gathered there in the firelight, in Guillaume Lebrun's cottage. They huddled close to the hearth, for it was the Ember Days, the bitter days after Christmas. Though there had been but little snow that year, and only a few icy patches still clung to the roof, there was a harsh wind blowing outside, troubling the chimney with sound and smoke. In one corner, Mistress Lebrun had set a small table for the Good Folk, decorated with apples she had saved in the cellar all winter. A thin candle burned on the table beside the apples, but aside from that the only light in the room came from the fireplace.

Francoise Chausse, fifteen years old, sat before the fire on a three-legged stool and stared at the floor. She was naked, her skin glistening. She was starting to sweat.

Ordinarily, Francoise was a cheerful girl, but tonight she was uncharacteristically solemn. More precisely, she was afraid. Tonight was to be her first journey with the Good Folk.

She wished her brother Pierre could be there, for she always felt safe with him. But none of the men from her family were present—in fact, Master Lebrun was the only male in the room. Her mother Lisette was there to see her set forth upon her journey. Francoise loved her mother and trusted her—there was no question of that. But Lisette Chausse could be a little bit...well, frightening at times, especially when possessed by the deep, impersonal detachment that came upon her when she herself was close to the Good Folk.

As she was tonight....

The ointment had been prepared by Marie Grandet, the oldest of them all, who had gone about the village wrinkled and bent with age for as long as Francoise could remember. Marie's daughter was a staunch Catholic who avoided her mother at all costs, and for some years Marie had complained bitterly that her knowledge of herbs was sure to die with her, since there was no one to pass it on to. But her granddaughter Jeanne (child of Marie's oldest son, not of her devout daughter) was showing an interest, and indeed, she had helped her grandmother mix the potion tonight, and rub it all over Francoise's body after she had stripped down.

And now Francoise was beginning to perspire in earnest, and the room was starting to spin, and the prayers to the Good Folk that Mistress Lebrun muttered as she knelt by the table were starting to take on a rhythm, a melody, a dreamlike incantatory quality....

"Mother...," called Francoise. She was beginning to spin away.

"It's all right," murmured Lisette. "It's all right."

"Mother!"

And now they could all hear the terror in Francoise's voice. The girl rose from her stool and walked a few unsteady steps toward her mother. But Lisette just stared dispassionately back at her. It was time for the girl to go on her own....

Francoise collapsed on the floor, her eyes staring wide into the Otherworld.

Then she stiffened up, and her mouth fell open.

Those with the sight saw the mouse, the little gray Spirit Traveler, emerging.

"It is good," whispered Marie. "She will fly...."

A young witch applying her flying ointment

Francoise crawled to her knees. Her eyes were still wild, but the fear had been replaced by a kind of ecstasy. Her lips, softly parted, trembled as she tried to speak to the Good Folk swarming around her.

"Now," commanded Marie Grandet.

Guillaume Lebrun had the broom at the ready, and though he had seen many a spirit journey—and was no mean traveler himself—he was still surprised by the strength and force with which Francoise grasped the broom.

Planting the broom hard on the floor, Francoise used it to raise herself up. She straddled it, clinging to it with her thighs, stroking the besom of willows as if it were a horse's mane.

Sweat streamed from her face. She spoke words, but none that anyone could understand. What they all saw was a naked girl, wrapped around a broomstick, thrusting up and down like a rider on a horse, her shadow dancing in the firelight.

Francoise raised one hand and arched her back as if in flight. The sounds coming out of her mouth were recognizable now; Francoise was meowing like a cat.

The little group around the hearth fire urged her on. Sitting in a circle, they stamped their feet on the floor in rhythm, humming a long, low wordless chant led by old Marie. Francoise rode on.

There was a wild gust of air as the bitter wind howled in the chimney.

Once again, Francoise collapsed onto the floor.

Guillaume Lebrun helped Lisette carry the girl to the bed, while Mistress Lebrun fussed around her, wiped her streaming brow with a cloth. Francoise was clearly in trance; or, more accurately, she had gone with the Good Folk. Everyone agreed that her first journey was turning out quite successfully. They agreed on the details as well— Francoise's soul had left her body in the shape of a mouse, allowing her to mount the spirit horse and fly. She had changed into a cat and flown away up the chimney.

Marie and her granddaughter Jeanne left a little while later; Lisette lingered with her daughter, speaking softly with Master and Mistress Lebrun as the night wore on. They spoke of the old days, when their parents and grandparents had gone visiting an Otherworld that—or so it seemed in memory—must have been much closer in those times.

But the Land of the Good Folk was never far away, at least not for those who believed. Francoise stirred a bit in the bed, and there appeared to be a smile on her lips. As the wind wailed through the village—the sound of the Wild Hunt, as anyone with sense would know—Mistress Lebrun kept casting her glance over to the little table in the corner of the room, watching the candle there gutter and flicker....

This, of course, is admittedly a fictional reconstruction, though based upon standard items from the testimony of the witch trials.

First, there is the nature of the journey itself. That the "flight" of the witches was, in fact, a shamanic trance—what we would presently call "astral travel"—is attested from many different sources. The ben-andanti, of course, journeyed to the Otherworld to "fight for the harvest" while remaining asleep in their beds. In fact, they believed that if they were to be turned face down, their souls would be unable to re-enter their bodies. The medieval satirist Jean de Meung noted (Chapter 3) that the "demented" individuals who believed themselves to be part of Dame Habonde's company *left their bodies*, passed right through the doors, and then went riding with the "good women" or entering people's houses.

Nider, the demonologist whose *Formicarius* accused witches of cannibalism, also had a few words to say regarding the spirit journey.[8] He tells of a woman who insisted that she habitually rode out with Diana in a large basket. The woman was watched, and witnesses reported that she didn't really go anywhere; she remained in the room but fell into a trance. When she awoke, she was convinced that she had been on a long journey.

THE FLYING OINTMENT

Margherita of San Rocco, at her trial in 1571, declared that her visits to "the games" were undertaken in the spirit, and that she left her body at home. Her companion, Polissena of San Macario, says that "I greased myself with the ointment I had brought with me...and was transformed into a cat, *left the body at home*, descended the stair, and went out by the door."[9]

Polissena's testimony is of interest, for here we find no less than three of the classic elements in shamanic travel:

- The use of a potion or "ointment;"
- The induction of a shamanic trance wherein one leaves one's body;
- A journey in the form of an animal.

That witches traveled to the Otherworld "in the spirit" has been demonstrated throughout the present work; and in the previous chapter, we examined the question of animal transformation among witches. It is time, now, to take a look at Polissena's "ointment" and address the issue of hallucinogenic drugs.

The topic, of course, lends itself to sensationalism. Two or three decades ago, academic researchers became very fond of the theory that the famous "flying ointment" of the witch trials was a derivative of the deadly nightshade family, and that, consequently, most of the phenomena recorded in the witchcraft trials could be explained as hallucinations resulting from the use of psychotropic chemicals. This was a theory that, at that time, was certain to make professors popular with their students, who were themselves ingesting most anything they could lay their hands on.

But does it really explain the spirit travels of the witches?

Yes, and no. Hallucinogens probably played a role in the activities of European witches, but that role has, upon occasion, been dramatically overstated.

The use of drugs by shamans to induce ecstatic forms of trance is common throughout the world. We have noted the use of "magic mushrooms" among the Maya and the Mound Builders, *yage* in the Amazon, and so on. The most commonly used hallucinogen among Siberian shamans was the fly agaric mushroom, with its red cap and white spots, and fly agaric may have been the principal ingredient in the divine *soma* that plays such a prominent role in the *Rig Veda*.

The concept of a divine, intoxicating substance that belongs to the gods but that may also bring spiritual ecstasy to mortals appears throughout European mythology as well—as the "poetic mead" of the Vikings and the Dionysian cult, and as the "ambrosia" consumed by the Greek gods. Though there is no hard proof that fly agaric was still employed by peasants of the late Middle Ages, there are, at least, some provocative hints. As noted earlier, a certain Billia la Castagna was said to have created a potion from "toad's excrement" that was used to initiate individuals into an heretical cult. Since mushrooms were often referred to either as "toad stools" or with other idiomatic expressions involving animal excrement, there is the possibility that Billia may have been preparing her own version of *soma*, used to induct witches into the techniques of the ecstatic journey.

Toads, in fact, commonly appear in the trial records in connection with "witches' brews" of all kinds, and, also mentioned in the previous chapter, some species of toads contain the psychotropic chemical bufotenin, so that licking or eating the toad itself may also induce an hallucinogenic state.

By far the most common elements in the "flying ointments" that appear again and again in the trial records, however, are herbs such as henbane and belladonna, members of the nightshade family that contain atropine chemicals. When combined into an ointment and rubbed on the flesh, these substances would indeed invoke a trance state characterized by a sensation of "flying."

It is possible that all these substances—fly agaric mushrooms, bufotenin, and the atropine drugs of the nightshade family—were used by witches in much the same way that hallucinogens have been used by shamans all over the world. However, many accused witches, especially the Italian benandanti, make no mention of ointments, and were apparently able to enter trance states without the use of chemicals. Those who believed that they had been born "under the sign" (i.e., with a caul) actually fell into trance involuntarily, whenever the Ember Days approached—or even on every Thursday. In the examples researched by this author, the "flying ointment," though mentioned fairly frequently, appears in a little fewer than half of the trial records where astral travel is implicit. In the end, it is fair to conclude that some of the back-country shamans accused of witchcraft did, in fact, induce their journeys with the Wild Hunt by ingesting hallucinogenic substances; the majority, however, probably did not.

THE BROOMSTICK

An even more common adjunct to spirit travel than the flying ointment is the broom, which is mentioned so often that it has become a
(sometimes comical) part of our folklore. The earliest portrait of a
"witch on a broom" is found in Schleswig Cathedral in Germany and
dates from about 1280; the witch in question is called "Frigga," who, in
Norse myth, is the wife of Odin and whose fertility associations have
provided the English language with at least one four-letter word. Even
earlier, a literary reference to witches flying on brooms can be found in
the Icelandic saga of *Burnt Njal* (which, in Chapter 3, also provided us
with a dramatic portrait of the Old Bone Goddess in multiple form as
the Valkyries). This would suggest that the actual image, or practice, of
witches riding on brooms is derived from Germanic or Teutonic elements in European Paganism, and perhaps had its origin in the Norse
rites of *seidr*.

Whether or not this is the case, the famous broomstick of witchlore can be related to an even broader context, for it has a long and
respectable shamanic ancestry. During shamanic rituals, a stick or staff
often served as a substitute for the spirit horse. When the Hungarian
shamans called *taltos* mounted to the sky, they placed a reed between
their legs and galloped away, as if on a horse. Among the Buryat, the
staffs of shamans were actually mounted with the image of a horse's
head. Similar staffs or scepters, also mounted with carved horse's
heads, are found in the earliest Indo-European sites in Europe, and
date back to circa 4,300 B.C.

The horse was unknown among the village farmers of Neolithic
Europe, but was a sacred animal among the Indo-European tribes who
poured into the European land mass mounted on horseback. From
India to Ireland, early Indo-European peoples practiced a rite known as
the "horse sacrifice," a form of which, as we have already seen, was still
common among Altaic shamans as late as the nineteenth century.

In Sanskrit, the horse sacrifice is called *asvamedha*, a very revealing
term: *asva* means "horse," but *medha* means "drunk with mead." We

think of mead as a form of fermented honey, though in this context, as among the Vikings and the worshippers of Dionysus, it may well have been a rather more potent concoction, containing the essence of the fly agaric mushroom. Thus the horse is connected, even in the earliest contexts, with ecstatic journeys induced by hallucinogens.

The Viking World Tree also has a rather revealing name—Yggdrasil means "horse of Ygg," and Ygg is a synonym for Odin. Thus the World Tree itself is "Odin's horse," the pathway upon which he rides between the worlds, mounted on the eight-legged Sleipnir.

In the shamanic world view, a simple stick, or broom, could have some very powerful associations. It was:

- The World Tree or *axis mundi*, up which the shaman climbs;
- The spirit horse upon which he makes the journey.

The practice of miming the spirit horse's transcendent journey has survived up until the present day. A "hobby horse," for instance, appears in England's Morris Dances, as well as in the Horned Dance of Abbots Bromley, which we shall examine in more detail later on. The most famous English hobby horse, however, is the one who plays the starring role in the May Day celebration at Padstow, in Cornwall. There are, in fact, two dancers elaborately dressed as horses, who ritually die and are resurrected in an apparent re-enactment of the shaman's initiatory death-and-rebirth experience.

In Kent there is a "Hooden Horse" comprised of a horse mask on a pole, carried by a man who is concealed in a sheet. The Hooden Horse is accompanied, among others, by a "jockey" who tries to ride on its back and a "Mollie," a man dressed in woman's clothes who carries, interestingly enough, a besom or broom. It has been suggested that the term "hooden" is derived from Woden or Odin, though it may equally well be associated with Robin Hood, another folk character with shamanic roots, whom we shall meet a bit later on. In Cheshire, a Hooden Horse is actually linked with the Feast for the Dead. On Halloween Night, a group of "soulers," accompanied by a Hooden Horse, goes from house to house with specially baked "soul cakes" and sings a begging song in which prayers for the dead are requested.

The presence of horse-headed staffs in 4,300 B.C., together with the persistence of "hobby horse" rituals in contemporary England, strongly suggests that such traditions remained alive and well throughout the intervening centuries, including the late Middle Ages. The most likely explanation for the folk image of the witch riding on a broom, therefore, is the use of brooms or besoms as surrogate spirit horses or World Trees.

Sifting through all the evidence for spirit journeys among the peasants accused of witchcraft in the Burning Times, we may arrive at the following question:

If witches, whether through natural psychic ability or with the help of hallucinogenic plants, climbed the World Tree or rode the spirit horse to the Otherworld, then what exactly did they find there?

It is time now to follow them into the Otherworld itself.

A witch and her cat familiar on broomsticks, from an old woodcut

135

SCRYING

Among those who frequently stood accused of witchcraft, scrying was a common way of gaining Otherworldly knowledge. In this book, we have encountered individuals such as Diel Breull, Wyprat Musin, and Giuliano Verdena, all of whom gazed into a bowl of water in order to see (or "scry") into the spirit world, and thus gain information about what was happening in that other dimension. Diel Breull, as we have seen, eventually "graduated" to the use of a crystal ball.

The mechanics of scrying are amazingly simple:

1. Find a surface upon which to gaze. Conventional "fortune tellers" have typically favored "crystal balls," and, though these are not as popular as they used to be, they are still seen on occasion. These large globes of leaded crystal are, however, rather expensive.

Native American shamans typically prefer a simple, uncut piece of quartz crystal. To the talented crystal gazer, the patterns inside the crystal take on an infinite variety of shapes, and form suggestive images and pictures. The Navajo Indians of northern Arizona and northwestern New Mexico actually recognize a whole class of shamans called "crystal gazers."

European witches, as we have seen, preferred the use of a simple bowl of water, though this, because it lacks the clouded depths of the crystal ball or the patterns of the typical quartz crystal, is probably, for all but the most advanced or talented practitioners, the most difficult method of scrying.

Since scrying probably has its mythological origins in the idea of gazing into the primordial Well of Memory and Fate, one can always go back to the source and simply find a pool of clear water somewhere in the woods. As with the bowl, this is a very difficult method. A clear spring of water or a peaceful pool formed by a forest stream may be restful, soothing, and conducive to a meditative state of mind, but the surface, once again, lacks the suggestive features of the quartz or crystal ball. Also, you have to take care not to be distracted by fish, colorful rocks, and so on.

2. Once you have chosen a surface, simply sit. Breathe deeply and rhythmically until all mental chatter disappears and the mind is clear of thoughts. If you like, use the technique outlined on page 26—imagine that you are sitting on a mountain peak, and that your thoughts are just clouds, blown to pieces by the wind.

   Then allow yourself to gaze, in a non-directive way, at the scrying surface. It is important not to focus intently on anything. The kind of seeing inherent in scrying arises on the margins of our consciousness, the periphery of our perceptions. Remember how you walked through the trees, looking for your own special tree without actually looking at it. This is precisely the same thing.

3. If you are successful, you will begin to see shapes, forms, and pictures in the interior of your quartz crystal, or on the surface of the bowl of water or forest pool. Now you are scrying.

   Does this sound simple? It is, in fact, the most difficult exercise included in this book. At one time in human history, we may all have had a ready and clear ability to "see" in this manner—and it is probable that this ability still remains within each and every one of us, sleeping in our unconscious. So much of this natural ability has been lost, however, that only those with a considerable amount of natural psychic talent, or those who work very hard at training their innate psychic faculties, can actually perceive vivid images from gazing on a scrying surface. Don't be disappointed if scrying turns out to be somewhere between difficult and impossible for you personally.

THE ASCENT UP THE WORLD TREE

This exercise is a guided journey to the deeper realms of your own mind, and the collective mind as well. In it, you will take a first look at the Otherworld. Your purpose, on this initial visit, will be simply to listen. Traditional shamans journey up the World Tree to receive messages from the gods, and this is what you, too, will do, whether you prefer to imagine the gods as real, distinct entities, or as archetypes within the collective mind. Either way, the wisdom spoken by "the gods" is real.

1. Sit with your spine erect, your eyes closed. Breathe in and out, deeply and with regularity. If you like, you may also use your drum, beating it in time to your breathing until you feel clear and calm.

   As in the exercise called "Growing the Inner Tree," imagine that your tree of power lies within you and that your spine is its trunk. See its roots reaching down into the earth beneath your feet, and its topmost branches swirling round the crown of your head. Breathe the energy up and down your spine, from heaven to earth.

2. When you are fully empowered with energy, mentally move your inner tree so that you see it in front of you, shining with light and power, enormously large. It seems to rise up forever, into the distant shining stars. Look up toward the North Star, which shines above the topmost branches. Your own inner tree has been transformed into the great World Tree.

3. For this next part of the exercise, you will need to use all your powers of imagination. See yourself rising up, walking away from your body as it sits there, on the floor or in a chair. See yourself approaching the great Tree.

   As you begin to climb, try to feel the cool bark scratching against your fingers and hands. Notice the comforting smells of wild Nature emanating from the Tree. Go slowly, from branch to branch, like Jack climbing the beanstalk in the old fairy tale.

4. Higher and higher you climb, until at last you find yourself surrounded by clouds. The mist swirls. The cool, damp air is bracing to your spirit. If you want to look down, go ahead. Don't be afraid—you cannot fall down from inside the sky of mind. Take a look at the world, the fields and cities and forests, shining below you with a golden glow, as if the whole world were magic—which indeed it is.

5. Now, at last, you burst through the clouds. Now, at last, you are among the highest branches of all, at the very top of the Tree.

   Find a branch to sit on, and look all around you. Below your feet is a canopy of clouds, shining with the light of the Otherworld sun or moon. So bright and vivid are these clouds, they seem to be the solid ground of this different world—silver cloud fields stretching on and on like the green fields of earth.

6. Now you are above the clouds; there is nothing to do but watch.

   What do you see? Are birds flying in the Otherworld sky? Do you see the glow of unfamiliar stars? Whatever you may see, don't be distracted by it. It is not yet time to go questing through the Otherworld—we shall take that journey soon enough. Right now, it is most important simply to listen.

   If you learn to listen, you will hear what you need to hear. It doesn't have to be dramatic; you need not expect some god or goddess to approach you and speak with a great shining voice. The words you need to hear are more likely to come quietly, through your own inner voice. Be assured; it is in fact the voice of the gods.

   When you have heard the message you came to hear, give thanks.

7. Now you may begin your return to the ordinary world. Bid farewell to the calm, shining landscape that lies all around you. Pleasant though it may be, you will not become attached to it. After all, it continues to exist, always, within you and around you, so you don't need to feel nostalgic about it. You can return at any time.

Climb down the Tree. Take your time. It is not wise to end an imaginary journey in a harsh and jarring manner, simply by calling it to an end and opening your eyes. Do it the natural way, by retracing your steps.

8. When you reach the bottom of the Tree, feel yourself returning to your body.

Breathing in and out, draw the great Tree back into yourself, placing its trunk along your spine.

Now open your eyes and return to ordinary consciousness.

CHAPTER 6

Otherworld Geography

COMPARATIVE OTHERWORLDS

There are many Otherworlds.

Different cultures maintain, and perhaps even create, their own mental geography of the world beyond. The Siberian shaman we accompanied in the previous chapter met Erlik Khan in a simple tent, not unlike his own. Similarly, Native American shamans traveled to Otherworldly wigwams or teepees.

In some cultures, the map of the Otherworld is highly elaborate. *The Popol Vuh*, epic of the Quiche Mayan people, tells the story of two hero twins who journey down a road that leads into the Underworld. The Lords of the Underworld look like skeletons, dressed in elaborate garments and smoking cigars. They force the twins to occupy different "houses," where they must successfully meet a number of magical challenges. Then the twins are taken to the ball court of the dead, where they play a life-and-death handball game with the Underworld Lords.

In recent times, Westerners have become familiar with the afterlife perceived by Tibetan Buddhists and outlined in what we call *The Tibetan Book of the Dead*, but which is more properly titled "The Book of Hearing on the After-Death Plane." According to Tibetan tradition, the soul travels after death through three *bardos* or "transitional states." In the first, there is light and bliss. In the second, the deceased undergoes a series of visions, some ecstatic, others demonic. The wandering soul is judged according to its deeds. In the third *bardo*, the soul hears the siren call of a new life, a new incarnation, and will surely follow one or another astral path back into this world, into rebirth.

The Maya and the Tibetans both practice spiritual traditions that owe a great deal to shamanism. Closer to our own cultural matrix, there is the so-called *Egyptian Book of the Dead*, which, like its Tibetan counterpart, is generally misnamed and which is more correctly called "The Book of Coming Forth by Day." Here, too, we find a detailed geography of the radiant world to which the soul travels after death, a

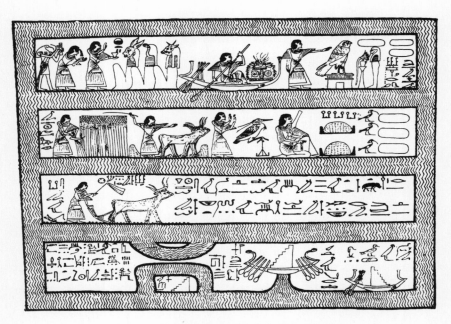

The paradise of the Egyptian Otherworld

world peopled by both devas and demons, and that, again as in the Tibetan tradition, postulates a judgment of the soul.

In our own time, the phenomenon of the Near Death Experience has revealed a contemporary map of the Otherworld—one that, we may note with fascination, seems still to be emerging from the mind of Western man and is founded as much upon metaphysical theosophy (including reincarnation) as it is upon more traditional Christian themes. The soul, at the moment of death, journeys down a tunnel of light, and may encounter many figures. Sometimes these are the figures of individuals he or she has known in life and who have themselves passed on, while sometimes they are benevolent or angry figures familiar to us from popular Christian iconography. As in both Egypt and Tibet, this contemporary Otherworld also includes a judgment of the soul.

It is well beyond the scope of this book to seek a precise definition of or explanation for these Otherworlds. They are, in any event, imprinted on the collective unconscious of the various cultures that produced them, and imprinted in a most powerful way. Even the ultimate transition, death, cannot eradicate them, for our recorded data on the process of dying reveals that we typically undergo that passage in terms of our own cultural Otherworld geography.

The Otherworld is, of course, a land of the dead. We shall all journey there at the moment of our deaths. Shamans, being the unique and sometimes bizarre individuals that they are, have the ability to journey there and back again while still living, but the Otherworld is also, in most traditional cultures, something more than a repository of departed souls. It is a separate dimension, lying close by our own and in many ways parallel to our own—though in another sense it is the polar opposite of our waking world, as night is the opposite of day.

Those who possess the requisite talents need not wait till death, but may enter this dimension at any time through an abnegation of the waking ego—an altered state of consciousness that is, in and of itself, a kind of temporary death. These talents are not the exclusive province of those who have been specially trained; they are not necessarily an indicator of holiness, or goodness, or even of particular intelligence. In ancient times, people were indeed trained to enter such states of consciousness, and such training was the business of shamans; but from the Middle Ages up until the present day, the ability to travel in the Otherworld has more often been a "wild talent," something we are born with, something we may not understand or even particularly appreciate. It's just there.

Mystics and occultists use the term "astral plane" to describe this other reality, a fluid reality built up by the thoughts and images of millions of people, but no less real than our own. Thus we may speak of "maps of the astral." There is a Tibetan map, and there was an Egyptian map. We believe that there is also a contemporary map. Magicians even create their own maps, such as the Tree of Life of the Kabbalists, and are able to travel at will in astral worlds, thus, according to magical doctrine, influencing the world around them by manipulating its collective astral imagery. It is to this astral plane that we travel when we undergo what is now termed an OBE or "Out-of-Body" experience. The Near Death Experience would seem to be another, if rather more profound, variety of OBE.

The peasants of late medieval Europe who were accused of witchcraft have emerged, in this book, as travelers in astral realms. Like shamans, they journeyed there to aid and assist their fellow villagers, both living and dead. Unlike more traditional shamans, many of them were untrained and hence occasionally mystified by their own experiences, and, like Otherworldly travelers everywhere, they journeyed to a land that was part of the unconscious spiritual geography of their own people.

Let us examine the astral maps and Otherworlds of the various European mythologies, and of the witches.

THE ROAD TO HEL

The members of the Orphic cult buried their initiates along with beautifully carved tablets—some of pure gold!—that were meant to guide them on their journey after death. A few lines from these tablets have already been quoted (Chapter 1). Along with the works of Classical Greek and Roman authors, they serve as a road map, a geography of the Greco-Roman Otherworld.

When people died, said the Greeks, they descended to the Otherworld by way of a grove of black poplars that led to the banks of the river Styx. Here the ghosts removed from their tongues the coins placed there by their pious relatives, and with them paid Charon, the ferryman of the dead. Across the dark river they sailed. On the other side was three-headed Cerberus, the hound of hell who guarded the Otherworld from unwelcome intruders.

Beyond the banks of the Styx lay the Asphodel Fields, where ghosts wandered in gray silence or flew chittering about like bats. These were the ranks of the ordinary dead. An offering of blood poured into the earth would give them a voice, so that they might speak with mortals still living.

Beyond lay the halls of judgment, where the three judges of the Underworld—Aeacus, Minos, and Rhadamanthys—held court, judging the souls of the newly arrived dead. Among other dwellers in this realm were the three Furies, whom it was best to call "the kindly ones," for these ancient gnarled crones heard all the outraged cries of humanity and took vengeance in accordance with the crime.

Still farther beyond lay the palace of Hades and his bride Persephone, king and queen of the dead. To the left of the palace stood a white cypress, beneath which lay the Well of Forgetfulness, the waters of which led souls to forget who they were; to the right stood a white poplar, and beneath it the Well of Memory, the waters of which could enlighten and initiate the souls of the departed.

Close to the Well of Memory lay the entrance to the Elysian Fields, where dwelt the happy spirits of the dead. Here there was eternal daylight, eternal summer, and the dead spent their time in feasting and revelry. Those who wandered there might choose at any time to be reincarnated on earth, and those who were three times reborn and three times had attained the Elysian Fields could go to the Fortunate Isles, where the feasts were even brighter and happier, presided over by the shades of beautiful Helen of Troy and the great Achilles. The Fortunate Isles were thickly wooded and rich in game.

This, according to the Greek poets, was the nature of the Otherworld. The portrait is not only vividly imaginative, it represents a marvelous spiritual-intellectual synthesis as well. In fact, it is a creative blending of two ancient traditions. For throughout the European mythologies, we find that there are actually *two* Otherworlds, and that they are very different in character.

One of these realms of the dead is a gloomy and dark-spirited place. According to the *Prose Edda*, it lies beneath the World Tree, in the cold, damp regions where the unpleasant creatures gnaw at Yggdrasil's roots. This dank and misty region is called Hel, after its dark queen, daughter of the trickster Loki. Here the dead dwell in undistinguished shades of gray.

The way to Hel is treacherous. Hermod and/or Odin, traveling thence, crossed a narrow and fearsome bridge beneath which the dark Resounding River raged. A ghostly woman, or in another version, a ferocious hound, stood guard there. Herein we may recognize both the River Styx and the hell-hound Cerberus, but there are other tones in this portrait as well. In the previous chapter, a Siberian shaman on his way to the netherworld also crossed a bridge that spanned a raging river; this bridge is well-known in Indo-European lore. Among the Zoroastrians of Persia, it was called the Chinvat Bridge, and the goodly found it a wide and spacious path, while the unrighteous found it as narrow as a sword blade and difficult to cross. The Irish hero Cuchulain, on his way to take instruction from the warrior woman Scathach, could enter her realm only by crossing a bridge as narrow as a hair's breadth.

This Otherworld, then, is a dark and gloomy place, entered by way of a treacherous bridge that spans a raging river and is guarded by a fierce hell-hound. The dead live there in a state of faceless gloom. A god and goddess, best typified by Hades and Persephone, rule there together, though in some traditions (notably the Norse) the goddess reigns alone.

This gray Otherworld survived well into Christian times, for it makes its appearance in a medieval British folk song called "The Lyke-wake Dirge." One suspects that the line "And Christ receive thy soul" must once have read "The gods receive thy soul."

> *This ae night, this ae night,*
> *Every night and all,*
> *Fire, and sleet, and candle light,*
> *And Christ receive thy soul.*
>
> *When thou from hence away are past,*
> *Every night and all,*
> *To Whinnymuir thou comest at last,*
> *And Christ receive thy soul.*
>
> *If ever thou gavest hosen and shoon,*
> *Every night and all,*
> *Sit thee down and put them on,*
> *And Christ receive thy soul.*
>
> *If hosen and shoon thou ne'er gavest none,*
> *Every night and all,*
> *The whinnes shall prick thee to the bare bone,*
> *And Christ receive thy soul.*
>
> *From Whinnymuir when thou may'st pass,*
> *Every night and all,*
> *To Brig o' Dread thou comest at last,*
> *And Christ receive thy soul.*
>
> *From Brig o' Dread when thou may'st pass,*
> *Every night and all,*
> *To Purgatory Fire thou comest at last,*
> *And Christ receive thy soul.*
>
> *If ever thou gavest meat or drink,*
> *Every night and all,*

The fire shall never make thee shrink,
And Christ receive thy soul.

If meat or drink thou ne' er gavest none,
Every night and all,
The fire shall burn thee to the bare bone,
And Christ receive thy soul.

This ae night, this ae night,
Every night and all,
Fire, and sleet, and candle light,
And Christ receive thy soul.[1]

The "whinnes" who prick the dead soul to the bone are reminiscent of the demons who dismember the shaman during his or her initiation ritual, a ritual that guides the initiate through a simulated death. "Brig" or "brigge" is a Middle English term for "bridge," and hence the "Brig o' Dread" in the song is almost certainly the razor-sharp bridge over which souls traveled to the Underworld.

The gloomy Asphodel Fields, where ghosts chitter like bats and which are entered by a fearsome boat or across a "bridge of dread," is not the only concept of the Otherworld that appears in European mythologies. There is also a world where joy, brightness, and feasting reign eternal, that happy Otherworld the Greeks called the Elysian Fields.

THE LAND OF YOUTH

Almost all European traditions contain some version of the Happy Feast in the Otherworld. Although the Norse placed most souls—the undistinguished dead—in a misty Hel ruled by a dark goddess, they also believed that the souls of brave warriors would travel to Valhalla, there to feast with Odin. The Valkyries would gather up their souls from the battlefields where they had fallen, and would carry them away to Odin's banquet hall in Asgard, where they would drink the divine mead and feast eternally. The Greeks, as we have noted, actually postulated two cheerful Otherworlds—the Elysian Fields, wherein all was joy and light, and, for the truly blessed, the Fortunate Isles, where the dead feasted with Achilles and Helen of Troy.

It is among the Celtic peoples that we may discover the most enchanting Otherworld of them all. From the time of the old Irish epics up until the present day, the Otherworld journey has formed one of the principal themes of Celtic literature and folklore. In many of these stories, the hero or Otherworld traveler simply walks into a fog or mist, to emerge in a magical, vibrant realm that lies in its own dimension, close by, but diametrically opposed to, our own. Sometimes, however, Celtic peoples perceived the Otherworld as an island (or islands) in the West, precisely as with the Greek Fortunate Isles. This Otherworld was called Tir-na-nog, the Land of Youth, or sometimes the Isle of Women.

The tale of Bran's voyage contains a vivid description of the Land of Youth, "a distant isle, around which sea-horses glisten," upheld by four pillars—like the shamanic cosmos of both the Norse and the Maya (Chapter 1). It is a silvery land "on which dragon-stones and crystals drop," while crystal hair drips from the mane of the sea. The traveler, upon arriving, will be greeted by a group of women, and will hear the music of singing birds.

The Celtic Land of Youth, then, is a glorious island, misty and silver, joyous with the sound of singing birds and inhabited by women. The fact that it is often called the Land of Women may remind us of the Land of the Shamanesses mentioned in the vision of the Samoyed shaman (Chapter 2).

We may remember how Cuchulain fell into a trance after trying to bring down two magical birds with his javelin. He journeyed in the spirit to the Otherworld, and there made love to the goddess Fand, consort of the Otherworld king, Manannan mac Lir. Here is what Cucuhulain saw:

> At the entrance to the enclosure is a tree
> From whose branches there comes beautiful and
> harmonious music.
> It is a tree of silver, which the sun illumines;
> It glistens like gold.

There are thrice fifty trees.
At times their leaves mingle, at times, not.
Each tree feeds three hundred people
With abundant food, without rind.

There is a well in that noble palace of the fairy-mound.
There you will find thrice fifty splendid cloaks,
With a brooch of shining gold
To fasten each of the cloaks.[2]

Cuchulain, then, was in the realm of the World Tree and the Primordial Well. In fact, Cuchulain's Otherworld contained 150 World Trees, a veritable forest! Another Celtic journeyer to the Land of Youth, King Cormac, noted nine World Trees and a Primordial Well that gave birth to five springs:

> *Then he saw in the enclosure a shining fountain, with five*
> *streams flowing out of it, and the hosts in turn drinking its*
> *water. Nine hazels of Buan grew over the well. The purple*
> *hazels dropped their nuts into the fountain, and the five*
> *salmon which were in the fountain severed them and sent*
> *their husks floating down the streams. Now the sound of*
> *the falling of those streams was more melodious than any*
> *music that men sing.*[3]

The Celtic Otherworld was typically ruled by a king and queen who dwelt in a palace within a fairy mound, just as Hades and Persephone ruled the Greek Underworld from their palace in Erebus. The Otherworld King is variously named. Most often he is Manannan mac Lir, son of the Celtic sea god, but sometimes he appears as Lugh, another god. As the Fisher King of the Grail Legend, he has a variety of names—Pelles, Brons, and in a very important sense, the Grail Knight Peredur or Perceval himself. And yet the Fisher King's names, too, fade into the older Pagan names of yet other Celtic Otherworld gods—Pelles into Pwyll, Brons into Bran, and Peredur into Pryderi.

During the great days of Celtic Paganism, the King of the Otherworld always reigned together with a queen. A visitor to the Otherworld often found her holding a cup—yet another image of the Well of Memory, the grail, or the witches' cauldron—from which the weary traveler might drink. It is she—under various names such as Fand and Rhiannon—who was remembered as the medieval Queen of the Elves for several centuries after her lord had been transformed into "the devil."

The Otherworld journey of yet another old Irish hero, Conn of the Hundred Battles, presents a fairly typical portrait of the queen. With some of his warrior companions, Conn rode across a Plain of Mist and emerged into a shining, Otherworldly landscape. He came to a golden tree, and a house thirty feet long with a ridgepole of white gold. He and his companions entered the house and beheld a woman, seated in a chair of crystal and wearing a crown of gold. Beside her was a vessel of gold and before her a golden cup. On the Otherworld throne was a king, who identified himself as Lug.* The woman was none other than the Sovereignty of Ireland, a figure who appears in Celtic lore as the primordial goddess of the land. She served Conn and his companions ale and food.

We can see that European peoples recognized two very different concepts of the Otherworld—one in which the dead traveled to a joyous land of eternal music and feasting, and one in which they became gray and nameless ghosts in a dank gray land. Marija Gimbutas theorizes[4] that the notion of dead heroes feasting in the Otherworld is essentially an Indo-European concept and should be linked with the Otherworld of darkness, while the Island in the West is a much older concept, dating back to the Neolithic era. Indeed, it is this happy Otherworld that is most clearly a "land of women."

Neolithic temples typically included their own workshops for creating votive vessels used in worship; typically these vessels are found in the same context as small female figurines. Gimbutas thinks that the vessels held food as offerings to the Goddess, and that the figurines

---

* Lug or Lugh, a Celtic god of light and power, is an unusual choice to act as Otherworld Lord; that distinction more typically falls upon the shoulders of one of the gods of earth and sea. Conn's tale is atypical in this respect, and was probably subjected to a fair amount of medieval muddling.

therefore represent various aspects of the Goddess.[5] This author considers it equally possible that the figurines represented departed (typically female) ancestors who had joined the world of the gods or fairies, and that the vessels filled with food and drink were set forth as part of the Feast for the Dead, a concept that should more properly be linked with the happy Otherworld and that is much older than the Indo-European invasions of Europe (circa 4000–2500 B.C.).

THE OTHERWORLD OF THE WITCHES

If we turn to the evidence of the witch trials, there to seek out the topography of the late medieval Otherworld, we shall encounter a very curious fact, and one that shows an actual shift in the collective unconscious of the European peoples.

Most of the examples we have studied, until now, bear the marks of shamanic practice—sometimes cast in the symbolism and imagery of European Paganism, sometimes with a veneer of Christianity tossed in. In the trial records we have reproduced here, we have focused upon folk beliefs from the period *just before* the actual persecutions, or upon the testimony of people whose association with the Burning Times was, like that of the benandanti, fairly marginal. In none of these examples have we discovered much in the way of Satan, or demons, or a riotous Sabbat that included orgies and the renunciation of Christianity.

If we look carefully at the Otherworld of the witches, we will notice a shift in direction, in imagery, in the very nature of the astral world itself. The medieval traditions, and those of the "marginal" benandanti, bear the imprint of a happy Otherworld, a Land of Youth, but, as the witch persecutions begin to increase in number and in vehemence, the astral journeys of the witches take on a darker tone, and their Otherworld geography is lit up with the hellish firelight of the conventional demonic Sabbat.

Why? Let us keep this question in mind.

Witches who were relatively unaffected by the persecutions still remembered, and of course visited, the Land of Youth. In popular Celtic folklore, from the Middle Ages until the present day, the

Otherworld most often lies inside the barrow mounds, the Neolithic communal graves that dot the landscape of the British Isles. Irish tradition holds that the old gods of Celtic myth, the Tuatha de Danaan, took up residence in the barrow mounds after people had ceased to believe in them; diminished in stature, they became known as the *sidhe*, the "people of the hills" or "the fairy folk," and the barrows themselves were "the fairy hills."[7] When one entered their kingdom within the mounds, one encountered a glorious feast. But if a mortal were to partake in such a repast, and eat the fairy food or drink their wine, he might discover, upon returning to the world of humankind, that a hundred years had passed.

It was to this familiar Otherworld of Celtic lore that Isobel Gowdie journeyed (Chapter 3). She had been "flying" in the spirit when she beheld a barrow mound—one of the traditional houses of the fairy folk or spirits of the dead—open up below her. And though it was night in the human world, it was bright daylight within the world of the barrow mound, and there was a feast going on. There were animals (elf bulls)

As shown in this sixteenth-century woodcut, the fairy hills were actually Neolithic barrow mounds

frolicking about, just as there were animals in the realm of Madonna Oriente, the astral goddess of fourteenth century northern Italy. Isobel met the King and Queen of the Elves, who bore a marked resemblance to the Otherworld king and queen encountered by Conn the Hundred Fighter, and she feasted with the fairies.

When Isobel flew away from her body to travel in the spirit, it was night. In the Land of Faerie, however, it was day. Herein lies a fact of great importance: the Otherworld is a mirror image of our own. Everything is the same, but seen as through a mirror, in reverse. The dead come forth to ride on the Wild Hunt when our world is cloaked in darkness; in their world, however, it is day, and hence time for riding. Though the hunger of the dead may call forth images of the hungry, chittering ghosts in the gray Asphodel Fields, and though the feasts set forth for them may remind us of the ancient Greeks pouring blood onto the earth so that the dead might drink and henceforth speak, there is another idea at work here as well—in their own world, the dead are eternally at feast, while in our world they are eternally hungry. The image in the mirror is reversed.

What happens to the shaman, or any other mortal, who journeys into the Otherworld? He partakes of a reality that is the reverse of his own; hence he returns with a different perspective. He is a bit out of joint with our own world—he is *asymmetrical*. Those who feast in the Otherworld, and who taste the food of the elves, may return to find that many years have passed, and that everyone they have known is dead. This is a folkloric way of pointing out the strangeness—the essential asymmetry—of those who have journeyed to the Fairy Hills. In an anthropological context, this explains why shamans often behave strangely, and manifest symptoms of what we would call psychological imbalance.

Now we know why Cinderella wears only one slipper. The girl of cinders, marked with the ashes of the Death Goddess, calls upon her totem animal, regenerates its dead bones, and uses its power to journey to the Otherworld—conceived, in the fairy tale, as a castle, like the Otherworldly Grail Castle of Arthurian myth. There she meets the Prince, the Otherworld Lord who will act as consort to the girl of ashes, and she returns to *this* world with only one slipper, for she has made the Otherworld journey—she's the asymmetrical girl!

Andrew Man, tried in Aberdeen in 1597, didn't exactly go to the Otherworld—it came to him. It was a summer's day during the harvest when Andrew saw a stag emerge from a sudden snowstorm—for our worldly summer is the Otherworld winter. The stag turned into a man called, almost unbelievably, Christsonday, which means "Sunday of Christ." This Christsonday was possessed of such a shining countenance that Andrew thought him an angel, the very equal of God. Elves stepped forth out of that magical snow to set a feast, having the appearance of human beings but much more insubstantial, like "shadows." Christsonday presided with his consort, whom Andrew called the Queen of the Elves.

Then comes the peculiar part. Andrew testified that Christsonday was in reality the Devil, and that he had called upon Andrew to kiss his behind.

Andrew went on to make passionate love to the Queen of the Elves, as Cuchulain had done with Fand, but the fierce shift in the European subconscious had broken through: the Otherworld King, in Andrew's account, has become the Devil.

In other parts of Europe, witches often traveled to the Mount of Venus. We may remember the tale of Zuan delle Piatte (Chapter 1), who, during his journey to the Venusberg, underwent an experience rich with all the symbolism of the mythological European Otherworld. He crossed a lake and encountered three Otherworld guardians—a friar, a serpent, and an old man named Ekhart. According to the legend of Tannhauser, those who reached the interior of the Venusberg spent their time in feasting, revelry, and love-making—a cornucopia of Pagan joys presided over by the goddess Venus herself.

The finest descriptions of the Otherworld the witches knew are found in the statements of the Italian benandanti, collected by Carlo Ginzburg in his now-famous book *Night Battles*. Paolo Gasparutto and Battista Moduco, in 1575, testified that they were called out upon their journeys by "an angel," who traveled with them, fought with them, and blessed them upon their departure. Paolo said that he and his companions crossed several bodies of water in a boat—including a local river, that, according to Paolo, turned turbulent and stormy, and frightened one of his fellow benandanti.

Having arrived "on the other side," Paolo found a landscape that greatly resembled certain familiar spots around his own village, but Menichino della Notta—who, we may remember, was initiated by a fellow villager while strolling down a country road one winter's night—saw a much different and less familiar landscape. Along with other benandanti, he "moved through the air like smoke" and "crossed over water like smoke." He traveled as if in a haze; he could neither see his companions nor make out the landscape below.

Presently, however, he began to smell the scent of roses. In time, he found himself in a place "wide, large and beautiful," that he called Josaphat's Field, a magical place where flowers and roses bloomed even in the winter. There the assembled company indulged in a number of medieval pastimes such as jousting and, of course, feasting. They "played, leaped about and rode various animals." According to Menichino della Notta, they also bowed their heads to a mysterious woman seated on the edge of a well—the Goddess seated by the Well of Memory.

Clearly, the benandanti were wandering in the Elysian Fields, the Land of Youth, the happy Otherworld of European mythology. This glorious realm was not without its perils, as we may discover from the testimony of other European shamans. Hundreds of miles away, in the Caucasus Mountains, Ossetian shamans traveled to a similar Otherworld as recently as the end of the nineteenth century. They found themselves in a field of flowers, as did Menichino, but it was believed that plucking these elvish flowers would cause illness when the shaman returned to the ordinary world. Instead, the experienced shaman ought to eschew the picking of flowers and gather up the seeds of wheat that promise a good harvest. This, too, was a perilous act, for the souls of the dead would pursue the astral wanderer bold enough to steal the germ of an abundant harvest.

The benandanti, after feasting in Josaphat's Field, engaged in combat for the sake of the harvest, much like Thiess the werewolf (Chapter 4). Their opponents were the "witches" (malandanti or "bad walkers" as opposed to benandanti or "good walkers"). There is some confusion as to the identity of these witches, as there is regarding the identity of Paolo's spiritual traveling companions. Sometimes the "good walkers" seemed to be the familiar, living inhabitants of Paolo's own village, and the "bad walkers" the citizens of neighboring villages, which, being several miles away, were regarded by Paolo as distant and therefore threatening. Other times, the malandanti are clearly the angry spirits of the dead, while the happy dead make an appearance on the side of the benandanti. The combats consisted of a general melee in which the benandanti carried fennel stalks as weapons, while the malandanti wielded sorghum.

If the benandanti won, the village crops would flourish; if they lost, it would be a bad harvest. (Trial records report that the benandanti frequently awoke from their spirit journeys sore, as if they'd been in a fight, though the bruises themselves were invisible.) As they traveled back through the spirit world into their own bodies, they stopped at various houses to eat—the favorite pastime of the hungry dead. The malandanti, who seem to have been present even then, were prone to urinating in the wine casks unless the benandanti prevented them.

In 1618, there occurred the interrogation of Maria Panzona, an accused benandante. Like Menichino della Notta, she had journeyed in spirit to the valley of Josaphat, which she, too, perceived as a field of flowers. She, like Menichino, had met the "abbess" who sat on the edge of a well. Maria went on to voice her suspicion that the abbess was really the Devil, and that the animals upon which she and her fellow wanderers rode were also demons and devils. She showed a similar confusion concerning the roles of the benandanti and their antagonists, the witches. At one point she insisted that the benandanti fought for the Christian faith and that it was the witches who forsook Christ and dedicated themselves to the Devil, while at another point she confessed that she herself had abjured her faith and given herself to the Devil!

Maria Panzona's lawyer argued to the court that his client had "few brains," and that the few she did have were scrambled by frequent epileptic seizures. Undoubtedly, this was true. But Carlo Ginzburg, who collected her story, believes that Maria Panzona's testimony shows an important shift in the way the benandanti were perceived by their neighbors and by themselves—the dark myth of the demonic Sabbat had intruded itself upon their astral battles for the sake of the crops.

The example of the benandanti comes very late in the game. By the beginning of the seventeenth century, the witch trials were already in full force in many other parts of Europe, and though the evidence gleaned from the testimony of the "good walkers" is instructive as regards surviving pockets of shamanism in Europe, it is almost a footnote to the trials themselves. In most parts of Europe, the transformation from the Elysian Fields to the "blasted heath" of the Devil's Sabbat had occurred much earlier. The flowering meadows of the Otherworld Goddess had already given way, in the collective European mind, to dark midnight gatherings where children were consumed, where witches coupled with demons, and where a horned devil, his touch as cold as ice, presided over the rites of the damned.

In other words, a shift—or perhaps a split—in the European unconscious had occurred, a split so massive that it changed the European "map of the astral," the very geography and character of the Otherworld.

What had happened? What was the Sabbat? And who was its dark lord?

Or, as Isobel Gowdie's judges wanted to know: What about the Devil?

OTHERWORLD JOURNEYS

During late medieval and Renaissance times, the village shamans of Europe traveled to the Otherworld by way of what we would now call an "out-of-body experience," the same experience that students of the occult call "astral travel." As we have seen, some shamans left their bodies due to the stimulus of hallucinogenic drugs, while others were able to travel astrally simply by virtue of natural (and sometimes uncontrollable) talent.

Most of us have the ability to travel astrally, even though we usually suspect otherwise. Although astral travel has been successfully taught to many individuals, we shall not attempt to teach it here. There are a few perils inherent in the process, and consequently it is a technique that must be taught in some detail—more than we have time for in the context of this work.

There is, however, another technique used to journey to imaginary realms and inner landscapes, one that may be safely and easily attempted by just about anyone. It was developed by Jungian psychiatrists, and it goes by the name of "active imagination." In active imagination, you allow your mind to drift freely while another individual guides it through an inner landscape. The primordial well of images is allowed to do its work, producing a mental geography in accordance with the words of the guide. Depending on how visual your imagination is, you may even be able to see that inner landscape with all the bright colors, tastes, and sounds of reality. Typically, one is encouraged to encounter other entities or beings in this inner landscape, and to communicate with them.

Following are two journeys designed for the practice of active imagination and employing some of the Otherworld imagery and geography we have studied.

Active imagination has only one real peril—it's easy to drift off and away through these inner landscapes. In other words, the technique can easily degenerate into idle daydreaming. This is why it is always best to work with another person, someone who can guide you through the journey and thus help you to keep your imagination focused.

What if you don't know anyone who might help you with this? Let's say you live in a mid-sized Midwestern town and you work at a bank, and that shamanism and witchcraft don't exactly constitute common topics around the employees' lounge. In fact, you don't know anyone who shares your private interests.

In this case, you may want to tape your own voice, giving instructions. Modify the descriptions in this book to suit your own purpose; guide yourself along the Otherworldly road.

JOURNEY TO THE LAND OF YOUTH

1. Sit comfortably, holding your drum in your hands. Visualize the North Star shining above your head.

2. Now use all of your powers of visualization and imagination to see and feel yourself walking along a deserted beach. You may walk in the light of day, or by moonlight—but no matter what your choice, be sure to hear the waves and smell the fresh salt air as vividly as you can.

   Fix your inner gaze upon the distant horizon. You will see a barge approaching you over the sea. As the barge sails closer and closer, you will see that it is moving of its own volition. It may even be unoccupied, though in many Celtic tales the Otherworldly vessel is associated with a female figure or figures—for instance, there were three queens in the barge that bore King Arthur off to Avalon. If the barge in your own vision should happen to be piloted by someone, just smile and proceed on your own. It's not yet time for conversation with the inhabitants of the Land of Youth.

3. At last the barge will beach itself softly upon the sand. Now you may step aboard. Breathe deeply as the vessel magically turns itself about and ventures back out onto the waves. Ahead of you looms the open sea.

4. Begin beating your drum. Let the drumbeat and the rhythm of your voyage be slow and stately, but at the same time cheerful and relaxed. This is not meant to be a somber occasion; on the contrary, it is a most joyful affair.

5. At last you will see land, rising before you out of the mist. Don't try to force this to happen; just keep drumming and traveling at your own pace until the Land of Youth appears quite naturally before your inner eye, all silver and green, shining with a mist as bright as crystal. As you step ashore, stop drumming.

6. Now it is time to reach as deeply as possible into the core of your creative imagination, for you are about to meet the inhabitants of the Land of Youth.

   It sometimes happens that the elvish being whom you have come to meet is waiting for you right on the beach, or you may have to walk a little ways through the beautiful landscape of the Land of Youth before you are approached by someone. If so, then enjoy your walk. The Land of Youth is a place of sweet-smelling meadows, of shining crystals embedded in the rocks and ground, of mist and dewdrops and trees. You will see apple trees and hazel trees in particular, and in some of these trees there will be birds singing joyfully and beautifully.

7. Sooner or later, you will meet with one of the beings of the Otherworld. Be advised that the inhabitants of this particular world—the old Celtic Land of Youth—always appear in human form. Although shamans may often communicate with various kinds of magical animals or astral entities, these are activities for a different sort of journey. Be clear about this. If you are approached by a non-human entity of any kind, simply dismiss it—gently, but with a firm will and intention. It is an astral phantom, and most likely a construct of your own subconscious mind. It is not necessarily harmful, but it has no place here.

   When at last you meet with a being from the Land of Youth, she or he will be exceptionally beautiful, and glowing with an inner light. The inhabitants of this Otherworld resemble the full-sized, transcendent elves of Tolkien's well-known fantasy novels, and you will feel only light and comfort in their presence. The old Celtic Land of Youth was inhabited primarily by female spirits, and you are more likely to meet with a woman than a man. This, however, is not a hard and fast rule.

Once you have encountered a being, there are several things that might happen:

- The being may have a message for you, or for someone you know. This message may take the form of a great spiritual truth, but it is much more likely to deal with something immediate and practical. For instance, you may be given information on how to solve a certain problem in your life. You may be given a message as to how to help someone else, although this is a bit trickier. Such messages, if they are true ones, never allow you to force your will upon other people by lecturing to them, or by practicing hands-on healing when a subject appears to be reluctant, or anything of that nature. Either you will be given practical information to help someone on a very basic level that cannot possibly do harm to anyone, or you will be instructed to help someone on a very spiritual, meditative level.

- Sometimes, however, the Otherworldly being won't simply come forth with information. You may have the choice to ask a question and receive an answer. What, then, should you ask? The best thing is to ask for help on some specific matter—preferably a matter that helps you to grow spiritually and thus be of service to others. For instance, you may certainly seek information on how to improve your health, stop smoking, or be more kind to others. The beings of the Otherworld always welcome such questions. If you ask for this kind of information in behalf of another person rather than yourself, remember that all the qualifications listed above will apply here too.

- Upon occasion, you may receive a gift. This may be a very "traditional" gift, such as a silver apple, a wand, or a crystal—or it may be something quite modern and unique. Whatever it is, accept it.

Sometimes, if your connection with the Land of Youth is very highly developed, you may experience a combination of the scenarios described above.

8. When the communication is finished, the being will withdraw. This is your cue to return to the beach, where the magical barge will be waiting for you.

9. Embark once again upon your ocean journey. Take up your drum and sing yourself back to the shores of our own world. Don't hurry; in exercises such as these, you must always retrace your steps. It took you a while to reach the Land of Youth; it is likely to take you just as long to get back.

When at last you reach that first, original beach, bid farewell to the barge. Watch as the magic vessel turns about and drifts away, back across the horizon.

Now you are ready to open your eyes and return.

JOURNEY TO THE LAND OF THE DEAD

Please be advised: *This is a much tougher exercise than the preceding one!* This one can unnerve you just a little bit, and might be emotionally very trying. Read through the example given here, and if you are at all bothered by it, don't attempt the exercise. Remember that certain kinds of shamans traveled only to the Land of the Gods, never to the Land of the Dead. You can get all the knowledge you need by climbing the World Tree or sailing to the Land of Youth. This journey is only for those who feel drawn to it.

1. Before you begin your journey, sit quietly for a while. Perform the exercise "Growing The Inner Tree" (page 29). The goal of this exercise is to fill yourself with power and energy, as well as with "an abiding sense of calm." These are the qualities, above all others, that you will need for the present venture.

2. When you have placed the World Tree within yourself and can feel yourself empowered with its energy, close your eyes and take a deep breath. Sink into yourself as far as you can go. Start beating your drum, very slowly this time. If you are practicing this exercise with a friend, let him or her beat the drum for you.

3. Now, in your mind's eye, you will see the mouth of a great cave looming before you. Mist rises from the ground, swirling across the dark opening. Go ahead and enter.

4. Now you will find yourself in a long dark tunnel. Far ahead of you, a dim glow is visible. Walk toward it. You may see beings flickering in the half-light to the right or left of you. You may hear noises, even voices. Disregard all of these. Just keep moving forward. Walk with courage and confidence.

5. Even before you reach the end of the tunnel, you will hear the crashing of waves. Now, as you emerge from the tunnel, you find yourself in a vast underground cavern. In front of you is a dark river, rushing

wildly through the blackness. Hear the pounding of its waves, the roar of its mighty current. This is that body of water the myths called the Resounding River.

Look straight ahead of you and raise your eyes. Now you see the bridge.

6. The bridge is like a silver thread arching over the river. It is as narrow as the blade of a sword. You cannot simply tromp across it; this bridge can be crossed only by walking in the spirit. Realize that the bridge represents your fears. Here is your terror of heights, or of airplanes; here are your anxiety attacks, etc. To cross the Bridge of Dread is to conquer fear.

IF THE BRIDGE ALARMS OR FRIGHTENS YOU, YOU MAY WISH TO TURN BACK NOW.

If you feel confident, let your friend know. Give a nod or some other signal, so that she or he may slow the drumbeat even more.

Breathe deeply. Walk slowly. Walk with grace and courage. Follow the beat of the drum. You will feel as if you are walking on air, for the bridge will be invisible beneath your feet.

When you reach the other side, you will feel a great sense of exuberance. After all, you have conquered some special and particular fear.

7. After you have crossed the bridge, the cavern will open gradually into a vast meadow. Here all is quiet, and all the colors are soft and muted. This is where the spirits of the dead roam.

It is not an evil place; it is not even a sad place, as we would define sadness, but there is an awesome neutrality here, and this can be a bit disorienting for some people. Remember that there is no reason for you to fear anything in this place; in any case, you have already crossed the Bridge of Dread and faced some of your fears.

You may notice the spirits of the dead first as gray shadows, drifting about. They may move away from you, as quietly as smoke. Some of them may gather round you, struggling to emerge. Never force them.

If no being emerges from the shadows, you may eventually turn around and go back, but it is more likely that someone will emerge. In many cases, this will be the spirit of someone you have never known, someone you have never met, but this may also be the spirit of someone who was once close to you. You may find yourself gazing into the face of your father or mother, your brother or sister, or a friend who has passed on.

Now is the moment to muster all your courage and all your inner calm. It is no crime to give way to tears and mourning, but a display of emotion won't help you much, either. If you meet someone with whom you once were close, and if that meeting elicits great emotion in your soul, you will simply have to regain your sense of calm, empowered detachment. It is best to hold on to that equanimity from the very beginning.

Now, let the soul know that she or he may speak.

When we give the dead the power to speak, they frequently ask for our help. This may simply be a matter of lighting a candle on your altar, or in some local church, or of saying a prayer, or meditating, but you may also be asked to help the departed spirit with unfinished business. Thus you may be asked to take a message or a gift to someone still living.

This is another reason you should **NEVER ATTEMPT THIS EXERCISE UNLESS YOU REALLY MEAN IT**. Once you have agreed to help the dead, you are under a certain obligation to actually do so. We will have more to say about this.

8. After you have received a message, the departed spirit will probably fade back into the mist. Now return to the upper world.

As with all shamanic exercises, it will be necessary to retrace your steps properly. Your friend should guide you back, through the fields and the cavernous tunnel. In this particular exercise, there is one thing that works a bit differently: You do not have to cross the Bridge of Dread again.

You have to make your passage through fear only once during every journey to the Underworld. It is true that you will face some new fear or phobia each time you enter the Underworld and come once again to the bridge, but you will always be allowed to leave much more easily than you entered.

So when you come to the Resounding River, just close the eyes of your imagination, take a deep breath, and exhale.

Open your inner eyes, and you will see that you have crossed the river. The tunnel looms before you now.

A few more words must be said about the shaman's obligation to help the dead. This often becomes an issue when you are approached by someone you once knew, someone with whom you shared immediate day-to-day realities in the upper world. You can't neglect to take a vital message to Uncle Fred simply because he might think you're a nut (let's assume he's an old codger with a John Deere tractor and doesn't often hear from dead relatives the way you do).

If you take on the duty to help the dead, then you have to do so faithfully. Even if they want you to do things like:

- Drive your cousin to the nearest alcoholism treatment center;
- Continue that work with the homeless in which your dear old mother was engaged in at the time of her death;
- Donate money to AIDS research in honor of a friend who has passed over.

Of course, you can always choose not to do it. This won't cause you any real harm. You will simply have proved to yourself that you were never cut out for this particular form of journeying, and that you should content yourself with other exercises more in line with your talents.

CHAPTER 7

Master of Animals, King of the Dead

SCOTLAND, 1662

"Tell us about the Devil," said Isobel Gowdie's judges.

And tell them she did....

Isobel had first met the Devil fifteen years ago, back in 1647. She had been going from one farm to the next, traveling over the downs where the ghostly shapes of barrows stooped in the wind. The Devil had come to her as a man dressed in gray, and Isobel had agreed to give herself to him right then and there. They met at the Auldearne church that very night, and the Devil stood in the pulpit with his black book in his hands, and he called upon Isobel to renounce the faith of Christ. And that was what she'd done.

There were others present, too, for there had always been witches in Auldearne, and one of them, Margaret Brodie, held on to Isobel while the Devil made his mark upon her shoulder. He sucked out her blood, spit it in his hand, and sprinkled it over her long red hair to baptize her.

And afterward, the Devil had taught her a great deal of magic. He had taught her to change herself into a crow or a hare, and given her a little spirit horse upon which she sometimes rode to the Sabbats. Each of the Auldearne witches had received a familiar spirit: Bessie Wilson's was named Rory, and was dressed in yellow, while Margaret Wilson and Jean Martin had spirits who were dressed in elvish green, and Jean's was a handsome young man not yet twenty. Isobel's familiar spirit was dressed in black.

The witches of Auldearne had enemies, many indeed, and the Devil had taught them some vengeance to work. They were particularly adept at blighting crops. "Before Candlemas we went be-east Kinross," Isobel said, "and there we yoked a plough of toads. The Devil held the plough, and John Young, our officer, did drive the plough. Toads did draw the plough as oxen, couch-grass was the harness and trace-chains, a gelded animal's horn was the coulter, and a piece of a gelded animal's horn was the sock." Another time they had dug up the body of an unchristened child and buried it in a farmer's manure heap to ruin his crops.

But that was not the worst. Once, they had made clay images of the children of the laird (the same one Isobel had missed when she flew through the sky shooting elvish arrows), and they had watered and baked the images till the children died.

Isobel proclaimed that the witches were organized in groups called covens (the first time her judges or anyone else had heard that word) and that there were thirteen members in a coven. The organization was strict and sometimes cruel. If anyone missed a meeting, she was stripped naked and beaten severely by the Devil. The witches met at Sabbats. The great Sabbat meetings were held four times a year, on the old Celtic festivals—Imbolc, Beltane, Lammas, and Samhain. In animal shape, or upon her spirit horse, Isobel flew to the Sabbats, where there was always plenty of dancing and where a favored witch was chosen as the Maiden. "The Devil always takes the Maiden in his hand next him when we dance gillatrypes; and when he leaps from place to place, he and she say 'Over the dyke with it.'" And that, added Isobel, was why the Maiden was nicknamed "Over the Dyke With It."

At the Sabbats, the Devil appeared most often as a big, black hairy man, though he sometimes became a bull, a deer, or a dog. At the Sabbat feast, the witches looked to the Devil, and, bowing to him said, "We thank thee, our lord, for this."

And then there was the sex. The first time Isobel made love to the Devil, it was a few days after her initiation; he had come to her at night. The Devil made love to all the witches at the Sabbat, and sometimes Isobel made love to his demons there as well. One night, she made love to a demon while lying in bed right next to her snoring, dim-witted husband....

The judges were enjoying this part. The sheriff and the pastor conferred with each other in brief whispers, and decided it would be well worth their while to strip Isobel down and search her thoroughly for Devil's marks.

"And what," asked the sheriff, "was this intercourse like? How did it feel?"

"The sperm of the Devil and his demons is cold as ice," said Isobel, "and their members cause a pain like childbirth."

"So it was not at all enjoyable," suggested the pastor.

"Oh, it was enjoyable," answered Isobel, and she smiled. "Very."

THE OTHERWORLD LORD

By the time Isobel Gowdie launched her public confession[1] in 1662, the image of the Devil was already well established in the minds of both the witch-hunting inquisitors and the European peasantry. He strides across the trial records of the Burning Times, big and black and hairy, appearing as often as not in the form of a goat or a stag, leading the wild dance of the Sabbat and poking holes in his devotees to bring them into his fold. Then he proceeds to trample a cross or two, get his bottom kissed by one and all, and copulate with every woman present.

The portrait of the Devil that arises from these records is a fairly consistent one:

- Though he sometimes appears as an ordinary mortal man, he is more often large, hairy, and black in color;
- He often appears in animal form, or at least with horns and hooves;
- He teaches his devotees magical techniques that involve crops or the harvest;
- He presides over gatherings called Sabbats that feature dancing, feasting, sexual license, and initiation ceremonies that include the renunciation of Christianity and the scarring of the initiate with a "Devil's mark."

Most academics have seen the Devil, at least in his late medieval form, as a creation of the inquisitors themselves, a collective fiction built up successfully over the centuries. And indeed, his beginnings were humble and obscure. He seems to have been entirely absent from early Judaism; he was an import, brought back to Palestine after the

Robin Goodfellow, a "horned god" of Renaissance England

Babylonian Captivity. In Babylon, the Jews picked up a number of new ideas, drawn mostly from Zoroastrianism. The Zoroastrians were strict dualists, recognizing an evil cosmic entity, Ahriman, whose power was almost (but not quite) as great as that of Ahura Mazda, the supreme god of light. The Jews gave Ahriman a new name, Satan, which means "the adversary," and they identified him with their own mythological Lucifer, angel of "the daystar, star of the morning," which is, of course, the planet Venus.

Though Satan seems not to have caught on altogether with the Jews, he certainly made an impact on the early Christians, who, like the Zoroastrians, were dualistic and divided everything in the cosmos into good or evil. They tended to perceive Satan as a cosmic dragon, one who would, in the days of the imminent apocalypse, be defeated in battle by Christ, who emerges here simply as one of many mythological dragon-slayers.

Upon such foundations, the monks who Christianized Pagan Europe added important elements of their own, notably horns, a goatish appearance, and the whole drama of the Sabbat, with its dancing, sexuality, and initiatory rites. Ever since Margaret Murray's time, folklore scholars have sought the origins of this specifically European Devil in one or another of the old Pagan earth gods, transformed into a demon by Christian monks who regarded all vestiges of Paganism as Satanic. Though the Devil's origins must indeed be sought, in large measure, in the earth gods of Paganism, our study of witchcraft as shamanism has revealed that the Devil of the witch trials may also be understood as the old shamanic Lord of the Otherworld.

Nor is there any real contradiction between the two concepts, for the Earth Father and the Otherworld Lord were, in many European regions, one and the same.

As we have seen, the Otherworld Queen most often ruled her astral realm in consort with an Otherworld King. Among Siberian shamans, this god was worshipped until quite recently as Erlik Khan, King of the Underworld, to whose yurt the "black" shamans traveled when they sought the souls of the dead. Among the earliest Indo-Europeans (circa 4,500 B.C.), the Underworld King seems to have been a younger, darker brother of the Sky God, one whose realm was not the starry heaven, but the dark places underneath the earth. His color was black, he rode a steed of black, and his totem was the serpent. Our ancestors felt his presence in whirlwinds and troubled skies. His adversary was the Thunder God, with whom he engaged in endless, cosmic combat—thus Zeus, wielder of the lightning, battles with the serpent Typhon, Thor with the Midgard Serpent, and Babylonian Marduk with the dragon Tiamat. And yet the Underworld Lord was himself a vital part of the cosmic order, and some of the names he bears give evidence that he was not only the Sky God's rejected younger brother, but his spiritual polarity, his cosmic twin.*

Even at such an early date, the Indo-European god of the Underworld bore a strong resemblance to the later Christian Devil. Like the Near Eastern Satan, he was associated with the serpent or dragon. He shared the totemic color black with the later Christian Devil as well, and a dwelling place beneath the earth. And though Christianity typically regarded the Devil as an affront to cosmic order, there were Christian Gnostics who actually believed that Satan was the twin brother of Christ.

In the beginning, when the Indo-Europeans first rode their horses into the heart of the European continent, there was only a goddess in the Otherworld, and she reigned alone, like the Norse Hel (who is in this sense a very archaic figure). How did this dark patriarch of the netherworld come to share her throne?

Sometimes, as in the earliest Near East, we can see how the Old Bone Goddess was forced to compromise with the newly arrived god. A Sumerian myth tells how Nergal, god of war and the scorching summer sun, invaded the Underworld, conquered the fierce Ereshkigal, a wild hag with leeches in her hair, and mounted the Underworld throne by her side. The Greek myth in which Hades kidnaps Persephone, though

---

* In Vedic myth, the Death God is named Yama, a name which appears in Zoroastrian lore as Yima, in Norse myth as Ymir, and among the Romans as Remus, brother of Romulus. The probable Indo-European root of all these names is yemos, meaning "twin."

much changed through the centuries, may once have been rather similar, and Persephone, far from being a gentle maiden abducted while gathering flowers, may once have ruled the Underworld in her own right, for her name means "she who is to be feared."

The same process of forcing the Old Bone Goddess to share her Underworld realm undoubtedly took place in western Europe as well, for we have already encountered this Otherworld Lord, seated on his throne in the palace of the Land of Youth, the goddess with her grail cup by his side. There were important variations, however, for in those western lands the Otherworld Lord sometimes wore a very benevolent face.

In many traditional cultures, the deities who rule the world below the earth are responsible for the earth's abundance. This spiritual metaphor of the earth's growth cycle is founded upon a natural perception, for plants, though warmed and nourished by the sun, grow upward from beneath the earth, vitalized and encouraged by a generative force below the surface. Though the Maya regarded the Lords of the Underworld as rather treacherous characters (gaudy skeletons with big cigars), their Underworld deities were not actually evil.

Rather, the Underworld Lords—tricksters though they might be—were to be revered because of their positive influence on all growing things. To Mayan shamans, the cardinal direction south is also symbolic of the direction "below," and just as warm summer winds come from the southern direction, bringing fertility and life-giving rain, so all worldly abundance comes from "below." (As part of their compromise with Christianity, the Maya have placed the southern direction under the rulership of a new deity—Mary Magdalene!)

THE HORNED GOD

The Otherworld Lord and Lady were associated with the fertility of the earth in Europe as well—the color black may easily be seen as an image of rich fertile soil rather than a symbol of evil. In Celtic myth, especially, the eternal round of the seasons found its metaphor in the myth of the Otherworld King. *The Mabinogion* tells us how Pwyll,

Prince of Dyved, was out hunting one day when he encountered the magical hounds of the Otherworld King, Arawn of Annwn (yet another leader of the Wild Hunt). Soon, Arawn himself appeared, and professed anger because Pwyll's dogs had interfered with his own. There was one way, said Arawn, that Pwyll could make restitution. The kingdom of Annwn was beset by an enemy named Havgan or "Summer White," and Arawn himself was too weak to fight against this formidable foe.

If Pwyll were to undertake the struggle, he could reign like a king in Annwn for a year and a day, magically transformed into Arawn's very shape, while Arawn would take the shape of Pwyll and reign in Dyved, and more, Pwyll would have the most beautiful woman anywhere, to do with as he pleased. Pwyll did as he was asked and slew Havgan, though he declined to sleep with the beautiful woman. The woman was, of course, the Otherworld Queen, and, after Pwyll's return to earth, Arawn chose to be kind to him and to his kingdom of Dyved because Pwyll had defended the Otherworld—and yet not slept with Arawn's wife.

A similar myth forms the story of the medieval poem "Sir Gawain and the Green Knight." In this tale, a wild green man, armed with a club of holly, appears at King Arthur's court on New Year's Day and challenges the knights to combat. Taking up the challenge, Sir Gawain quickly decapitates the green man, who then picks up his severed head, announces that Gawain must meet him in one year's time at a place called the Green Chapel, and departs. Sir Gawain sets forth upon his winter quest and comes to a castle ruled by a lord who shares his domain with his beautiful wife and her companion, a loathly old woman. While the lord goes out hunting day after day, Gawain is left alone with the wife, who tries to tempt him into a love affair. He resists her out of courtesy to the lord of the castle.

On New Year's Day, Gawain rides forth from the castle to meet the Green Knight at the place called the Green Chapel, which turns out to be a Neolithic barrow mound! The wild green man, however, now appears in different guise as the lord of the castle, and the combat ends with professions of friendship. The lord of the castle tells Gawain that

176

the loathly old woman accompanying his wife is none other than the enchantress Morgan le Fay, whom he also refers to as "Morgan the Goddess."

The pattern of the two stories is remarkably similar. In the Otherworld realm, called Annwn or the Green Knight's castle, an eternal combat goes on, representative of the seasons of the year. The Otherworld Lord manifests in two principal aspects: he is both the Summer King and the Winter King. This is clearly seen in the story of Pwyll, whose antagonist is called Havgan or "Summer White." Pwyll, then, is the Winter King defeating the Summer King at the summer solstice, when the days begin to grow shorter. Gawain's combats with the Green Knight take place on New Year's Day, another solstice, and the Green Knight's club of holly may well be a symbol of winter.

We have heard much, of late, about the Earth Mother, who appears in so many different guises in so many different spiritual traditions, but in ancient Europe, there was an Earth Father as well, and his myth is the myth of the earth itself, of its seasonal changes. The Earth Father is known by many names, for he succeeds himself again and again, as the seasons succeed each year, always different but always the same. His latest incarnation, transformed into a (more or less) Christian legend, is the Grail King of the Arthurian cycle.

As we noted in the previous chapter, the Grail King has a number of names, such as Brons, Pelles, and Peredur, that can be traced back to earlier Celtic myth—Bran, Pwyll, and Pryderi. All these figures, characters in *The Mabinogion*, are part of a mythological family called the Children of Llyr. Though Llyr himself makes no appearance in *The Mabinogion*, he is generally regarded as the old Celtic god of the ocean, and his children as deities associated with earth and water. Bran was one of his sons, and another was Manawyddan, who appears in Irish lore as the sea god Mannanan mac Lir, King of the Otherworld.

The Otherworld Lord, then, is a deity of earth and sea. His names are legion, for, like all good shamans, he dies and is reborn, again and again, even as the fruits of the earth die and are reborn with the seasons. Because he rules over the abundance of the wild earth, he is a god of the forests and the woods, and thus he may appear as the Green

Man, as in the tale of Sir Gawain and the Green Knight. Because the animals dwell in those woods, and because the animal kingdom is part of the world of vast Nature, he is a Lord of the Animals as well.

This, then, is the god who rode forth on Halloween, or during the Ember Days, to lead the Wild Hunt. In the Otherworld, the dead, or at least the male dead, spent their time in hunting as well as feasting (as if ancient and medieval Europe had its own version of what Native Americans called "the happy hunting grounds"). On nights when the dead rode forth, led by their king and queen, most medieval peasants stayed safely indoors, for fear of meeting them—except, of course, for the witches, who happily joined them in their travels.

To meet up with the Lord of the Wild Hunt was not necessarily an inauspicious thing, for the Otherworld Lord was not evil, but such a meeting might constitute a rather harrowing encounter with the unknown. In time, however, the ecclesiastical doctrine that identified the Otherworld Lord with the Christian Devil took its toll, and the Lord of the Wild Hunt came more and more to be feared. We have already heard the story (in Chapter 3) of the priest who encountered the Wild Hunt one night, led by an enormous and terrible being with a club, which of course was the favored weapon of the Green Knight.* In his fierce glowing eyes and barbaric countenance we may sense the transformation that was even then occurring, of the Wild Hunt's Lord—whether Arthur, Odin, or Herlechin—into the Satan of the witch trials.

As a Master of Animals, the Otherworld Lord occasionally wore horns, and it is these horns, more than any other physical feature, that have had the greatest impact on our picture of the Devil. The original Lucifer or Satan of the Near East had no such headgear—the horns are linked clearly and incontestably with old European deities of the woods and the animals. Thus, modern neo-Pagans have made much of the old Celtic deity Cernunnos, the Horned One, though it must be

---

* The earliest Tarot deck on record, dating from 1425 and originating in the Visconti court of Milan, features a "wild man" with a club instead of the usual Tarot Fool. The familiar cosmic Fool of the Tarot, then (and as distinct from the Devil), would seem to have his origin in the Lord of the Wild Hunt.

admitted that Cernunnos himself never actually appears by name in the records of the witch trials. Nevertheless, he is a typical incarnation of the Otherworld Lord.

A relief sculpture from France, during the Gallo-Roman period, depicts him as Lord of the Underworld. Crowned with antlers, he is encircled by a serpent. At his feet is a cornucopia—for, as we have seen, all abundance flows from the Underworld, and the cornucopia is yet another metaphor for that inexhaustible source we have called the cauldron of death and rebirth. In similar fashion, Cernunnos appears on a ritual vessel called the Gundestrup Cauldron, a bronze masterpiece discovered in Denmark but obviously fashioned in some Celtic country. Here Cernunnos sits in lotus posture with his serpent in his hand and his horns spreading proudly. He is surrounded by animals. Also included in the scene is a cauldron into which bodies, apparently dead warriors, are being tossed.

The myths that once told tales of Cernunnos are lost to us now, but a few tantalizing fragments remain. Most scholars agree, for instance, that Cernunnos makes an appearance in a tale entitled "Owain, or the Countess of the Fountain."* In this story, Kynon, a knight of King Arthur's court, tells Owain how he was wandering in the wilderness when a mysterious man directed him upon the next stage of his quest:

> ...take the right hand path and continue until you come to a great cleared field with a mound in the centre, and on that mound you will see a great black man, no smaller than two men of this world. He has one foot, and one eye in the middle of his forehead, and he carries an iron spear which you can be certain would be a burden for any two men. Though ugly, he is not an unpleasant man. He is keeper of the forest, and you will see a thousand wild animals grazing about him.[2]

---

* This tale, included in *The Mabinogion*, has some marvelous mythic features. Owain and another knight battle for the hand of the Countess who tends the magical fountain, and Owain, upon winning the combat, becomes her champion in his turn. This would seem to be yet another version of the same old story: the Summer King battling the Winter King for the sake of the goddess who sits by the Well of Memory and Fate.

Kynon rises in the morning and continues on his way. At last he comes to the clearing where the black man resides, and finds him sitting on the mound. He is far bigger than Kynon expected him to be, and the iron spear which was to be "a burden for two men" seems to Kynon to be too huge for four warriors to lift—and yet the black man holds it easily in his hand. When Kynon greets him, he replies rudely, and when Kynon proceeds to ask him what sort of power he has over the animals, the black man takes his cudgel and strikes a stag; the creature roars, and a host of wild animals, "like stars in the sky," appears, including serpents and lions. The black man commands them to begin grazing peacefully; they bow their heads and instantly obey.[3]

In summary, we may say that the Lord of the Otherworld was a fierce wild man, sometimes black, like the dark forester of the Owain story, and sometimes dressed in elvish green, like the Green Knight who challenged Gawain. His typical wand of office was a primitive club. As ruler of all that lay beneath the earth, he was concerned with the fecundity of growing things, and thus carried a distinctly sexual connotation.

He was Lord of the Animals as well, and as such appeared either with horns or in animal disguise. By medieval times, he was remembered chiefly as the leader of the Wild Hunt, in which he roamed at night with a host comprised both of animals and of the souls of the dead. As his legions feasted in the Otherworld, so the members of the Wild Hunt sought food in this world.

The Otherworld King often traveled with his consort, that medieval descendant of the old shamanic Bone Goddess who was called Perchta or Diana in the Wild Hunt tales of the German witches, or the Queen of the Elves in Celtic lands. The leader of the Wild Hunt bore many names, some of which reveal his true identity—Odin was a shamanic god of the dead who, like the black forester of the Owain tale, possessed only one eye; and Arthur, who was carried off to the Land of Youth by that enchantress whom the anonymous Gawain poet called "Morgan the Goddess," is clearly returning from that Otherworld Avalon when he appears as leader of the Wild Hunt.

It is clear that the Otherworld Lord has a great deal in common with the Devil of the witch trials:

- He may appear as a large black man, as in the Owain tale;
- He is a "wild man," associated with the wilderness;
- He may appear in animal form, or as the leader of a pack of animals or, very often, with antlers;
- As lord of the realm below the earth, he is associated with the growth of crops or the harvest, and hence, by implication, with sexuality.

But do these elements from myth and folklore really add up to the Devil?

An American folktale[4] recounts the story of a miser named Tom Walker, who was walking in the woods near Boston one day when he encountered a "huge black man" with an ax on his shoulder, curly black hair, and a face that looked as if it had been smeared with soot.

"Who are you?" asked Tom.

"I go by many different names," answered the black man. "Some call me the Wild Huntsman, others call me Old Scratch. Still others call me Satan. Here I am known as the Black Woodsman."

THE RITES OF THE HUNT

That our familiar portrait of the Devil was drawn, in large part, from the old Otherworld King seems clear, but we are still a long ways from the Witches' Sabbat of demonological lore. How was the Otherworld King worshipped? And did the rites held in his honor bear any resemblance to the conventional picture of the Witches' Sabbat?

The Animal Master may well be one of the oldest deities known to man. A painting on the walls of the cave of Trois Freres in France seems to depict a shaman, wearing a mask made from a deer's head complete with antlers, engaged in a dance. So, at least, thought the great Abbe Breuil, archaeologist of the caves and authority on Ice Age art, who reconstructed the famous scene from a very faded original.

Some would say that the original is too faded, and that we cannot be sure it represents a shaman at all. But there is other, better evidence that Stone Age shamans wore headdresses of antlers when they performed their magic rites of the hunt, for a Mesolithic settlement at Star Carr in Yorkshire, England, has yielded a pair of antlers notched in such a way that they could only have been used as headgear.

Worship of the Animal Master is not only incredibly ancient, it is also nearly universal. As we have seen, shamanic journeys up the World Tree gave birth to yoga; and to discover Cernunnos, a Celtic god, seated in full lotus as he is on the Gundestrup Cauldron, reminds

A dancing shaman, from a Paleolithic painting found at
Caverne des Trois Freres, France

A horned god found on a seal from the
Indus Valley civilization, circa 1,500 B.C.

us of this connection. A seal from the Indus Valley civilization, dating from about 1,500 B.C., shows a scene that is virtually identical to that sculpted on the Gundestrup Cauldron a millennium and a half later— a man, wearing antlers, sits in lotus posture surrounded by animals. Scholars believe that the Indus Valley seal represents a deity who was ancestral to the Hindu god Shiva, who was also "Lord of Animals" (*pasupati*), and who was often envisioned as a wild man. As a deity of yoga, metaphor for the kundalini power, Shiva is connected with the power in the spinal column, the internal World Tree; the Samoyed shaman who, in his initiatory vision (Chapter 2), spoke with the Lord of the Tree, may well have been speaking with a prehistoric Animal Master who is the original archetype of both Cernunnos and Shiva.

Whenever Stone Age shamans traveled to the Otherworld to beseech the gods for a good hunt, or whenever the benandanti of later times traveled to Josaphat's Field to fight for a good harvest, they were in spiritual communion with the Otherworld King. Such ecstasies were the business of shamans, and ordinary people were content to worship the gods through seasonal rituals and celebrations. Though

183

early Christian missionaries in Europe had a special horror of the Master of Animals, and consequently tried their best to eradicate both the practice and the memory of his rites, a few hints have come down to us regarding those ceremonies, and they cast a fair amount of light on the origins of the Sabbat. The medieval Feast of Fools, for instance, was devoted to ritual license and chaos in honor of the New Year and the winter solstice, for it took place during those Ember Days between Christmas and Epiphany which have proved to be important in witchlore as a time when the Wild Hunt was most active.

More important to our own theme, there was a tradition of hunting festivals that took place during the Ember Days (on January 1, to be precise), and that included dances wherein the participants wore animal masks. These festivals also featured men dressed as women, and processions of carts upon which ritual objects were drawn. The early records of such festivals attribute these activities primarily to Roman soldiers of late Imperial times, but by the beginning of the sixteenth century it was more often than not a troop of male children who wore the animal masks, and who were understood to be impersonating the dead (this, of course, is the origin of our own Halloween custom of children in "spooky" costumes). Tables of food were set for nocturnal divinities during these festivals.

"What rational person could believe that he would find men of sound mind who would wish to change themselves into a stag or other wild beast?" asked Caesarius of Arles (died 542).[5] But, Caesarius to the contrary, the battle waged by the Church against these Pagan winter ceremonies was, in the main, unsuccessful, and rites that had once involved the Lord of the Animals, and that featured singing, dancing, eroticism, banquets in honor of nocturnal divinities, animal disguises, and a ritual king survived well into the Middle Ages. And though it may be rash to conclude that the whole origin of the Devil's Sabbat is to be found in such festivals, we may at least suspect that the inquisitors drew some of their cannon fodder from such rites.

That ceremonies reminiscent of the rituals once performed for the Otherworld King still took place during the time of the witch trials, and in the same locations, is clear. In the 1530s, Protestant Swiss

reformers[6] were complaining about the *stopfers* or "piercers," also
known as *punchiadurs*, who, armed with large clubs, went from village
to village, jumping up and down and colliding with each other. Their
behavior was understood as a form of ritual combat (not unlike the
"stick dances" performed by British Morris Dancers) to obtain a more
abundant harvest. Here we may note several familiar features:

- A ritual combat, like that associated with the Celtic Lord of
  the Otherworld or with the activities of the benandanti;
- The use of clubs, a typical symbol of the Green Man;
- Actors who are called "piercers," and who, like the
  "whinnes" of the "Lyke-Wake Dirge," function as
  shamanic initiatory demons.

As late as the nineteenth century, in Austria and Bavaria, groups of
"beautiful Perchtas" and "ugly Perchtas" enacted similar ritual combats
during the Winter Carnival; the "beautiful Perchtas" generally prevailed. (We may remember that Perchta was the name by which the
Goddess of the Wild Hunt was known in those regions.) Some vestiges
of these rites have survived until the present day; during Carnival, a
group of men called *schurtendiebe* ("thieves in short skirts") come forth
from the woods surrounding Swiss villages. They are clothed in sheep-
skins, with cowbells around their waists, and their faces are masked.
They steal things from the other villagers as part of their ceremony.
The *punchiadurs* of the sixteenth century wore similar cowbells and
made similar mischief.

Another sixteenth-century account comes from a Lutheran pastor,[7]
this time in Frankfurt, who complained of a "Pagan" ceremony in
which youths pushed a large cart covered with leaves through the town,
singing songs and predicting the future. The youths were said to be
symbolic of "Eckhard's Army," (i.e., the Wild Hunt). Such carts certainly formed part of the January hunting festivals in honor of the Animal Master, and they have a long mythological ancestry.

The Norse god Freyr, who was associated with fertility and the
earth, was the brother of Freya, a goddess of sexuality, whose priestesses practiced the shamanic *seidr* rites and whose totem animal was

the cat. Several clues from the works of the medieval Icelandic poet Snorri Sturluson suggest that Freyr was a vegetation deity who died and was reborn with the seasons. We may suspect that Freyr and Freya were yet another Otherworld King and Queen (indeed, both are associated with the boar, which, at least in Celtic lands, was an Underworld creature).

Freyr was frequently carried about in a ritual cart (in earlier days, so was a goddess called Nerthus). The cart may also be found in a context that includes the ritual combat, though in a most unexpected time and place: in Boston, in the 1760s, Guy Fawkes Day was celebrated by two groups of men, each with their decorated wagon or cart, who met in the fields near town for a "ritual" battle that all too often turned into a dangerous brawl. It was from these fierce companies of Guy Fawkes Day brawlers that Samuel Adams recruited his Sons of Liberty, who, we may remember, were goaded to wild action by dancing around "the Liberty Tree."

Dancing around sacred trees—local images of the shamanic World Tree—was a part of the May Day festivities in England, and May Eve (also known as Walpurgis Night after the obscure German martyr, Saint Walpurga, whose feast day it was) is another day that is frequently associated with the Witches' Sabbat. In Elizabethan times, The King and Queen of the May were often called Robin Hood and Maid Marian. Robin appeared dressed in his traditional green and crowned with antlers and, hand in hand with Maid Marian, led the villagers in the May Day dances. Witchcraft scholars, from Margaret Murray onward, have noted some of Robin Hood's Pagan associations—he dresses in green, lives in the wild, and sometimes wears antlers. In fact, he may well be a folkloric descendant of the Lord of the Animals.

In the British Isles, as in the Alps, many of the customs associated with the Animal Master have shown remarkable persistence. At the village of Melbury Osmond in Dorsetshire, a wooden mask called the Dorset Ooser was preserved until the beginning of this century, when it was stolen from its owners. A surviving photograph shows a terrifying,

The Dorset Ooser, a wooden mask from the village of
Melbury Osmond in Dorsetshire

semi-human face crowned with bull's horns and featuring wild, pro-
truding eyes. Interestingly enough, no record of any ceremony involving the Ooser has been preserved, though its similarity to shamanic
masks from the Americas, or to Stone Age artifacts such as the horned
crown of Star Carr, is striking.

We have already noted (Chapter 5) some of the hobby-horse rituals still being practiced in England today; but the most wonderful of all
the ancient festivals (at least for our purposes) is the Horned Dance,
which takes place at the village of Abbots Bromley, Staffordshire, each
September.

Six pairs of antlers are kept in the village church of Abbots Bromley, and are removed only on the day of the festival. There are twelve
participants—six men who wear the horns and six other characters in
the pageant. The other characters are: the Hobby Horse (again, see
Chapter 5), Maid Marian (a man dressed as a woman, reminding us of
the ritual transvestism practiced at the January hunting rites), a Fool,
Robin Hood, and two musicians (a boy with a triangle and a man with
an accordion). The dancers make a twenty-mile circuit, stopping at
various houses to perform the dance—a journey which, considering

that the antlered headpieces weigh about twenty pounds each, must have been a difficult task in the old days, but which is now made easier by loading the antlers onto a trailer while the dancers walk. In the dance itself, the horned men form two rows and prance back and forth, almost locking horns. This suggests the typical ritual combat for the harvest, and the fact that the Horned Dance was, in the seventeenth century, performed "around Christmas" marks it as a direct descendant of the animal dances and hunting rituals condemned by Caesarius of Arles in 542.

The Horned Dance at Abbots Bromley, Staffordshire

THE MYSTERY OF THE SABBAT

Throughout Europe, rituals and festivals dedicated to the old Earth Father continued to be practiced throughout the Middle Ages. These festivals included many features that were later attributed to the Witches' Sabbat:

- Dancing and feasting;
- Sexual license;
- A ritual king;
- Animal disguises (e.g., masks);
- As with the astral journeys of the benandanti, ritual combat for the sake of the harvest.

It would be simple indeed to conclude (as many witchcraft scholars have done) that the Sabbats were merely harmless folk festivals, transformed into demonic orgies solely through the twisted perceptions of the Inquisitors.

But nothing is as simple as we might wish. The mere fact that such folk festivals were still observed, and that some of them included elements similar to those of the Sabbat, doesn't actually prove that real Sabbats, attended by "real" witches, ever existed. There are three opinions on the matter:

1. The Sabbat was wholly imaginary, a mental construct of the inquisitors, who "invented" it in their minds out of the popular literature of heresy and demonology. This is the argument of Norman Cohn.[8]

2. Folk festivals, like the ones we have described, were practiced throughout Europe by villagers who were still essentially Pagan, until the Inquisition, branding such harmless customs as demonic Witches' Sabbats, finally descended upon the peasants with fire and sword. This is the argument of Pagan apologists, from Murray onward.

3. The Sabbats, like the gatherings of the benandanti, can be shown, in most cases, to have occurred when the witches *left their bodies* and undertook astral journeys. The astral landscapes through which they traveled were collective, in the sense that the same basic features were agreed upon by most individual travelers. These landscapes included elements from ancient shamanic practice, as well as from existing folk festivals. This is the opinion of Carlo Ginzburg, to whose work this volume owes so much.

As we have seen, the witches were primarily shamans—village shamans, if you will—who still remembered and practiced spiritual techniques of incredible antiquity. Again and again, we have seen that Ginzburg is essentially correct, and that many of the spirit journeys undertaken by witches were astral rather than physical (i.e., they were shamanic journeys to the Otherworld).

So, does this mean that the Sabbats never really took place in any *physical* sense?

If there were never any Sabbats, what provoked the great witch hunt and the horrors of the Burning Times?

Throughout the Middle Ages, peasants continued to celebrate their folk festivals, set tables for the dead, and journey with the Wild Hunt. Though the Church disapproved of such customs, it never persecuted the peasantry. Then, in the late 1300s and early 1400s, the Church decided that a whole new sect of heretics had arisen, and that these heretical "witches" constituted a grave threat to the spiritual security of Christendom.

And so the witch trials began. So powerful and so intense were their effects that the whole nature of the European unconscious went through a dramatic change. Though the Old Bone Goddess, the Otherworld Queen, tends to predominate in the earliest testimony, she soon disappears, along with her fairy cohorts; her consort, once the Earth Father, steps into the starring role, but transformed into Satan, with his elvish hosts reclassified as demons.

What had happened?

There have been so many explanations: the Church hated women, the Church hated the folk festivals, the people themselves were looking for scapegoats. None of these theories really solves the mystery. The Church had always looked down upon women—but why, at the dawn of the scientific age, should it suddenly take up arms against them? Similarly, the Church had always complained against the folk festivals—so why, just when the doctrine of reason was sweeping Europe, should it suddenly try to eradicate them by destroying large portions of the general population? (Let us remember that many churchmen, and even a few inquisitors, came from peasant stock themselves, and had been raised in the country. They probably had parents and cousins who took part in folk festivals and astral journeys.) And, though the "social scapegoat" theory may be applicable in isolated cases (it works fairly well for *part*, though by no means all, of the Salem trials), it cannot quite serve as a blanket explanation for a holocaust of such magnitude.

In order to hazard a guess as to whether or not the Sabbats were physically real, and to understand the forces at work behind the witch trials, it will be necessary to examine more closely the world in which the witches lived.

EARTH HEALING

The rituals dedicated to the Lord of the Animals and King of the Otherworld all had the same purpose—to heal and renew the earth. This has always been part of the business of shamans, for shamans must care for the health of the tribe in all its totality—which includes the entire environment in which the people live and breathe and have their being.

One of the most common, and most powerful, shamanic techniques for healing the total environment is the creation and projection of a spirit body, or body of light. As explained earlier, we shall not actually attempt to teach the techniques of full-scale astral projection in this book. Instead, we shall use a method of projecting the body of light that has become popular in present-day workshops and seminars on shamanism.

First, sit quietly. Build your inner World Tree. When the World Tree is vibrating within you and you are fully empowered, you are ready to project yourself outward into the great world.

In "The Ascent Up the World Tree" (page 138), you learned to project your inner tree outside of yourself, to see it standing before you. This is the same technique; the only difference is that it is your own "spirit body" that is to be projected outward. See it, in your mind's eye, as a glowing body of light, a shining and radiant image of yourself. This body of light is capable of merging with other beings, other entities. Let us say that you choose to become one with a great boulder on a beach near your home. You may either go to the beach and contemplate the boulder itself, or you may build an imaginary picture of it in your mind. It doesn't matter. The important thing is to extend the body of light and "see" it entering that boulder, infusing it with a glow of shining energy. Watch as the light becomes part of the boulder. Then know that you are yourself within the boulder, and that your perceptions, accessed through meditation, arise from that source.

With your body of light, you can enter into and become one with anything, and by so doing you will be able to feel the essence of the thing. Is it healthy? Does it need healing? Can you help?

Let us take a few examples from the natural world.

Perhaps the easiest place to start is with the very air you breathe. After building your inner World Tree, go and stand outside. Feel the wind blowing and gusting around you. Let it rustle through your hair, touch your face. Then project your body of light outward. Imagine it merging with the wind; feel it grow and extend and become so light that it merges with the air.

By the same token, you can project yourself into the consciousness of an animal. If you have the opportunity to wander or hike through wild nature, this is an excellent form of meditation for your rambles. Of course, it can also be practiced upon a family pet or, if you're really desperate, you can go to the zoo. Project the body of light into an animal. Learn to feel its essence. If your critter is sick, get inside of it and fill it with healing light and energy.

Plants are easy to work with because most of us have them at home and, in a sense, we already know them. Projecting your spirit body into a plant is a wonderful way to learn what it likes—its special music, how often it likes to be watered, and so on. And from plants to trees is only a short jump. In a sense, you already know how to project yourself into the spirit of a tree, for this was part of our very first exercise. But you can work with trees at long distance, too. Choose an image. If you want to work with endangered forests, as in the Amazon, take a picture out of a book or magazine and concentrate on that picture until you can actually see it and feel it in your mind's eye. Use all your senses—feel the humidity, smell the jungle smells, hear the voices of birds and insects in the cloud forest, and so on. Then project your light-body into that scene and fill the forest with all the healing energy and power at your disposal.

You can learn to feel the essence of water by sitting on a beach or by the shores of a river or lake, then projecting your body of light into the water. If you understand the essence of water, you can understand what water needs in order to experience healing, when it, like all natural things, occasionally falls out of balance. Is there a drought in your area? Link your body of light with the spirit of water. Call the essence of water and feel it accumulate there, in your body of light, until you grow heavy, dense, pregnant with rain.

If you can learn to increase the essence of water, you can also learn to decrease the energy of fire. Let us suppose that you hear about a forest fire on the evening news. Use the same techniques that allowed you to enter into an environment such as an Amazon rain forest—let the image from your television screen become imprinted on your inner vision, so that you can project yourself into it. Sailing above it all, you can become the energy of fire. Then feel yourself fading, diminishing, trailing away into embers, then nothingness.

If you project your energy into the rocks, you can actually feel the crystals growing. You can gain intuitive knowledge and wisdom about the way gems and minerals are nurtured in the earth.

You can practice these techniques with human beings as well, especially those who are sick or sad or otherwise in need of healing. Of course, all the restrictions that require you to obtain permission from the ailing individual apply here.

PART II

Ghost Dancers

We shall live again!
We shall live again!

Sioux Indian
Ghost Dance Song, 1890

CHAPTER 8

The Origins of the Sabbat

THE SURVIVAL OF THE OLD GODS

Shamanism is not a religion; it is a technique of spiritual practice. As such, it is far older than any "formal" religion on the planet. Its heart and soul—the ecstatic journey to the Otherworld in quest of wisdom—transcends the names, formulae, and doctrines that are characteristic of organized religions. Any religion may include elements of shamanism, and most of them do, but shamanism itself cannot be contained within the confines of any single religion. Time and again, it has slipped through the cracks and loopholes of doctrine and dogma, and remained itself. This is what it *must* do, for it answers a deep human need: the need for contact with that other dimension which lies all around us, which interpenetrates our own, and which holds within it the souls and spirits of all those who went before us.

Because it is founded upon experience rather than dogma, shamanism tends to survive the rise and fall of formal religions. Pontiffs and prophets come and go; shamanism stays the same.

It is clear that the religion of Paleolithic man was, at least to some degree, shamanistic, for shamanism is older than the migration of human beings into the Americas, as we may see from the fact that the first New World settlers brought their shamanism with them out of the Old World. Whether or not the religion of Neolithic Europe was shamanic may never be known; but the many votive vessels found alongside of female figurines suggest that Neolithic people honored their female ancestors at a Feast of the Dead, and the rituals involving ancestral bones that seem to have taken place in the forecourts of the great megalithic tombs (which faced west, toward the Land of Youth) intimate that the Old Bone Goddess held sway in the mythology of Neolithic Europe, as she continued to do in later mythologies.

The Indo-European peoples who began moving westward from the Russian steppes around 4500 B.C. practiced a religion that was almost certainly shamanic. We have already seen how the spirit horse of the witchcraft trials may be traced to their influence, and how Greeks, Celts, and Vikings alike recognized a shamanic cosmos with the World Tree at its center. In fact, it is likely that shamanism played a major role in *all* the pre-Christian religions of Europe, and that it was not until the advent of Christianity that shamanic practice was seriously challenged.*

Traditional scholarship has always maintained that the Christianization of Europe was thorough and complete, while Pagan writers have claimed that many European peasants continued to practice their ancient faiths as a kind of medieval underground religious movement. Both of these views are extreme. The truth probably lies somewhere in between.

---

* There was even a shamanic component in early Christianity. We have already noted how Christ's crucifixion and descent into hell follow the classic pattern of the shaman's initiation on the World Tree and his journey to the Otherworld to help the dead. Gnostic Christians produced a whole literature involving journeys through vivid and colorful heavens—until they were declared heretical. St. Paul found it necessary to speak out against independent Christian leaders—usually women—who "spoke in tongues" and experienced visions— though in this case it seems that actual *possession* by spiritual beings (rather than *ecstatic journeys* to spiritual realms) is indicated (i.e., Voudoun as opposed to shamanism).

The conversion of Northern and Western Europe may have been thorough, but in many ways it was only skin deep. Let us remember that ordinary European peasants could neither read nor write. They went to the church because they were told to; there they heard a ceremony conducted in a language (Latin) they did not understand, delivered by rote and without explanation. Sermons were sometimes delivered by village priests, but the priests who ministered in rural regions were frequently of peasant stock themselves, and sometimes almost as illiterate as their fellow villagers.

Medieval village priests were hastily taught a catechism and the rudiments of the Mass, and while understanding perhaps enough written Latin to make their way laboriously through the service, they had some notions about Christianity that were, to say the least, peculiar. (In 1281, the priest of Inverkeithing in Scotland led his parishioners in a merry Easter dance round a phallic fertility figure.) Thus ancient Pagan ideas and practices continued to linger in the minds of European peasants, blending with Christian teaching in a rich and vivid tapestry of belief that was altogether new. The technical name for such a blend is *religious syncretism*.

Most religious scholars don't care much for syncretism. They seem to regard it as a process of bastardization, wherein the "pure" stream of a religious tradition is muddied by outside influences. But this attitude itself shows the imprint of the Judeo-Christian outlook. It is as if these academics were seeking something as pure and austere as the deserts that produced the Abrahamic religions, something which can be reduced to a single vision or revelation, something which can be properly "nailed down." Syncretism, by definition, slips through one's fingers, for it blends any number of spiritual influences into a new, colorful whole.

What happens when a faith imbued with shamanism gets syncretized with a more austere, formally organized religion like Christianity? The Maya of Central America constitute an outstanding example of this process. As we have seen, Mayan religion was a highly elaborate spiritual tradition with a powerful shamanic foundation. Christianized in the sixteenth and seventeenth centuries by fire and sword, the Maya, like medieval Europeans of the previous millennium, were forced to sit and listen to doctrines preached in a language they scarcely understood and backed up by mysterious rituals that were seldom fully explained. Because they lived in isolated jungle or mountain areas, the Maya were frequently without the strong organized Catholic structure that predominated in the larger cities. They evolved their own, syncretistic blend of Christianity and Mayan shamanism.

For instance, the contemporary Maya of Guatemala recognize a Trinity, but it is a Trinity all their own, comprised of God, Holy Earth, and the Ancestors. In the word "God," they include the whole Catholic Trinity as well as Mary and all the saints. "Holy Earth" is none other than the old shamanic Lord of the Underworld, and it is to this "person of the Trinity" that Mayan shamans are especially devoted. The Mayan Calendar, which, contrary to what some New Age writers would have us believe, is still a vital divinatory tool among the Quiche Maya, is believed to be *his* calendar, while the Christian calendar rules over an entirely different dimension of reality. Sometimes the Otherworld Lord or Holy Earth is called St. Maximon, and in the village of Santiago Atitlan there is an idol of this peculiar "saint" dressed in black peasant clothes with a wide-brimmed hat and clutching a bottle of brandy—and, like the old gods of the Underworld, he smokes a big cigar.

As for the third "person" of the Trinity, the Ancestors are, of course, the Good People, the dead who were once invoked by kings in the rituals of the Classic Maya and who still, in Mayan thinking, remain all around us.

Note that the sky gods and heavenly deities of the Classic Maya seem to have disappeared altogether, replaced by Christ and all the Catholic saints. Rather, it is the cult of fertility and the dead that has remained alive with its shamanic components intact. Gods of the sky are cerebral creatures, and Christianity, with its austere dogma, has traditionally sought to speak to that rarefied portion of the human soul. What Christianity has historically failed to address is the need for contact with the earth, with the twin polarities of sensuality and death, with the growth of the soil and the world beyond. This was the human need the Maya could answer only by continuing, somehow, to revere the old shamanic god of death, fertility, and the Otherworld.

This author believes that a similar process took place in Europe. The white-bearded patriarchal god of the medieval theologians and his son, "the king of heaven," came to rule in the sky of the European mind early on, and hence the gods of light and thunder were probably the first to vanish under the new dispensation. Jesus and Jehovah, because they addressed metaphysical concepts like law and order, were names that could easily be substituted for Lugh or Tyr (or even Odin, if we consider him in his occasional role as ruler of the gods rather than in his more chthonic role as a shamanic Lord of the Dead.) St. Michael came to slay dragons on high, thus serving as an effective substitute for other dragon-slayers, such as Sigurd and Thor.

But Christianity had no gods, no saints, to replace the Lord and Lady of the Otherworld, the deities of earth and water who gave life to animals and crops and who watched over the dead with a gentle concern that was altogether foreign to the scowling Christ of the medieval Judgment Day. Peasants knew that one ought not to forget the Lord and Lady, for without them one's ancestors might go hungry in the Otherworld, and one might go hungry in this world as well, for the Lord and Lady of the Otherworld had dominion over all the earth's growing things, and without their help the crops might fail and the animals sicken.

And so medieval peasants continued to worship the Old Bone Goddess and the Master of Animals. Though the old names could not be spoken aloud, the deities themselves could still be worshipped under other, less overtly Pagan names. The great goddess Hel became Mother Hulda with her big teeth, and Odin became Herne the Hunter, leader of the Wild Hunt. Irish deities like Mannanan mac Lir and Fand were no longer called the gods of the Otherworld—rather, they were the King and Queen of the Fairy Folk, or of Elfland, as were their British counterparts such as Manawyddan map Llyr and Rhiannon.

The old deities, with their new names, continued to rule over the kingdom of souls, which constituted the Otherworld and which was now called Faerie or Elfland. For if the elves were, in one sense, nature spirits who existed on a less dense, more elemental level of reality than our own, they were also the spirits of the dead, for it is part of shamanic tradition that our ancestors, after death, merge into the collective mind, and that their individuality, over time, dissolves into and becomes one with Nature and its spirits, and ultimately, with the gods.* When one went to visit the King and Queen of the Elves, one did so by entering one of the barrow mounds, which were, after all, graves, and the British folk tradition of the Hosting of the Fairies is clearly recognizable as yet another version of the Wild Hunt, the riding forth of the spirits of the dead.

Nature spirits, like Nature itself, can be wild and tricky, and the dead live by rules that are sometimes the reverse of our own. It is always best, under the circumstances, not to make them angry. One must speak of them with exceptional kindness; thus elves and ancestors alike were known as "the good folk" and "the good people." It was a matter of both wise policy and religious reverence to feed one's dead, for they were certain to be hungry when they came riding upon the Wild Hunt to visit our world. Thus tables were set forth for them.

There were various times when the ancestors came forth upon their riding. Most people in central and northern Europe believed that the Ember Days between Christmas and Epiphany were such a time, and some of them believed that the dead rode forth every Thursday—which, speaking astrologically, is the day of Jupiter or Thor. The Celts believed that Halloween was the time of the Hosting of the Fairies, and this belief survives to the present day. Though real, genuine belief in Halloween as a "doorway between the worlds" may be fading in the British Isles, it is still quite alive in Mexico during the Days of the Dead.

The Ember Days were important because they constituted the turning of the year, when the light awakened after its winter sleep and

---

* In ancient Hawaiian religion, rituals are performed by which the *aumakua*, or higher self, of a deceased family member becomes part of one of the gods. A similar process exists in Haitian Voudoun, wherein the spirits of the dead become merged with one of the *loa*, or gods.

the days grew longer. The Otherworld Lord as Summer King had slain his other, aging self, the Winter King, and the doorways between the worlds stood open in the interval. During such times, the people celebrated their ancient rites for the Otherworld Lord. The Church watched with disapproval, but did nothing. The festivals consisted of dancing, feasting, and various mischief made by men and boys in animal masks. Sometimes groups of men, dressed as animals, fought ritual battles for the sake of the harvest—just as the Otherworld Lord fought his battle for the Earth Goddess twice a year, as Summer King and Winter King. At such times, "official" morals became lax and sexual license was common. Later in the year, similar festivals occurred, and those held on May Day included a dance around a Maypole or some sacred tree, a memory of the great World Tree upon which men traveled to visit the Otherworld itself.

Of course, the Otherworld King was no longer called by his ancient name, and if, in many places, he was regarded primarily as the King of the Elves, he might also be known as Robin Hood or Puck, or

A celebration of ancient rites in a churchyard,
from a seventeenth-century engraving

the Green Man. In other regions his rites were simply called The Feast of Fools.

Though most people were content simply to take part in the festivals and perhaps set a table for the dead, there were others who acted as community shamans, though the word itself would have been foreign to them. When the doors between the worlds opened, these individuals went into a trance and left their bodies. They rode with the fairies, traveled with the Wild Hunt. Most of them were women, and in early medieval times it was usually the Queen of Fairies rather than the King who was acknowledged as the principal leader of the Wild Hunt, and to whom the "witches" paid their devotions. Some, those who possessed great natural talent, simply fell into a trance, while others probably used fly agaric mushrooms or belladonna to assist them in their journeys. In vision, they rode a broomstick or spirit horse to the Otherworld. Some of them took the shapes of animals, and indeed, many such individuals kept household pets of various types, their "familiars" who assisted them in their journeys.

The Wild Hunt itself was not unlike one of the folk festivals. There was dancing and feasting aplenty on those astral journeys, and witches often went with the dead to visit houses throughout the village, taking part with the good folk in their spirit feasts. And when they returned to their bodies, they brought back a special kind of knowledge, the same knowledge sought by shamans everywhere, in all cultures. They learned about the fate of the dead, and thus were able to comfort relations still living, letting them know their departed loved ones were happy in the Otherworld, or, if the need arose, instructing them as to how they might serve their dead and better their condition. Even during those times when the doors to the Otherworld were not fully open, the village shaman or witch could "scry" into that world by gazing into a bowl of water—thus imitating the Norns who peered eternally into the Well of Memory. By so doing, they could keep informed about events in the Otherworld, and thus serve the community as a whole.

To serve the dead was to serve the living. Medieval Europeans believed in a symbiosis between this world and the Otherworld that necessitated caring for both worlds at once. The harvest upon which all villagers depended was itself dependent upon activities in the Otherworld, where the Master and Mistress of Earth and Animals had their dwelling. The so-called witches served the living directly, too, for useful knowledge such as herblore was given to them during their astral journeys.

What heals may, of course, also harm. Shamanic talent does not necessarily imply goodness or wholeness of heart, and some individuals almost certainly used their knowledge and abilities to inflict illness, blight an enemy's crops, and so on, but there were groups like the benandanti to help one deal with such problems.

And so it went, for centuries. This syncretistic blend of Christianity and Pagan shamanism, which explains the seemingly "pious" visions of individuals like Chonradt Stocklin, persisted from the beginnings of Christian missionary work in Europe (circa A.D. 400) until the close of the Middle Ages (circa 1400). As Europe became more densely settled, more urbanized, the old shamanic practices lost their hold on many people, especially those who lived in the cities. The old ways survived most powerfully in the isolated parts of Europe, the wild mountain reaches of the Alps and the Pyrenees. The Church looked the other way; it had failed to eradicate the winter festivals, and it could easily dismiss astral participation in the Wild Hunt as a collective dream or fantasy, a mere hallucination, and though there were a few isolated trials for *maleficium* or sorcery, there were very few instances in which the old folk beliefs were persecuted (a rare exception being the execution of Madonna Oriente's followers in 1390).

Then, in the latter half of the fourteenth century, the delicate balance that had lasted nearly a millennium was suddenly shattered.

What happened?

THE ALPINE WITCH CULT

Let's return to the *Formicarius* of Johannes Nider, the German Dominican who couched his theology in terms of a comparison between men and ants. Nider obtained his information on witches while attending an ecumenical council held in Basel, Switzerland. It was there that he spoke with several men, and one in particular, who were just beginning to execute large groups of peasants for the crime of witchcraft.

Nider's principal informant was one Peter von Greyerz, a secular judge (not a Church inquisitor) from the region of Bern in Switzerland. Greyerz appears to have been something of a paranoiac—whenever he fell down the stairs, he was convinced that witches, traveling on the astral, had pushed him.

They would have had good reason, too, for Greyerz was dedicated to the extermination of what he believed to be an especially perfidious sect of heretics; he called them witches.

According to Greyerz, this particular sect was but newly established. In conversation with Nider about 1435, he stated that it had begun some sixty years previously, which takes us back to the year 1375. Much later, in 1500, an inquisitor named Bernardo Rategno, working on the Italian side of the Alps, wrote that the sect of witches had begun to expand rapidly around 1350.

Was the fanatical Greyerz, then, correct in his assumptions? Did peasants band together, in the late 1300s, in a group, or in various groups, dedicated to the practice of the old shamanic ways?

The records of the witch trials presided over by Greyerz no longer exist—all we have is the second-hand information provided by Nider.[1] Greyerz's principal victim seems to have been a peasant called Stedelin, from the village of Boltigen, whose trial must have taken place somewhere around the year 1400. From Stedelin, Greyerz learned that the sect of witches had been founded, at least in that part of Switzerland, by a man named Scavius, a great caster of spells who had the ability to change himself into a mouse. History is silent as to the fate of this Scavius, though Greyerz, thirty-five years later, was still complaining to Nider that the leaders of the sect had eluded his policemen by turning themselves into mice and skittering away (or sometimes by emitting a foul smell that left their pursuers incapacitated). So perhaps Scavius slipped through the good judge's net.

Stedelin was tortured into confessing that he had practiced sorcery against a neighbor's farm, rendering the cattle infertile and causing the farmwife to suffer seven miscarriages; he had accomplished this by burying a lizard beneath the threshold. In consort with other sorcerers, he had caused storms. He and his cohorts had gathered in a field and begged the "prince of all demons" (or the Otherworld Lord?) to send them a particular demon from out of his legions. Then they had repaired to a crossroads, sacrificed a black cock, and thrown it into the air—whence it was snatched up by their demon helper, who then proceeded to make hail storms and cast thunderbolts. The storms were intended to devastate the crops of the witches' enemies, and the thunderbolts to strike and kill the enemies themselves. Alas, said Stedelin, though the storms came and the lightning struck, they didn't always devastate the right farms or strike the right people.

Greyerz proceeded to arrest and torture some of Stedelin's compatriots, thereby securing the confession, mentioned by Nider, that was noted in Chapter 2: how children were killed by magic, and how their corpses were dug up and boiled into an ointment that served either to assist the transformation of witches into animals or to be consumed in initiation rituals. These rituals took place at the village church, very early on a Sunday morning (before the priest came in to bless the holy water). They consisted of renouncing Christ and pledging oneself to a demon known as "the little master," who appeared in human form. After consuming the initiatory potion from a skin flask, the witches experienced a sudden sensation of receiving and preserving within themselves "the image of the art" and the principal rituals of the sect.

Greyerz was a secular judge, but Nider's other principal informant was a church inquisitor, from the region of Lausanne, also in Switzerland. He told essentially the same story. The magical activity that Greyerz and the Lausanne inquisitor noted around 1400, and that apparently began in the Alps, was not eradicated by the burning of the peasants involved.

In 1409, Pope Alexander V issued a bull directed to the Inquisitor General for a vast area including parts of Switzerland, southern France, and the Italian Alps. The Pope, apparently acting on information supplied by the Inquisitor General, complained of new sects, established by renegade Christians and Jews, that practiced witchcraft, magic, and forbidden rituals. In typical medieval fashion, the Pope laid most of the blame on the Jews, who probably had nothing to do with it, aside from inspiring later inquisitors to use the term "Sabbat" for witches' gatherings. The Pope sent the Inquisitor General a nice gift of money to assist him in his efforts.

The papal campaign against this "new sect" of witches came to its dark fruition in 1428. The Bishop of Sion, again in Switzerland, persuaded the peasant communes of the Valais district that anyone accused of witchcraft by more than two people should be arrested, that anyone so arrested should be tortured, and that anyone so tortured should be burned on the strength of a confession attained by such means!

A witch hunt began that same year, and another "sect of witches" was duly discovered in the nearby valleys of Henniviers and Herens. The accused confessed (under torture, of course) that they were members of a society of witches and that they had been taught to induce illness and death by magical means. The Devil appeared to them in the shape of a black bear or a black ram, while they themselves could transform themselves into wolves and devour cattle. They consumed herbs that rendered them invisible, and thus they flew to their gatherings on brooms or other sticks. On their way home, they stopped in the wine cellars of their more prosperous neighbors, drank the best wine, and then shat into the barrels. Of course, they had renounced Christ and the Church; they were now some seven hundred strong and, had they not been caught, in one more year they would have become the masters of the countryside, ruled by their own king.

As a result of the Valais trials, more than one hundred men and women were burned at the stake.

Throughout the next decade, the persecutions gathered force. On the French side of the Alps, in the Dauphine, a host of poor people were accused of witchcraft. They were, it was affirmed, members of an organized sect of witches. Most instructive is the case of Pierre Vallin, tried for *maleficium* in 1431 and then again in 1438. During his second trial, he was tortured into confessing that he had been led astray some sixty-three years ago (the year 1375 again!) by a woman, now dead, who had encouraged him to trample on the cross and renounce Christ. He had obtained a demonic master called Beelzebub, whom he had kissed upon the thumb and who taught him to raise storms and practice other types of *maleficium*. He confessed, again under torture, to sacrificing his six-month-old daughter Francoise.

This sect of Dauphine witches was involved, said the Inquisitors, in a wide range of nefarious activities. They invoked demons, which sometimes appeared in animal form—a black rooster, black dog, black cat, black crow, pig or dog—but more often in human guise. The human shapes taken by the Dauphine demons typically involved the color black—a knight in black armor, a huge man in black, or a black man—though sometimes a demon might appear as a little boy or a small dark man. The Dauphine witches met at Sabbats, usually on Thursday, but sometimes on Tuesday or Saturday. They were transported thence by the Devil over long distances, riding on black horses, red mares, or upon sticks they had anointed. At the Sabbat they danced, held orgies, and had frequent intercourse with demons (Vallin's demon Beelzebub pleasured him by taking the form of a twenty-year-old girl). Sometimes they had sex with the Devil—who, in the Dauphine trials, makes his first definite appearance at the Witches' Sabbat. He took the form of a black cat or a man with terrible shining eyes, crowned and dressed in black garments. The Dauphine witches paid homage to him and kissed his behind.

In prison, the Dauphine witches maintained that the Devil came to them, even there, to strengthen them against torture, or, if all else failed, to help them commit suicide.

With the Dauphine trials, the stereotype of the malevolent witch became complete. The Burning Times had begun.

It seems clear that *something* happened in the Western Alps around the year 1375. Some kind of a sect or society of "witches" was formed and grew with a fair degree of rapidity. But was it, in fact, a devil-worshipping association of heretics? Or can we discover the traces of archaic shamanism in this so-called "new sect"?

Let us take a look at the earliest example, that of Peter von Greyerz and his persecution of the suspected witch Stedelin. Between Stedelin himself and the report published in Nider's *Formicarius* we have several layers of obscurity:

- The confessions were extracted under torture to;
- Meet the expectations of the fanatical Greyerz, who;
- After pondering the matter for some thirty years, related his own version of the story to;
- Nider, who wrote it down in his own words rather than those of Greyerz.

All the examples quoted here were subject to a similar garbling. At such a distance in time and human consciousness, we can only guess at what was real and what was a product of the judges' expectations. Let us at least make the attempt:

- These early witches were members of a sect that stood in stark opposition to the status quo, for they hoped to create their own rebellious social structure, complete with their own king. In the countryside near Bern, this sect had been organized by an individual named Scavius, who operated about 1375 and who was said to be able to transform himself into a mouse. In shamanic terms, we may suspect that the mouse was Scavius' totem animal, for it was a common belief that the soul made its exit from the body in the form of a mouse at the beginning of an astral journey. There were other leaders of the sect as well, and they were apparently pursued by the local authorities. These authorities said that the leaders of the witch cult were capable of vanishing into thin air, leaving only a foul smell—a detail which itself "smells" of the judges' expectations about heretics and demons.

- The witches revered a figure whom the judges identified as the Devil, but who bears many of the symbolic attributes of the Otherworld Lord. He frequently appeared in animal disguise, he had blazing eyes (like Herlechin, a common name for the leader of the Wild Hunt), and his Sabbats bore a strong resemblance to the hunting festivals and folk rituals celebrated in honor of the Otherworld Lord and Animal Master.

- The witches believed that they traveled in the spirit to the Sabbats of their master, where they participated in orgiastic activities. On their way home, they visited peoples' houses, ate the food put out for the dead, and defecated into the wine barrels of stingy neighbors. All of this is reminiscent of the tradition of the Wild Hunt, just as "the Devil" is reminiscent of its leader.

- The members of the sect were initiated in a ritual that involved entering the village church and drinking a potion from a skin flask. Whether or not they actually renounced Christianity is difficult to say, for this was part of the collective inquisitorial fantasy. Even more fantastical is the notion that the witches dug up corpses and used them in the preparation of their potion. This, as we have seen, was a very ancient notion, used over the centuries to defame any heterodox or unusual religious group. However, testimony to the effect that those who drank the potion gained a transcendent and sudden understanding of the magical art suggests that some sort of hallucinogen—whether belladonna, bufotenin, or fly agaric mushroom—may have been involved.

- After being inducted into the sect, the members learned how to transform themselves into animals. They also learned to cast spells and make magic, most of which involved agriculture. The judges were interested solely in *maleficium*, sorcery intended to harm other individuals. But shamans and herbalists were traditionally healers, and we may suspect that a great deal of witchcraft was actually oriented toward healing. The judges, of course, had no use for such data—we may remember that King James VI actually classified the curing of diseases among "base things."

Now, it is clear that some of the witches' meetings described in these trials were out-of-body experiences, for they bear a strong resemblance to the Wild Hunt. There are, however, significant differences between the Wild Hunt tradition and the Sabbats which arose in the Alps during the last few years of the fourteenth century:

- Early accounts of the Wild Hunt are concerned primarily with women, and name a goddess as leader of the hunt. In the Alpine trials, however, the Old Bone Goddess has more or less disappeared, replaced by the Otherworld Lord.
- The Sabbats themselves sound suspiciously like the hunting festivals that were celebrated in his honor, traces of which still remain, and in the same part of Europe.

Did the winter solstice rituals in honor of the old god of Earth and the Underworld become the focal point for the development of a new sect? Though many early witch gatherings took place as astral or out-of-body experiences, there are other indications in the trial records that describe experiences that surely took place in the real world—for instance, entering a church in the small hours of the morning to drink a psychedelic brew from an ordinary skin flask. It is difficult to see why a secular judge—even a fanatic like Greyerz—would be overly concerned about the activities of a group of people whose "heresy" was practiced while they were asleep in their beds.

We have examined a great deal of medieval material that insists that the devotees of the Wild Hunt left their bodies when they traveled with the spirits of the dead; and yet it was also believed that at least some individuals were enacting the rites of the "good folk" in more earthly ways—even in dishonest ways. A fourteenth-century folktale tells of a group of larcenous peasants who dressed up as members of the "good society," then went through the houses of those who had set

tables for the dead and walked off with all the furniture, cheerfully pro-
claiming that they would "Take one and give back a hundred." Need-
less to say, the victims of this little hoax received no such blessing.

If the Alpine witches were sometimes operating on the astral, they
were sometimes operating in reality as well, and the yearly festivals in
honor of the Otherworld Lord may well have served as places where
peasants could meet, practice their ancient traditions, and band
together without being too closely observed.

If this *is* what happened, then we must still answer the question:
Why did it happen?

CHAPTER 9

Hunting for Souls in a Country of Ghosts

SOUTH DAKOTA, 1890

They had gathered from all over, from one reservation or another, and pitched their tents in a circle around the dancing ground. The white observers and curiosity seekers—and there were many of these—arrived in wagons or on horseback, noting that the collection of teepees stretched far beyond the dancing ground itself, and that there were at least three hundred of them drawn up in a circle around the central pole. The pole itself was a pine tree, hung with multi-colored cloth, eagle feathers, claws, and horns.

Early in the morning, those who had fasted and prayed rose and washed themselves in the river. Then they gathered around the central pole. The medicine men began the ceremony, chanting and marching round the circle of teepees. Behind them danced those who had seen visions. They had spoken with the ancestors, and the ancestors had told them of the great truth, the great apocalypse: the spirits

215

of the Lakota dead would come forth from the ground, and the whites would be banished from the land.

When the procession had ended, the shaman stood by the center pole once again. All the people came to hear him; they put on their ghost shirts and threw away all the ornaments they had acquired from the whites. The shaman spoke, and then everyone stood up—there were several hundred of them now—and formed a circle. Each stood directly behind the other, his hands placed upon the shoulders of the dancer in front of him.

They shuffled in a circle and chanted. The white observers blinked, uncomprehending. Those who spoke some Sioux said the words of the chant were, "Father, I come."

Finally, the dancers stopped. Standing in the circle, they began to wail and cry out. The whites found the noise fearful, and the actions of the dancers even more bizarre. The Sioux gathered handfuls of dust and covered their hands and faces with it, casting the soft fine dirt into the brisk autumn sky. They called out the names of their relatives who had died.

Mesolithic painting of dancing women

Let us speak, let us speak. Let us talk with each other again....

But the sky never broke its silence. At last the dancers sat down, still in a circle, and the shaman told them how the prophet had come, far away in the west, among the Paiutes. The prophet had told them that the dead would surely rise again, and surely the whites would go.

Then everyone joined hands and began to circle around. Faster and faster they danced, their bodies swaying back and forth, their hands swinging up and down. The dust began to rise, and covered them in a haze like the veil of the Otherworld. "Father, I come," they called out. "Mother, I come. Brother, I come."

And then, exultant: "Give us back our arrows."

Faster and faster they whirled. Now they were in a trance. Some were old; when they began to falter, the younger dancers held them up, kept them swirling. Some were ailing and had come here seeking healing; the young and strong sustained them in the dance.

And then they began to see....

One woman broke away from the ring. Her hair flew wildly about her face, and her eyes stared into another world. Her breathing came in great ragged gasps; she fluttered birdlike, then fell. She writhed and twisted on the ground.

Then there was another, and another. In the end, nearly one hundred men and women lay on the dusty earth, staring into the spirit world, speaking with their dead.

When the shaman's assistants had roused them all, and brought them back to the world of here and now, they sat and talked. They talked about their visions.

Later in the day, they would dance again, but now, they would share the wisdom the ancestors had bestowed upon them.

Listening to all those Indians babble in their own tongue made the whites feel bored. They got in their wagons and went home.

CRISIS CULTS

The phenomenon of the Ghost Dance, as recorded by early observers,[1] forms a spectacular example of what religious scholars call a *crisis cult*.

A crisis cult is a spiritual movement that arises in response to a political or social crisis. When faced with historic forces beyond its control, a culture or a people often responds by reaching out spiritually, seeking a new vision of reality to make sense of the chaos that lies all around.

In the late 1880s, for example, it was becoming clear to most Native Americans that the whites had finally prevailed. Even Geronimo had surrendered, and there were no more "free" Indians; Indian life and reservation life had become one and the same thing. Then, in Nevada, a Paiute medicine man had a vision. He saw a great change coming, an apocalyptic shift in the American axis. The ancestral spirits or "ghosts" of the Native American peoples were about to rise again. The whites would be overthrown; their reign would be ended; but in order for this to happen, Native Americans would have to return to their roots. They would have to be kind to each other, and turn aside from all violence, and they would have to shed the accoutrements of white culture like an illness, ridding themselves of clothes and trade goods that had come from the dominant race.

But most of all, they would have to dance the Ghost Dance, a shamanic ritual that brought them into living, immediate contact with the spirits of their departed ancestors.

History had another, sadder fate in store for the Ghost Dancers. The white administrators of reservations in the northern plains saw the dance as a threat, the beginning of a potential rebellion. The machinery of government moved; the first casualty was Sitting Bull, murdered in his home when reservation police came to arrest him. Native hopes of spiritual regeneration ended in December of 1890, when a starving band of Sioux Ghost Dancers was slaughtered at Wounded Knee.

What happens when a crisis cult fails? What does such a disaster mean for the spiritual life of a culture that has struggled so valiantly for regeneration through a return to the ancient ways?

We shall attempt to answer this question a little later on.

First, however, let us note another example of a crisis cult. In 1847, the Maya of Yucatan erupted into rebellion against the government of Mexico, inaugurating a Caste War that was at least partly successful—large portions of the Yucatan Peninsula fell into the hands of the Maya. Their desire to drive out the whites and reclaim their native land was fueled by a crisis cult that, in 1850, rose up deep in the jungles of Quintana Roo. A simple wooden cross, erected in the wilderness by Mayan rebels who must have professed, at least, a kind of lip service to Christianity, was said to have spoken. In fact, the cross was "speaking" through the medium of an interpreter or shaman who gave forth prophecies—and historical prophecy, of course, had always been an integral part of Mayan spirituality.

The Speaking Cross proclaimed a new era in which the whites would be driven out and the Maya would once again be masters of Yucatan. Like the prophets of the Ghost Dance, the interpreters of the Speaking Cross urged the Maya to return to their ancient ways. By so doing, a great political and social change would take place. The first would become last and the last would become first, and although the Mayan rebels did not quite succeed in achieving a complete revolution, they continued to rule part of Yucatan until the 1920s and 30s. This time the crisis cult did not altogether fail.

Sometimes, in fact, a crisis cult may be very successful. Let us go back yet a little farther in time, and examine the Haitian revolution of 1791. Throughout more than two hundred years of European colonialism, the black slaves of Haiti had been trying desperately to hold on to their native African traditions. Inasmuch as it had been brought to the Caribbean from various parts of Africa, the slave population was comprised of people from very different cultures; for two hundred years they had traded rites and mythologies, evolving a new way of looking at the old religions. In the midst of atwo hundred-year spiritual crisis, they were developing a crisis cult of considerable power and vividness. There was another component as well—when black slaves escaped from their masters, they ran away to the jungle, where they came into contact with Carib Indians, another tribal people in the midst of a spiritual crisis. At last, all the various streams of tradition *syncretized* into a mighty torrent called Voudoun.

In 1791, a ceremony was held in Haiti that had a great impact on the future history of the island. It was conducted by a Jamaica-born Voudoun priest called Boukman, who urged the slaves to revolt against their colonial masters. The souls of all those who died in the attempt would, he promised, return to Africa.

In the midst of the ceremony, a great storm arose. An elderly black woman stepped into the circle of the firelight, holding a knife over her head and trembling violently. She danced a wild and furious dance, and, when she was done, used the knife to cut the throat of a black pig. Everyone present drank of the blood of the pig and swore their allegiance to Boukman.

A week later, the revolution had begun. In 1804, Haiti became a free nation—the second such nation in the Western hemisphere.

The crisis cult had prevailed....

Voudoun, of course, has become one of the most important forms of spiritual expression among black people in the New World. Like Santeria and Candomble, it is a *syncretic faith*, for it blends elements of many different religious traditions into a coherent and powerful whole. Sometimes, then, a crisis cult survives to become a major religion.

In all the examples we have studied, we can see the same processes at work. A society that has hitherto relied upon its native traditions experiences a crisis so intense as to actually foreshadow the end of the tribe, the people, or the culture. Collectively, the members of such a society constellate a new form of spiritual expression, one that has strong roots in the past, but that also includes new and different elements—elements that address the chaotic situation of the present. In some cases, as with the Sioux and the Caribbean slaves, this new spiritual impulse is expressed through ecstatic dance. The dance is a reaching out, a search for the power and sense of vision that may restore the endangered culture unto itself. Sometimes the dancers prevail, as in Haiti. Sometimes, as in South Dakota, the outcome is more tragic.

But no matter what the outcome, the underlying pattern of the crisis cult remains the same. In fact, it is so specific that we can easily summarize it in a table (see Table 2). But how does this relate to our investigation of the witch trials?

CRISIS CULTS			
A Traditional Society:	Native Americans	Maya	Black Slaves and Carib Indians
Experiences a crisis:	Reservation life	Political subjugation	Slavery
Responds by developing a crisis cult:	The Ghost Dance	The Cult of the Speaking Cross	Voudoun
Comprised of a return to tradition:	Shamanic communication with the spirits of the ancestors	Shamanic communication with the spirits of the ancestors	Spirit possession
Mingled with new or syncretic elements:	The ideas of imminent apocalypse (Christian)	The symbol of the cross (Christian)	The worship of saints (Christian) and the idea of the shamanic World Tree (Carib Indian?)
Dedicated to radical social change:	The end of white dominance through apocalypse	The end of white dominance through revolution	The end of white dominance through revolution

Table 2

THE BREAKDOWN OF MEDIEVAL SOCIETY

We have seen how the original Alpine witches abandoned an oppressive faith to seek their traditional shamanic roots, and, in an ecstatic dance with the Otherworld, whether performed in reality or as an astral experience, they proclaimed the birth of a radically new social order, declaring that they themselves would be the forerunners of a new society. Was the "sect of witches" that arose in the Alps around 1375 actually a sort of crisis cult?

And if so, to what crisis were the witches responding?

We are used to thinking of a world made up of different nations or states, but medieval Europe was a cultural entity unto itself. A large portion of the continent was part of the so-called Holy Roman Empire, with the Emperor supposedly subject to the Pope in Rome. There were other kingdoms outside the confines of the Empire, such as England and France, but the kings who reigned there were more like overgrown feudal barons than contemporary heads of state, and their kingdoms more like exceptionally large fiefdoms than nations as we know them. Medieval Christendom was a monolith.

Then, beginning around 1300, the world fell apart. At the beginning of the fourteenth century, a group of rebellious peasants known as *Pastoureux*, or shepherds, marched through France pillaging and destroying everything in their path until a French army stopped them at Carcassonne. Their battle cry was the same one that would be sounded by the Valais witches a century later—that the peasants were to overthrow their noble masters and that the last would become first.

But it was the noble masters themselves, rather than the rebellious peasants, who sent medieval Europe into its great downhill spin. Philip IV of France became embroiled in a political quarrel with Pope Boniface VIII and sent his emissaries, along with an army of mercenaries, to try to persuade the pontiff to his own way of thinking. One of the leaders of the embassy punched the Pope in the face; Boniface VIII was an old man and died a month later.

The incident shocked all of Christendom. To strike a Pope was tantamount to striking a divinity. Even more disturbing, Philip IV failed to get himself blasted by righteous lightning—in fact, he prevailed over the papacy. In 1309, a new pope, Clement V, made himself Philip's tool by moving the papacy from Rome to the French city of Avignon. There the pope remained for sixty-eight tumultuous years, while Philip himself went on to commit further outrages by perpetrating a religious persecution that, in many ways, foreshadowed the Burning Times—the heresy trials of the Knights Templar in 1310.

The Hundred Years War between England and France began in 1340. In time it would bring France to its knees, and, also in time, be responsible for the rebirth of that country as a whole new kind of political entity—a modern nation state. But during the first decade of that struggle, the emergent idea of nationalism, fashioned and shaped in mystic fire by Joan of Arc, a convicted witch, was not even a pipe dream. One thing, and one thing alone, seemed clear to the rank and file of European humanity: the world was falling apart. As the authority of the Church dissolved and Europe slipped into conflict and chaos, a philosophic melancholy seized the poets and philosophers of Christendom. Things were so bad, they proclaimed, that it couldn't get any worse.

They were wrong. Things could, and did, get much worse. In October of 1347, twelve Genoan galleys, homeward bound from Constantinople and the Black Sea, disembarked in the Sicilian port of Messina. There were dead and dying men at the oars, for among their trade goods was an unnoticed but deadly cargo—rats who carried bubonic plague. The Black Death had arrived.

From Sicily, the Black Death spread all over Europe. Although the terrible plague seemed to abate after two years, its disappearance was an illusion. The disease simply went through cycles and was to continue to ravage Europe for more than a century.

Nothing shook the faith of Christendom quite like the plague. If poets and philosophers had previously been afflicted with a trendy melancholia, everyone from the Pope to the peasants was now gripped by apocalyptic terror and despair. Medicine and prayer were alike ineffectual against the spread of the disease, and while theologians debated—was it God's judgment against a sinful humanity or simply the result of a conjunction of Saturn and Mars in Aquarius?—the people died.

That was when the dancing began....

The plague years were characterized by a number of social disruptions that took the form of dance. Historians call them "dance crazes." The dancers were generally peasants or poor townspeople, much like the "witches" of the next generation. Many of them, again like the witches, were unmarried women whose husbands had died during the plague or who—because the Black Death seems to have taken more male than female victims—could never hope for an ordinary life as wives and mothers. The dancers would gather wherever they happened to be, whether at home, in the streets, or even in church. They stripped themselves half naked, and danced hand in hand, in pairs, or in a circle. They went on for hours, finally passing out from exhaustion. Those who still remained on their feet danced on the bodies of the fallen until they too collapsed. Sometimes the dancers twisted themselves into grotesque contortions and called out senseless things the clergy believed to be the names of demons; on occasion, they fell into convulsions. The Church didn't persecute them; rather, it tried to exorcise them with prayers or heal them. A later dance epidemic was named for St. Vitus because his church at Strasbourg was believed to be a place where the mania could be effectively cured.

The dances began in 1350, in southern Italy, with the Tarantella. They continued until 1418, by which time the witch trials were already under way. Medieval Europeans responded to the breakdown of their civilization much as Sioux Indians responded to the same crisis—they danced themselves into an ecstasy above and beyond the world.

The shamanic dance, common to many crisis cults, should not necessarily be seen as an escape from "reality." The dance serves a spiritual purpose, for it brings the dancers into close contact with the world of the ancestors, and it is from that great wellspring, that primordial source, that traditional peoples seek wisdom to guide them through their crises.

The burning of Joan of Arc

Sometimes the voice of wisdom speaks with a tongue of fire, as in Haiti, where the Voudoun gods called for rebellion, or in Yucatan, where the Speaking Cross prophesied a violent end to the established order. We have no records to tell us what voices came to those Europeans who danced the Tarantella or St. Vitus' Dance—the clergy believed that the peasants were calling on "demons," but this is highly unlikely.

However, there were other, more worldly, voices that raised the familiar battle cry: Let the first become last and the last become first.

In 1358, the merchants of Paris booted out the Dauphin and took over the city. Encouraged by the revolt of the middle classes, the peasants, too, rose up in bands called *jacqueries*, and expressed their rage against the nobility. They seized castles, cut the throats of the nobles, and raped their highborn wives—dressing their own wives in the finery of the violated noblewomen. And, like the spirits of the Wild Hunt, they raided the pantries and wine cellars of the wealthy, and ate like the hungry dead. In the end, the Dauphin's forces destroyed them in a series of bloody battles.

Then, in 1374, a new dance epidemic broke out, this time along the lower Rhine, whence it spread through Germany, Holland, and France. Like the Tarantella of twenty-five years before, or St. Vitus' Dance some forty years later, it was ecstatic, convulsive, visionary, and practiced by the poor, the unlettered, and the otherwise disenfranchised. This time it was called St. John's Dance because the dancers claimed to be dancing in honor of St. John (St. John's Day was June 23, almost exactly coincident with the old Pagan summer solstice festival).

According to Peter von Greyerz, it was at this exact time, and less than a hundred miles away, that Scavius, the mouse shaman, formed a new sect—one based around folk magic and an hallucinatory ritual conducted in village churches.

Scavius and his colleagues behaved like the peasant revolutionaries of the *jacqueries*, using both magic and cunning to stay a few steps ahead of Greyerz and the law. Did they gather at the old hunting and fertility festivals in honor of the Otherworld Lord? Did they dance, as others were dancing, all over Europe?

We don't know, but we know that "witches" who practiced similar rites and spells claimed they were dancing the Sabbat dance in the Valais and the Dauphine some fifty years later.

Did Scavius and his followers, again like the *jacqueries*, call for a reversal of the established order—a Christian order that had failed to save them from political abuse as well as from the ravages of the Black Death? We don't know, but the Valais witches of 1428 certainly held such beliefs.

Seen against the background of its own time, the Alpine "sect of witches" bears all the marks of a crisis cult, responding to the break-down of medieval civilization in a way that would be characteristic of the Mayans, Haitians, or Sioux. The phenomenon of the "witch cult" fits the crisis cult pattern so well, in fact, that we may easily place it in the context of our table of crisis cult characteristics (see Table 3 on page 228).

If this is, in fact, the case, then the Witches' Sabbat was much more than a fantasy concocted by the inquisitors, far more than a collective astral experience of the European peasantry.

It was the last desperate Ghost Dance of European shamanism.

It resulted not in the overthrow of the traditional order, but in almost three hundred years of mass executions known as the Burning Times. For if the peasants who lived in Europe's most rural and "primitive" regions sought to dance their way into the Otherworld in their quest for meaning amidst the chaos, there were others who sought to still forever the spirit voices whispering in the well of their collective souls.

When the security of an orderly existence crumbles all around us, we may either embrace magic or attempt to impose a new, more immutable order. The shaman is able to lift the veil of apparent real-ity and gaze upon the face of chaos with a joyous smile—he is, after all, the asymmetrical man, and loves the wild free spaces beyond the edge of the real. But such an embrace of images and dreams—the social solution offered by the witches—was already beyond the ability of most Europeans. Practitioners of a faith that sought to raise the sky of logic far above the vivid chaos of the earth, the Church and the

A MEDIEVAL EUROPEAN CRISIS CULT	
A Traditional Society:	The European peasantry
Experiences a crisis:	The breakdown of the Medieval world order
Responds by developing a crisis cult:	The Witch Cult
Comprised of a return to tradition:	Shamanic communication with the spirits of the ancestors (i.e., the Wild Hunt or Hosting of the Fairies)
Mingled with new or syncretic elements:	Folk Christianity (e.g., Joan of Arc and Chonradt Stocklin)
Dedicated to radical social change:	The end of aristocratic dominance through magical and social revolution

Table 3

feudal aristocracy were already bringing a new world into being—a world quite different from what the witches sought, and that, in time, proved to be the scaffolding of our own "modern" society. Faced with chaos, they struck back with logic, and built upon that fragile edifice a world where magic ceased to play a part. Afraid of being overcome by the dark, they sought to make of the rational mind a kind of beacon, a saving light.

In order to do so, they had to still the wild wind that blew from the Otherworld, the land where vision reigned supreme over reason, and to still the voice of that wind, to dissipate the Otherworld mist, they had to rid themselves of the shamans.

We have been misled by the belief that the witch trials were "medieval." They were not. They began, as we have seen, around 1428, when the Renaissance was just starting to gather momentum in Italy. They continued through the 1500s, the years of the Protestant Reformation, the years when the "scientific spirit" was growing.

We have also been misled by a prevailing belief that the witch trials were orchestrated almost entirely by the Catholic Church. They were not. The new Protestant states that were born during the Reformation proved to be every bit as fierce as the Catholics when it came to persecuting witches. In fact, the earliest witch hunter we have noted in these pages, Peter von Greyerz, was a civil rather than an ecclesiastical judge. It is a sad fact that some of the worst witch persecutions were perpetrated by civil courts; the ordinary townsmen of Europe cherished their orderly urban lives and feared the winds of the Wild Hunt that blew just beyond the edge of town.

That splendid darkness at the edge of town was various and multi-textured. For if we agree with Margaret Murray and Gerald Gardner that witchcraft was "real," we must disagree with their belief that there was a single, organized witch cult spanning all of Europe and dedicated to preserving a doctrinaire Paganism. In these pages, we have met with many witchcraft "cults," most of which were small and regional—the followers of Madonna Oriente in northern Italy, the benandanti of the Friuli region, the cult instituted by Scavius in the Alps. Some of these groups, like the benandanti, professed themselves to be Christians, though their practices were more genuinely Pagan in character. Other groups, like the Alpine witch cult of 1375, may have had no link with Christianity whatsoever. In the end, the Burning Times did not eradicate an organized witches' religion that had survived since the Neolithic; it eradicated many small witch cults founded upon shamanism and differing widely from one another in practice and belief.

The "scientific spirit"—the spirit by which we define our very culture—grew in direct proportion to the continuing eradication of Europe's shamans. The light of reason replaced the flickering glow of the Otherworld, which faded more and more deeply into the Well of Memory and Forgetfulness. The first wave of persecutions was aimed at peasant societies that sought to heal the crisis of Western civilization through a return to shamanic traditions. But in time, the persecutions became so widespread that Europeans were striking out at every factor in their society that contained even the faintest glimmer of Otherworldly light, including every social group—whether of women, peasants, or the mentally disturbed—on the "outs" with the prevailing mode of thought; they reminded people too deeply of a spiritual dimension that, being "irrational," had become uncomfortable.

By 1563, the Flemish physician Johann Wier wrote to beg the princes of Europe to put an end to the witch trials because their victims were simply old women and mentally ill individuals who had nothing to do with sorcery or magic. Dr. Wier was a pupil of the great Hermetic magus Cornelius Agrippa, and thus certainly a man who believed in magic and took it seriously. To read between Wier's lines brings us to the following conclusion: by 1563, the persecution mania had become so general that even the magicians knew it no longer had anything to do with magic.

THE WIND THAT BLOWS FROM THE OTHERWORLD

Carl Jung believed that the Grail Legend represented the last, most recent flowering of European mythology. In the Grail myth, a questing knight stumbles into an enchanted landscape dominated by a magical castle. The lord of the castle is a wounded man called the Fisher King—who, as we have seen, is none other than the King of the Otherworld. Not only is he sick unto death with a magical wound, his kingdom has become sick as well. It is a wasteland. The Otherworld itself has become blighted and sterile, and though the authors of the Grail myth were active about two hundred years before the witch trials, they had some prophetic inkling that Western society, even then, had turned in a direction that would lead inexorably to the stifling of the Otherworld music.

Thus the failure of Europe's shamanic crisis cult has had an immeasurable effect upon all of us, for we live in a world wherein the sky has replaced the earth altogether, wherein the spirits of our ancestors, no longer loved and fed, have drawn away from us into an almost unimaginable distance—their voices, and their wisdom, silent now. We are no longer conscious of the Otherworld all around us.

What, then, happens to a society when tradition has died, when no one walks the North Star Road any longer, and the voices of the Otherworldly dimension have been stilled?

An anthropologist who studies such societies would speak of "loss of soul." When the last shamans have passed away with no one left to receive their knowledge, when the gods themselves have died, a culture loses it soul.

The symptoms are many, and they are consistent: listlessness, depression, alcoholism, and a general spiritual malaise that has no other name save loss of soul. Many tribal peoples, all over the globe, are struggling with the disease. Australian aboriginal medicine men, saddened at the end of their way of life and finding no one among the younger generation capable of preserving the ancient ceremonies, simply walk off into the outback and die. Many native tribes in North America have been reduced to a diet of beer and junk food, a soul-crushing alcoholism, and a spiritless, unfocused anger. Let it be said, also, that there are many who are reclaiming their traditional belief systems and, consequently, their souls, in a vital—and highly syncretic—attempt to render the old ways meaningful in a new world.

Western peoples have been blessed, or cursed, with a higher degree of technology than other cultures, thanks in large measure to the fact that we elevated reason to a god by thoroughly eradicating our native shamans. Yet the symptoms of spiritual malaise, of loss of soul, are present in our own culture, and have been ever since the Burning Times. How, otherwise, could we have been capable of taking up arms against so many traditional cultures around the world and, in the name of righteousness, attempting to destroy them? Some have suggested that there is something innately perverse, or downright *wrong*, with that large collectivity of human beings who are of European descent—and yet our destruction of shamanic cultures all over the planet may more logically be attributed to our own radical loss of soul, made possible only because we had first destroyed our own shamans. If, in the process, we have transformed our physical environment into a technological wasteland, it is because the Otherworld within us is a wasteland as well.

And now we feel spiritually empty. Our doctors no longer play the role of shamans, for they inspire a profound mistrust in many (or perhaps most) of us, and as members of the scientific community they have joined their voices with those who cry out that the Otherworld does not exist. Our psychologists are as much figures of satire and derision as they are of respect. Neither our physicians nor our psychologists can believably fulfill the shamanic function, that of society's healers. The North Star Road no longer echoes with the sounds of our footsteps.

The late Joseph Campbell[2] said that our artists have become our shamans. Though this is an inspiring and hopeful thought, it is not, in every case, an especially comforting one. Many of our artists, like Rimbaud and Jim Morrison, seem to have gone mad, and can succeed in seeking the Otherworld only through addictions to drugs or alcohol that eventually destroy them. Deprived of a living contact with the vibrant force that is the Otherworld, we are left without a sense of spiritual continuity to inform our actions and lend us wisdom. In shamanic terms, we are hunting for souls in a country of ghosts, seeking through a wasteland, a blighted Otherworld, for any voice that might be borne on the winds of spirit.

Many of us, especially in the United States, have hoped to hear that voice speaking in the traditions of the Native American peoples around us. They, however, retreat into a well-founded mistrust and ask us: Why do you come here to raid the last thing we have left? Why can you not find what you seek among your own spiritual roots?

Why indeed?

Some seek the Otherworld voice through the practice of Eastern religions, but the images and dreams that move through those wells of memory are vastly different from our own; and though such faiths may historically be more tolerant and open-minded, Westerners have too often twisted them beyond all recognition by seeking to render them as dogmatic as our own Judeo-Christian faiths. We seem conditioned to hunger for one final doctrine, one great guru, one faith to quench the absolute once and for all. This misguided quest has led to little except a glut of phony, sex-crazed gurus and fanatical devotees who stockpile guns. As Jung affirmed, Eastern religions have never rested comfortably with the Western unconscious—and Christianity, in fact, was but another Eastern faith imposed upon the Western spirit.

Does this mean that we are, spiritually speaking, doomed? Are the doors of the Otherworld closed to us forever?

No. For in the final analysis, the ability to communicate with the Otherworld is integral to the human condition. It is as natural—and as necessary—as sleeping or dreaming. This is why shamanism, in some form or another, continues to persist. This is why it slips through the net of dogmatic assertions and carefully structured theologies, because the need it answers is essential to the human spirit, and can never be fully eradicated, no matter how fierce the flames or how sterile the doctrine.

The North Star Road still beckons from our own doorsteps. The Otherworld still lies all around us. We touch it in myth, in fairy tales, and even in more recent productions of fantasy, be they film or science fiction. And it lies all about us in the small incidents of our daily lives as well. As Dostoyevsky wrote: "Life is paradise, and we are all in paradise, but we refuse to see it. If we would, we should have heaven on earth the next day."3

To perceive life as such—to hear in every bird song, every stream, the voice of the Otherworld, and to see its green and silver meadows in every city street or backyard—is as good a definition of true witchery as there is. We need not seek for one final and ultimate answer, for the answer lies everywhere. The "original" witches—like modern practitioners of Afro-Caribbean traditions or like the inhabitants of the New Mexico pueblos—took their inspiration wherever they found it, whether the sources were Christian, Pagan Indo-European, derived from the matriarchal Neolithic, or whatever. Contemporary Pagans, who sometimes seek for a "pure" tradition of witchcraft or Wicca, would do well to remember the spiritual openness of their ancestors.

A healthy syncretism recognizes the spirit, the sacredness, in all things living. Let us, then, have an "impure" paganism, the kind that celebrates the magic inherent in everything.

Now that we have finished with our study of so much magic and lore, shamanic and medieval, we might well ask: What, after all, is magic?

Filmmaker Steven Spielberg once defined magic as "a childlike sense of wonder," and a sense of wonder is what we must have if we are to see the hand of the Otherworld in all things, and if, with Dostoyevsky, we are to be in paradise this minute.

The Otherworld is everywhere. Every breeze that blows carries with it the rich fragrance of elvish feasts, and it is a fragrance we have need of. Our need for it is eternal and everlasting, but it is also immediate. Like the witches of late medieval and early Renaissance Europe, we live in a world that is crumbling, where pollution and pandemics threaten us equally, and where nothing is secure. Only a childlike sense of wonder can save us.

It matters little what tools we use to dance our way into the Otherworld, for the tools are everywhere. What matters, if we are to find our souls in this ghost-world, is that we open our Otherworldly eyes, sense the wonder of life, and dance the joy of it into being.

Let the dance begin.

From a medieval woodcut

ENDNOTES

INTRODUCTION: WITCHES AND SHAMANS

1. Magnus Magnusson and Herman Palsson, trans. *The Vinland Sagas: The Norse Discovery of America* (Baltimore: Penguin, 1965), 81–3.

2. Carlo Ginzburg, *Night Battles: Witchcraft & Agrarian Cults in the Sixteenth & Seventeenth Centuries* (New York: Penguin, 1985).

3. See, for example, *Witchcraft and Black Magic* (New York: Causeway Books, 1974).

4. Norman Cohn, *Europe's Inner Demons: An Enquiry Inspired by the Great Witch-Hunt* (New York: Basic Books, 1975).

5. *The European Witch-Craze of the Sixteenth and Seventeenth Centuries and Other Essays* (New York and Evanston: Harper and Row, 1967).

6. *The Witch-Cult in Western Europe* (London: Oxford University Press, 1921), and *The God of the Witches* (London: Oxford University Press, 1970 edition).

7. (New York: Farrar, Straus and Giroux, 1974 edition).

8. (San Francisco: Harper and Row, 1979).

9. See *Night Battles*, cited above, and especially *Ecstasies: Deciphering the Witches' Sabbath* (New York: Pantheon Books, 1991).

10. See his classic study, *Shamanism: Archaic Techniques of Ecstasy* (Princeton: Princeton-Bollingen, 1972).

Chapter 1: The Shaman's Cosmos

1. Ake Hultkrantz, *Belief and Worship in Native North America* (Syracuse, NY: Syracuse University Press, 1981), 235–63; and Hultkrantz, *Native Religions of North America* (San Francisco: Harper and Row, 1987), 66–76.

2. Other old Norse poems identify it as a yew.

3. R. C. Hogart, trans. *The Hymns of Orpheus* (Grand Rapids, MI: Phanes Press, 1993), 33.

4. Ibid., 33.

5. Philip Stubs, *Anatomie of Abuses*, quoted in Joseph Strutt, *The Sports and Pastimes of the People of England* (first published in 1801, reprinted in Detroit: Singing Tree Press, 1968), 277.

6. Wilfred T. Jewkes and Jerome B. Landfield, *Joan of Arc: Fact, Legend, and Literature* (New York and Burlingame: Harcourt, Brace & World, 1964), 10–11.

7. Ibid., 44.

8. Ibid., 47.

9. Ibid., 45–6.

10. Ginzburg, *Ecstasies* (New York: Pantheon Books, 1991), 108–9.

11. Ibid.

12. Most writers, following Kabbalistic scholar Gershom Scholem, have regarded The Kabbalah as essentially Gnostic in origin, hence dating from the Hellenistic Period (circa 200 B.C.–A.D. 400). Moshe Idel, in his *The Kabbalah: New Perspectives* (New Haven: Yale University Press, 1981) argues that The Kabbalah actually retains very ancient ideas and spiritual techniques. This writer agrees with Idel and believes these ancient elements to be primarily shamanic.

13. *Yoga: Immortality and Freedom* (Princeton: Princeton-Bollingen, 1970).

CHAPTER 2: INITIATION RITES

1. George Catlin, *Letters and Notes on the North American Indians*, ed. Michael MacDonald Mooney (New York: Clarkson N. Potter, Inc., 1975), 199–206.

2. John G. Neihardt, *Black Elk Speaks* (Lincoln: University of Nebraska, 1979), 20–2.

3. Eliade, *Shamanism*, 38–42.

4. *The Quest for Merlin* (Boston: Little, Brown, 1985).

5. Quoted in H. R. Ellis Davidson, *Gods and Myths of the Viking Age* (New York: Bell Publishing Co., 1981), 143–4.

6. Ginzburg, *Night Battles,* 52–3.

7. Jewkes and Landfield, *Joan of Arc*, 6–7.

8. Ibid., 11.

9. Ginzburg, *Night Battles*, 75–6.

10. Ibid., 154.

11. Quoted in Ginzburg, *Ecstasies*, 69–70.

CHAPTER 3: THE OLD BONE GODDESS

1. Marija Gimbutas, *The Goddesses and Gods of Old Europe, 6500–3500 B.C.: Myths and Cult Images* (Berkeley and Los Angeles: University of California Press, 1982).

2. Marija Gimbutas, *The Language of the Goddess* (San Francisco: Harper and Row, 1989), 209ff.

3. Quoted in Gimbutas, *Language of the Goddess*, 209.

4. Clarissa Pinkola Estes, *Women Who Run with the Wolves: Myths and Stories of the Wild Woman Archetype* (New York: Ballantine Books, 1992), 27–32.

5. The version of her story given here has been compiled from several sources: Murray, *God of the Witches*, 57–8, 62; Ginzburg, *Ecstasies*, 96–7; and Colin Wilson, *Witches* (New York: A & W Publishers, 1981), 97–8.

6. *Fasciculus morum*, English, 1320, quoted in Jeffrey Burton Russell, *Witchcraft in the Middle Ages* (Ithaca and London: Cornell University Press, 1972), 175.

7. Quoted in Russell, *Witchcraft in the Middle Ages*, 76.

8. Quoted in Ibid., 134.

9. Quoted in Ginzburg, *Night Battles*, 48–9.

10. Quoted in Russell, *Witchcraft in the Middle Ages*, 211.

11. Trial records quoted in Russell, *Witchcraft in the Middle Ages*, 212–5, and Ginzburg, *Ecstasies*, 92–3.

CHAPTER 4: TOTEM ANIMALS

1. John (Fire) Lame Deer and Richard Erdoes, *Lame Deer: Seeker of Visions* (New York: Washington Square Press, 1972).

2. See Eliade, *Shamanism*, 190–7.

3. Quoted in Paul Devereux, *Shamanism and the Mystery Lines* (St. Paul, MN: Llewellyn Publications/Quantum, 1993), 174–5.

4. Quoted in Summers, *Witchcraft and Black Magic* (New York: Causeway Books, 1974).

5. *Ynglinga Saga*, quoted in Eliade, *Shamanism*, 381.

6. Quoted in Ronald MacDonald Douglas, compiler, *Scottish Lore and Folklore* (New York: Beekman House, 1982), 137–8.

7. Recorded in Ginzburg, *Ecstasies*, 153–7.

Chapter 5: Traveling in the Spirit

1. In Eliade, *Shamanism*, 201–3.

2. Gimbutas, *Goddesses and Gods of Old Europe*, 102.

3. Tolstoy, *The Quest for Merlin*.

4. Gerald of Wales, *The Journey Through Wales and The Description of Wales*, trans. by Lewis Thorpe (Harmondsworth: Penguin, 1984), 246–7.

5. Quoted in Ginzburg, *Ecstasies*, 188.

6. Quoted in Ginzburg, *Ecstacies*, 106–7.

7. Quoted in Emmanuel Le Roy Ladurie, *Montaillou: The Promised Land of Error* (New York: Vintage Books, 1979), 288.

8. Quoted in Russell, *Witchcraft in the Middle Ages*, 235.

9. Quoted in Ginzburg, *Night Battles*, 19; the italics are his.

CHAPTER 6: OTHERWORLD GEOGRAPHY

1. "A Lyke-Wake Dirge," in W. H. Auden, and Norman Holmes Pearson, eds., *The Viking Portable Poets of the English Language, Vol. I: Medieval and Renaissance Poets* (New York: Viking Press, 1961), 428–9. I have modernized the spelling a bit.

2. Tom Peete Cross and Clark Harris Slover, eds., *Ancient Irish Tales*, (New York: Barnes & Noble, 1969), 189.

3. Ibid., 505.

4. In Gimbutas, *The Civilization of the Goddess: The World of Old Europe* (San Francisco: Harper Collins, 1991), 399–400.

5. Ibid., passim.

CHAPTER 7: MASTER OF ANIMALS, KING OF THE DEAD

1. See Murray, *God of the Witches*, 36, 69, 88, 109, 114, 135; Wilson, Colin, *The Occult: A History* (New York: Random House, 1971), 417, 419; and Wilson, Colin, *Witches*, 97–8.

2. Jeffrey Gantz, trans., *The Mabinogion* (London: Penguin, 1976), 196.

3. Ibid., 196–7.

4. Recorded in Hubert J. Davis, *The Silver Bullet and Other American Witch Stories* (Middle Village, NY: Jonathan David Publishers, 1975), 151.

5. Quoted in Russell, *Witchcraft in the Middle Ages*, 58.

6. Such as Gilg Tschudi and Durich Chiampel, cited in Ginzburg, *Ecstasies*, 192–3.

7. P. C. Hilscher, in *De Exercitu Furioso* (1688), cited in Ginzburg, *Ecstasies*, 182.

8. In Cohn, *Europe's Inner Demons*, op. cit.

CHAPTER 8: THE ORIGINS OF THE SABBAT

1. Summarized in Norman Cohn, *Europe's Inner Demons*, 204–5; and in Ginzburg, *Ecstasies*, 69–71.

CHAPTER 9: HUNTING FOR SOULS IN A COUNTRY OF GHOSTS

1. See James Mooney, *The Ghost-Dance Religion and the Sioux Outbreak of 1890* (Originally published—Washington: American Bureau of Ethnology, 1896; reprinted—Glorieta, NM: Rio Grande Press, 1973).

2. Joseph Campbell and Bill Moyers, *The Power of Myth* (New York: Doubleday, 1998), 85.

3. Fyodor Dostoyevsky, *The Brothers Karamazov* (New York: Signet, 1957), 264.

BIBLIOGRAPHY

Bosley, Keith. *The Kalevala*. Oxford: Oxford University Press, 1989.

Bord, Janet and Colin. *Earth Rites: Fertility Practices in Pre-Industrial Britain*. London: Granada Publishing, 1982.

Briggs, Katharine, "The English Fairies." *Folk-Lore*, 68, 1957.

———. "The Fairies and the Realm of the Dead." *Folk-Lore*, 81, 1970.

Budge, E. A. Wallis. *The Egyptian Book of the Dead*. New York: Dover Publications, 1967.

Campbell, Joseph, with Bill Moyers. *The Power of Myth*. New York: Doubleday, 1988.

Carrasco, David. *Religions of Mesoamerica: Cosmovision and Ceremonial Centers*. San Francisco: Harper & Row, 1990.

Catlin, George. *Letters and Notes on the North American Indians*. Ed. Michael MacDonald Mooney. New York: Clarkson N. Potter, Inc., 1975.

Cohn, Norman. *Europe's Inner Demons: An Enquiry Inspired by the Great Witch-Hunt*. New York: Basic Books, 1975.

Cross, Tom Peete, and Clark Harris Slover, eds. *Ancient Irish Tales*. New York: Barnes & Noble, 1969.

Davis, Hubert J. *The Silver Bullet and Other American Witch Stories*. Middle Village, NY: Jonathan David Publishers, 1975.

Deren, Maya. *Divine Horsemen: Voodoo Gods of Haiti*. New York: Chelsea House Publishers, 1970.

Devereux, Paul. *Shamanism and the Mystery Lines*. St. Paul, MN: Llewellyn Publications/Quantum, 1993.

Douglas, Ronald MacDonald, ed. *Scottish Lore and Folklore*. New York: Beekman House, 1982.

Eliade, Mircea. *Shamanism: Archaic Techniques of Ecstasy*. Princeton: Princeton-Bollingen, 1972.

————. *Yoga: Immortality and Freedom*. Princeton: Princeton-Bollingen, 1970.

Ellis Davidson, H. R. *Gods and Myths of the Viking Age*. New York, Bell Publishing Co., 1981.

Ellis Davidson, H.R. *Myths and Symbols in Pagan Europe: Early Scandinavian and Celtic Religions*. Syracuse, NY: Syracuse University Press, 1988.

Estes, Clarissa Pinkola. *Women Who Run With the Wolves: Myths and Stories of the Wild Woman Archetype*. New York: Ballantine Books, 1992.

Evans-Wentz, W. Y. *The Fairy-Faith in Celtic Countries*. New York: Citadel Press, 1990.

————. *The Tibetan Book of the Dead*. London: Oxford University Press, 1972.

Freidel, David, Linda Schele and Joy Parker. *Maya Cosmos: Three Thousand Years on the Shaman's Path*. New York: William Morrow and Co., 1993.

Gantz, Jeffrey, trans. *The Mabinogion*. London: Penguin, 1976.

Gerald of Wales. *The Journey Through Wales and The Description of Wales*. Trans. by Lewis Thorpe. Harmondsworth: Penguin, 1984.

Gimbutas, Marija. *The Goddesses and Gods of Old Europe: 6500–3500 B.C.: Myths and Cult Images.* Berkeley and Los Angeles: University of California Press, 1982.

———. *The Language of the Goddess.* San Francisco: Harper and Row, 1989.

———. *The Civilization of the Goddess: The World of Old Europe.* San Francisco: Harper Collins, 1991.

Ginzburg, Carlo. *Night Battles: Witchcraft & Agrarian Cults in the Sixteenth & Seventeenth Centuries.* New York: Penguin, 1985.

———. *Ecstasies: Deciphering the Witches' Sabbath.* New York: Pantheon Books, 1991.

Graves, Robert. *The White Goddess.* New York: Farrar, Straus, and Giroux, 1974.

Graves, Robert. *The Greek Myths.* Baltimore: Pelican Books, 1964.

Grillot de Givry, Emile. *Illustrated Anthology of Sorcery, Magic and Alchemy.* New York: Causeway Books, 1973.

Grimm, Jacob and Wilhelm. *Grimm's Complete Fairy Tales.* Garden City, NY: Nelson Doubleday, Inc., n.d.

Hogart, R. C., trans. *The Hymns of Orpheus.* Grand Rapids, MI: Phanes Press, 1993.

Hollander, Lee M., trans. *The Poetic Edda.* Austin: University of Texas Press, 1962.

Hultkrantz, Ake. *Native Religions of North America.* San Francisco: Harper and Row, 1987.

———. *Belief and Worship in Native North America.* Syracuse, NY: Syracuse University Press, 1981.

Idel, Moshe. *The Kabbalah: New Perspectives.* New Haven: Yale University Press, 1981.

Jewkes, Wilfred T., and Jerome B. Landfield. *Joan of Arc: Fact, Legend, and Literature.* New York and Burlingame: Harcourt, Brace & World, 1964.

Johnson, Kenneth, and Marguerite Elsbeth. *The Grail Castle: Male Myths and Mysteries in the Celtic Tradition.* St. Paul, MN: Llewellyn Publications, 1995.

Jung, Emma, and Marie-Louise von Franz. *The Grail Legend.* New York: G. P. Putnam's Sons, 1970.

Ladurie, Emmanuel Le Roy. *Montaillou: The Promised Land of Error.* New York: Vintage Books, 1979.

Lame Deer, John (Fire), and Richard Erdoes. *Lame Deer: Seeker of Visions.* New York: Washington Square Press, 1972.

Magnusson, Magnus and Herman Palsson, trans. *The Vinland Sagas: The Norse Discovery of America.* Baltimore: Penguin, 1965.

Mallory, J. P. *In Search of the Indo-Europeans: Language, Archaeology and Myth.* London: Thames & Hudson, 1989.

Matthews, John. *Taliesin: Shamanism and the Bardic Mysteries in Britain and Ireland.* London: The Aquarian Press, 1991.

Mooney. *The Ghost-Dance Religion and the Sioux Outbreak of 1890.* Glorieta, NM: Rio Grande Press, 1973.

Murray, Margaret. *The Witch-Cult in Western Europe.* London: Oxford University Press, 1921.

———. *The God of the Witches.* London: Oxford University Press, 1970.

Neihardt, John G. *Black Elk Speaks.* Lincoln: University of Nebraska, 1979.

Perera, Sylvia Brinton. *Descent to the Goddess: A Way of Initiation for Women.* Toronto: Inner City Books, 1981.

Russell, Jeffrey Burton. *Witchcraft in the Middle Ages.* Ithaca and London: Cornell University Press, 1972.

Sandoz, Mari. *Crazy Horse: The Strange Man of the Oglalas.* Lincoln, NE: University of Nebraska Press, 1960.

Schele, Linda and David Freidel. *A Forest of Kings: The Untold Story of the Ancient Maya.* New York: William Morrow & Co., 1990.

Starhawk. *The Spiral Dance.* San Francisco: Harper and Row, 1979.

Starkey, Marion L. *The Devil in Massachusetts*. New York: Time Incorporated, 1963.

Strutt, Joseph. *The Sports and Pastimes of the People of England*. Detroit: Singing Tree Press, 1968.

Summers, Montague. *Witchcraft and Black Magic*. New York: Causeway Books, 1974.

Tedlock, Dennis, trans. *Popol Vuh: The Mayan Book of the Dawn of Life*. New York, Touchstone, 1985.

Tolkien, J. R. R., trans. *Sir Gawain and the Green Knight: Pearl and Sir Orfeo*. New York: Ballantine Books, 1980.

Tolstoy, Nikolai. *The Quest for Merlin*. Boston: Little, Brown & Co.,1986.

Trevor-Roper, H. R. *The European Witch-Craze of the Sixteenth and Seventeenth Centuries and Other Essays*. New York and Evanston: Harper and Row, 1967.

Wilson, Colin. *The Occult: A History*. New York: Random House, 1971.

———. *Witches*. New York: A & W Publishers, 1981.

ILLUSTRATIONS

INDEX

251

White Wife, 22, 59
Wicca, xix, 58, 233
Wier, Johann, 230
Wild Hunt, xvi, 74-76, 78, 83, 99, 103, 106,
    124-126, 130, 132, 154, 176, 178, 180,
    184-185, 190, 201-202, 204-205, 211-212,
    226, 228-229
William of Auvergne, 76
Wilson, Margaret, 170
Wilson, Bessie, 170
Winter Carnival, 185
Winter King, 177, 179, 203
witchcraft, witches
    Alpine witches, 103, 106, 206, 212-213, 222,
    227, 229
    Alpine witch cult, 206, 227, 229
    astral journeys of, 45, 90, 98-99, 130, 132,
    144, 152, 156, 158, 173, 188-191, 204-206,
    210, 212-213, 222, 227
    flight of, 4, 92, 99, 130
    modern, xix, 87, 178, 223, 227-228, 233
    Otherworld of, 5, 43-45, 51-52, 66, 76-77,
    79, 90, 92, 102-103, 106-107, 118, 120,
    123-124, 126, 128, 130-131, 135, 141, 144,
    146, 148, 150-152, 154-159, 162, 171, 173,
    176, 178-181, 184, 190-191, 202, 204-205,
    207, 210-213, 222, 226-230, 232-234
    witch trials, xvi, xvii, xviii, xix, xx, xxi, 8,
    14, 16-17, 21, 24, 41-45, 48-49, 52, 58-59,
    61, 64-65, 69, 75, 78-79, 87, 95-97, 102-
    106, 111-112, 123, 130-132, 152, 158, 171,
    173, 178-181, 184, 190-191, 198, 205-206,
    208-210, 212, 220-224, 228-230

Witches' Sabbat, xviii, 19, 21, 41, 43, 48,
    101-102, 104, 152, 157-158, 169-173, 181,
    184, 186, 188-191, 199, 205, 207-213, 226-
    227
Witekind, Hermann, 105
World Mountain, 4, 19-24, 38, 99, 116-118,
    125
World Tree, 4-11, 13-16, 18-24, 29, 35-36,
    38-41, 49, 55, 57, 62-63, 88, 91-92, 109-
    110, 113-114, 116-120, 126, 134-135, 138,
    146, 150, 165, 182-183, 186, 192-193, 198,
    203, 221
Wounded Knee, 218

-Y-

Yggdrasil, 8-10, 40, 120, 134, 146
Ymir, 8, 174
yoga, 4, 23-24, 28-29, 36, 53, 117, 182-183
Yorkshire, 182
Young, John, 170
Yucatan, 219, 226
Yugoslavia, 98

-Z-

Zeus, 49, 174
Zoroastrianism, 173

☾ LOOK FOR THE CRESCENT MOON

Llewellyn publishes hundreds of books on your favorite subjects! To get these exciting books, including the ones on the following pages, check your local bookstore or order them directly from Llewellyn.

ORDER BY PHONE

- Call toll-free within the U.S. and Canada, 1-800-THE MOON
- In Minnesota, call (612) 291-1970
- We accept VISA, MasterCard, and American Express

ORDER BY MAIL

- Send the full price of your order (MN residents add 7% sales tax) in U.S. funds, plus postage & handling to:

  Llewellyn Worldwide
  P.O. Box 64383, Dept. K379-4
  St. Paul, MN 55164–0383, U.S.A.

POSTAGE & HANDLING

(For the U.S., Canada, and Mexico)

- $4.00 for orders $15.00 and under
- $5.00 for orders over $15.00
- No charge for orders over $100.00

We ship UPS in the continental United States. We ship standard mail to P.O. boxes. Orders shipped to Alaska, Hawaii, The Virgin Islands, and Puerto Rico are sent first-class mail. Orders shipped to Canada and Mexico are sent surface mail.

International orders: Airmail—add freight equal to price of each book to the total price of order, plus $5.00 for each non-book item (audio tapes, etc.).

Surface mail—Add $1.00 per item.

Allow 4–6 weeks for delivery on all orders.
Postage and handling rates subject to change.

DISCOUNTS

We offer a 20% discount to group leaders or agents. You must order a minimum of 5 copies of the same book to get our special quantity price.

FREE CATALOG

Get a free copy of our color catalog, *New Worlds of Mind and Spirit*. Subscribe for just $10.00 in the United States and Canada ($30.00 overseas, airmail). Many bookstores carry *New Worlds*—ask for it!

Visit our web site at www.llewellyn.com for more information.

THE GRAIL CASTLE

*Male Myths & Mysteries
in the Celtic Tradition*

Kenneth Johnson & Marguerite Elsbeth

Explore the mysteries which lie at the core of being male when you take a quest into the most powerful myth of Western civilization: the Celtic-Teutonic-Christian myth of the Grail Castle.

The Pagan Celtic culture's world view—which stressed an intense involvement with the magical world of nature—strongly resonates for men today because it offers a direct experience with the spirit often lacking in their lives. This book describes the four primary male archetypes—the King or Father, the Hero or Warrior, the Magician or Wise Man, and the Lover—which the authors exemplify with stories from the Welsh Mabinogion, the Ulster Cycle, and other old Pagan sources. Exercises and meditations designed to activate these inner myths will awaken men to how myths—as they live on today in the collective unconscious and popular culture— shape their lives. Finally, men will learn how to heal the Fisher King—who lies at the heart of the Grail Castle myth—to achieve integration of the four archetypal paths.

1–56718–369–7, 224 pp., 6 x 9, illus., index   **$14.95**

SLAVIC SORCERY

Shamanic Journey of Initiation

Kenneth Johnson

In Eastern Europe and European Russia, the spiritual world of primordial hunters is still alive, even though their hearth-fires are long cold. Until now, few scholars were even aware that a magickal tradition still existed in the land now inhabited by Slavic peoples.

Author Kenneth Johnson presents his true-life experiences with the living practitioners of a magickal discipline extending back into pre-Christian times. Johnson traveled to Russia and studied with several Slavic sorcerers, one of whom took him under his wing and put him through extensive training in Pagan Earth Magic.

Slavic Sorcery serves as a course in authentic shamanic practices. For Pagans or individuals of Slavic descent, this book also serves as an introduction to the mythology and lore of the Slavic peoples, covering the seasonal festivals, cosmology, the gods, the Otherworld spirits, and beliefs about the ancestors.

1-56718-374-3, 224 pp., 6 x 9, illus., index   **$12.95**

JAGUAR WISDOM

Mayan Calendar Magic

Kenneth Johnson

The Mayan people and their Sacred Calendar continue to be a subject of fascination and speculation. *Jaguar Wisdom* presents, for the first time, an accessible introduction to the spiritual teachings and practices of the ancient *and* contemporary Mayan people. Since the Sacred Calendar remains the foundation of the Mayan spiritual tradition, *Jaguar Wisdom* introduces its complete magical system including correspondences, ritual, astrology and divination.

Make your own Mayan altar, celebrate the Day of the Dead, create a traditional Mayan amulet for protection, concoct Mayan herbal remedies, observe the five major Calendar ceremonies, find your own personal Mayan birth sign, and create your own "Tree of Life" astrological reading. In addition, you will learn how to make a typical Calendar diviner's medicine bag and practice divination with seeds and crystals.

1-56718-372-7, 288 pp., 6 x 9, illus., softcover $14.95